Church, Communion, and Culture

Church, Communion, and Culture

Samuel Seabury and the Fate of Global Anglicanism

Martyn Percy

Foreword by Ian S. Markham

CASCADE *Books* • Eugene, Oregon

CHURCH, COMMUNION, AND CULTURE
Samuel Seabury and the Fate of Global Anglicanism

Cascade Books
An Imprint of Wipf and Stock Publishers
199 W. 8th Ave., Suite 3
Eugene, OR 97401

www.wipfandstock.com

PAPERBACK ISBN: 979-8-3852-2932-1
HARDCOVER ISBN: 979-8-3852-2933-8
EBOOK ISBN: 979-8-3852-2934-5

Cataloguing-in-Publication data:

Names: Percy, Martyn [author]. | Markham, Ian S. [foreword writer].

Title: Church, communion, and culture : Samuel Seabury and the fate of global Anglicanism / Martyn Percy ; with a foreword by Ian S. Markham.

Description: Eugene, OR: Cascade Books, 2026 | Includes bibliographical references and index.

Identifiers: ISBN 979-8-3852-2932-1 (paperback) | ISBN 979-8-3852-2933-8 (hardcover) | ISBN 979-8-3852-2934-5 (ebook)

Subjects: LCSH: Seabury, Samuel, Bp,—1729–1796. | Anglican Communion. | Anglican Communion—History—Colonies—18th century. | Episcopal Church—Connecticut—History—18th century. | Anglican Communion—United States—History. | Anglican Communion—History.

Classification: BX5005 P47 2026 (paperback) | BX5005 (ebook)

VERSION NUMBER 02/12/26

Contents

Foreword

The Very Revd. Dr. Ian Markham,
Dean of Virginia Theological Seminary

As Edmund Burke reflected on the French Revolution, he penned these words: "In history a great volume is unrolled for our instruction, drawing the materials of future wisdom from the past errors and infirmities of mankind."[1] As a conservative theorist, he was especially alert to the significance of change. He felt that all social change had to be managed with some care. The unanticipated consequences of any moment can be momentous.

As the settlers made the journey to America in the early seventeenth century, they brought with them the Church of England. In Virginia it became the established church. After the Revolutionary War, the American church started to create its own identity—one theologically linked with the Church of England yet separate in terms of formal organization.

Theologically, the apostolic succession—the unbroken chain of bishops from the apostles to the present day—is clearly essential. This means that we need at least one Anglican bishop (ideally two or three) to lay hands on an American priest for that person to become a bishop. One would imagine that the simple task of consecrating a bishop for the American church would be one of those incidental details of history which at best would be no more than a footnote to a broader narrative.

In this pioneering study, Martyn Percy illustrates that the moment is pivotal. He makes the striking claim that "the consecration of Samuel Seabury marked the beginning and end of the Worldwide Anglican Communion." Now how can the consecration of a bishop be so significant? With skill and careful analysis, Percy argues that the Seabury consecration was both the start of the Anglican Communion (after all, the new bishop in America was made possible by a non-English province providing the bishops and therefore different provinces of Anglicanism were emerging) and the end of the Anglican Communion (because the Old World of Europe, England, and the Church of England could not adapt to the changing realities of Anglicanism).

All of this is set against a backdrop of the British Empire and, in particular, the horrendous evils of the trade of enslaved persons. Too often Anglican historians forget how horrendous the trade was; we recognize it was there but we choose not to dwell on it. We are all so familiar with this reality that we tend to overlook the extraordinary narrative that Christians—with their commitment to the imago Dei and the resolute emphasis in Scripture on justice and love—can perform the sinful intellectual somersaults to affirm the acceptability of the evil trade in human beings.

For Percy, the setting of empire and the trade in enslaved persons is central. Embedded in this setting is the complex identity of Britishness. This Britishness is embedded in class and racism that generates a problematic attitude at the heart of English Anglicanism. English Anglicanism thinks of itself as superior; the result is a hubris that culminates in a state of degeneration.

The consecration of Samuel Seabury, a man who had enslaved people, becomes a symptom of a deeper, more pervasive crisis within Anglicanism. The monarchic deference given to bishops in the Church of England leads to a credited expertise that makes tragic mistakes in "safeguarding" cases. The relationship with the Communion is marred by the historic patronizing attitude. With the decline of the Church of England goes the decline of the Anglican Communion.

Pan-national organizations are all fragile. Brexit was a decision of the United Kingdom to extricate itself from the European Union. America First with Donald Trump is challenging every single pan-national organization from NATO to the United Nations. The Martyn Percy thesis about the Anglican Communion has, perhaps, wider implications. Percy's argument is that embedded in the very design of the Communion was a set of obsolete assumptions around power and empire that obscures sin (for example, the trade in enslaved persons) and that made the Communion intrinsically unstable.

One way, then, to look at our historic moment is to recognize that many of these transnational organizations emerging from the Second World War were in a similar way building on obsolete assumptions grounded in European hegemony and power. There is, after all, something a little odd in 2025 that the five permanent members of the United Nations Security Council still count France and the United Kingdom. The world has changed a great deal since the end of the Second World War. So, then, Percy's thesis about the Anglican Communion could also be extended to the United Nations.

Overall, this book is an invitation to deep "truth telling." In this respect, Percy is making a theological claim. We need to strive to have a sense of the past that is as full as it possibly can be. Our narratives of our past tend to oversimplify and be personally satisfying. So, for the Church of England the oversimplified and satisfying narrative runs as follows: In the nineteenth century, the British brought the beauty of Anglican worship to different parts of the globe and the result is a global family that shares a liturgical structure and a distinctive ethos. Percy points out that this is an oversimplification that overlooks the trauma of enslaved people, the cruelty of empire, and the deep ambivalence that the Global South has with England. Now, this tendency of oversimplification and personally satisfying narratives applies also to the Episcopal Church in the United States. Our narrative runs thus: Although many Anglicans supported the British in the Revolutionary War, we responded with determination to rebuild our tradition for the fledging American state and did so by Samuel Seabury making the hazardous journey to Scotland to ensure that a distinctive Anglican tradition could flourish on these shores. Percy points out that you cannot overlook the reality that Seabury was an owner of enslaved people, and this embeds at the heart of the founding of the Episcopal Church in the United States a certain inherited ethos that continues to haunt the Episcopal Church today.

God alone has the full knowledge of the truth concerning our complex past and the ways in which that past is responsible for challenges in the present. And the invitation from Martyn Percy in this extraordinary book is to set the divine knowledge as our standard in judging all our smug, self-satisfied, often self-congratulatory, narratives. It is not that we will ever obtain the divine perspective, but by setting that perspective as our standard, we are much more likely to eliminate the most damaging and most misguided narratives. This is the Percy project. He wants us to understand our past so we can realistically confront the challenges of the present.

The challenging of our narratives of the past is hard work. This book is not an easy or enjoyable read (save for those delicious and occasional humorous illustrations that Percy cannot help sharing). Instead, it is holy work. It is a work of Lent in preparation for Easter. May God use this book to shed light on the Anglican Church as we seek to witness to the liberating power of the gospel.

Ian S. Markham
Christmas 2025

Preface

Church: Consecration and Culture

THIS BOOK USES THE life and times of Bishop Samuel Seabury to reflect on the beginning and the end of the Worldwide Anglican Communion. It is not a book that takes on the air of a reverential hagiography or some deferential biography. Instead, we are offering a blended form of social, theological, and historical study, which offers a cultural approach to church life, theology, and ecclesiology, and draws on the social sciences. In order to embark on this venture, we will take a journey through the life and times of Samuel Seabury, and use his history as a lens through which to see more clearly.

As readers will detect, what is excavated in this book is an established Anglican/Episcopalian tendency towards actions founded in "consecrated pragmatism." That is to say, the expedient becomes sacralized and the practical is theologically legitimized, precisely because the ecclesial and spiritual framework is born out of necessity and hybridity.

The emergence of Samuel Seabury as America's first bishop bears testimony to this modus operandi. Although this book is largely concerned with Samuel Seabury's ecclesial legacy in terms of the wider Anglican Communion, readers interested in the broader picture are directed to my *Crisis of Colonial Anglicanism* and other writings, which flesh out the cultural-theological approach to ecclesiology and congregational study.[2]

In the writing of this book, I have been blessed with rare access to original handwritten notes, prayers, and journals from Samuel Seabury, not to mention the licenses for his ordination and consecration, and other precious documentary evidence that chart the origins and birth of the American Protestant Episcopal Church. Seabury's *The Efficacy of a Mother's Prayers* (1791), some of his sermons, and his handwritten prayers for commending sick children to God's care, or for a person about to venture on a transatlantic sea voyage, were profoundly moving to encounter. Likewise, Seabury's sermons and other writings, his work on time and liturgical calendars since the Reformation, and his pro-British pre-independence tracts (written under the pseudonym of W. A. Farmer) were invaluable.

I was fortunate to be able to review the original minutes of the first gatherings of post-1776 Episcopalians—the General Convention of the American Protestant Episcopal Church. In all of this, the archives of General Theological Seminary (New York—GTS) and those of Virginia Theological Seminary (Alexandria, VA: VTS—neighboring Washington DC) have proved to be invaluable—a veritable treasure trove for research. So I wholeheartedly and sincerely thank the governors, faculty, librarians, and other staff for their assistance. Particular thanks are due to Dean Ian Markham for his own personal and inestimable assistance in this project.

I am also profoundly grateful to those writers who have crafted exceptional historical and biographical accounts of Samuel Seabury. Paul V. Marshall, Anne W. Rowthorn, and H. Boone Porter, amongst others, have offered invaluable insights and vignettes that illustrate the richness of the life and times of the first American Anglican bishop.[3] Their accounts have been read alongside other accounts of this period and Seabury's particular context.[4] I have also paid particular attention to the inherent inequalities of a society that ran on the proceeds of slavery. Gary J. Kornblith's work, and a host of others, have been extraordinarily helpful.[5] I have not attempted to replicate these works and their achievement. This book sets about the topic and issues in a different way.

Yet without wishing to preempt what follows, nothing prepared me for the days I spent reading through the well-preserved original newspapers of the time, dating from the 1750s to the early 1800s. For sure, it was fascinating to see how, just months after 1776, developments in Britain were briefly touched upon as "foreign affairs," and run together in a roundup of news from France and other European countries. I was intrigued that the diplomatic relations being fashioned between America and the new republic of France were warmly welcomed in the coverage. The French Revolution was not mentioned much. American newspapers tended not to use the term "revolution" about themselves either.

However, it is the small details—the small advertisements and notices in the newspapers—that remind us that the past is a foreign country. There were advertisements requesting tutors to help with schooling, dancing, and music. There were tutors offering such services, but who lacked the community space to provide their education. Yet nothing could prepare me for the shock of the small ads offering $10 rewards for "runaway slaves" and "missing negroes." Every newspaper I read carried several such advertisements.

In these old newspapers, one is immediately confronted with this awful and unforgiveable atrocity: the trade in human trafficking, which was legal and normal. In the 1700s in this New World, before and after becoming independent, people of all ages, and because of the color of their skin, were bought and sold as chattels. They had no rights, and as far as those posting these advertisements were concerned, these people were, quite literally, lost property. If you were to find such lost property, you could return him or her to the owner, and be paid $10 for your trouble. Some of the advertisements listed "domestic" (i.e., female) slaves, and their children too—also lost property. Some of the slaves who had been bought and were now to be sought were not even adults, but mere juveniles.

Samuel Seabury was a slave owner, as was his father, from whom he had inherited some. Slavery was "baked into" the social and economic life of the thirteen Eastern Seaboard colonies that started to break away from Britain in 1776. In neither the New World nor the Old World was slavery considered criminal or immoral. Slavery was part and parcel of the social ordering of society and the social and theological construction of reality. Churches understood themselves to be divinely appointed and the followers of Jesus to be entitled in their subjugation and ownership of others, especially from a different race, continent, or ethnic background. Had God not sanctioned such in the Old Testament? Had anyone in the New Testament so much as condemned the practice of slave ownership? No.

Does this make the racism, slavery and abuse of the past in any way forgivable? Some would say so, and argue that this was just the times in which people lived. But I beg to differ. The Enlightenment—with writers, philosophers, and inventors—was well under way with the likes of James Watt, Adam Smith, Francis Hutcheson, John Playfair, and Benjamin Franklin (a founder of the US Constitution). With the right to freedom, equality, political voice, and reform so clearly on the agenda, the lack of attention to systemic economic and punitive racism is shocking beyond comprehension. Slavery is a crime against humanity. George Washington was also a slave owner. Many Episcopalians north and south of the Mason-Dixon line were slave owners too.

In encountering such difficult history, and its systemic legacy in racism and generations of economic detriment, there are few signs of genuine remorse, reparation, and change. When one does come across them, however, they shine out as exemplary. Virginia Theological Seminary (VTS) was, for much of the nineteenth century, more associated with Confederate sympathies than support for the Union. On the day the American Civil War broke out, contemporary accounts record some students and faculty leaving their desks, books still unfinished, and signing up to fight for the South. However, during the war, the Union Army commandeered the seminary for use as a military hospital, catering for 1,700 wounded soldiers.

In preparation for its bicentennial (1823–2023), VTS commissioned a study of its history in respect of slavery some years back. As it turned out, the seminary had never owned slaves, at least directly. But it had employed them, or rather used them for labor, since local slave owners had hired them out to the seminary for labor. And, of course, it was the slave owners who were remunerated, not the workers. A number of the early benefactors of VTS were slave owners. All of this was hiding in plain sight in the small classified advertisements of the newspapers from the time.

To the great credit of the seminary, and its dean, the Very Revd. Dr. Ian Markham, the initiative for reparation was unique, ground-breaking, and generative. Many of the living ancestors of the enslaved were traced. They are now being paid a modest annual annuity by the seminary, in perpetuity. Furthermore, they have been made incorporated members of the seminary, and can dine there and use the facilities—for free.

For some contacted through this initiative, this was a painful reminder of enslaved ancestors, only a few generations apart. It also reminded many of the agonizing journey over the last few centuries to secure equality. There was a segregated college for Black students—Bishop Payne Divinity School—that ran from 1878 to 1949. Virginia Theological College was segregated until 1951, when its first African American student, John Thomas Walker, enrolled to train for ordained ministry. Walker would later go on to be bishop of Washington. The first full-time Black seminary professor was the Revd. Dr. Lloyd Alexander Lewis, who began teaching in 1978. Change has come, and increasingly the progressiveness has been proactive, not reactive.

That said, there can be no authentic change without a reckoning that the wider ecclesial culture has been structurally racist, and that the slavery and forced indentured labor were crimes against humanity, an affront to human dignity and basic human rights, and a blasphemy against God.

It is because the truth of this history has been faced, owned, and repented of, that Dean Ian Markham's reparation initiative could move forward. It avowedly testifies to a basic Enlightenment principle, and a basic gospel principle too. Namely, giving all people the freedom to self-determine in their lives in the here and now, and not to dictate how a sinful past and its current legacy should be atoned for.

In terms of proceeding, this book is divided into five parts, comprising an introduction and conclusion, and three parts in the middle. Our introduction sets out some thoughts on the contribution that cultural theory can make to the study of churches and denominations. Part one is concerned with Seabury's social world and his life and times. Part two explores the culture and context in more detail. Part three examines the cultural consequences for worldwide Anglicanism. Our conclusion offers some thoughts on the journey that lies ahead for Anglicanism in the twenty-first century.

Readers familiar with my method in the study of ecclesiology will know that I adopt a critical-cultural approach to polity and theology. I choose to do so because the shape of ecclesial life is deeply *determined* by the contextual ground in which it is located, and as the socio-sacred synergies grow and develop over time, so we discover new patterns of polity emerging that could not have been easily foreseen. Moreover, these new and emerging patterns require careful explication. What seems apparent on the surface often requires deeper reading to understand the shape and dimensions of ecclesial life. I often refer to this as "ecclesial *terroir*." Terroir is a single Gallic term that denotes all the contextual elements—soil, weather, human know-how, geography, topography—that give a wine, tea, or coffee its distinctive flavor. All churches and denominations are rooted in contexts and cultures they did not initiate and, to some extent, do not control.[6] What follows in this text, therefore, is an assemblage of pen portraits, vignettes, cultural and theological reflections, samplings and illustrations. In so doing, I have adopted an intentionally variegated cultural approach to the study of Anglican ecclesiology.

Correspondingly, in part three of this book, we examine a specific case study in Anglican polity, namely Sydney, Australia, which lies outside the English-monarchical and American-democratic dialect. The case study affirms the blended theological–social science approaches I adopt in the development of "grounded" and contemporary ecclesiology, thereby eschewing "purist" accounts of the church in favor of more intentionally syncretic interpretative methods. While I appreciate that the Sydney excursus in this book could also function as a stand-alone analysis, it rightly belongs in this study, since we are primarily concerned with how history and culture form churches, and how congregations and denominations grow out of distinctive cultures. Since this book is also concerned with the dialectics between monarchy and republic, or democracy and theocracy in ecclesiology, the critical-cultural theory applied to Sydney Anglicanism serves to remind readers that all ecclesiology is, ultimately, a kind of cultural theory. It is just that denominations choose to vest themselves in particular theological clothing as they emerge from their nascent cultural groundings. Or, as in the case of Sydney Anglicanism, it forgets its Brethren-style roots. Rightly, we pay attention to what has been put on and cast off as denominations seek to narrate their identities in the twenty-first century. Whether in the Church of England, the Episcopal Church of the USA, or in Sydney Anglicanism, ecclesiology is ultimately the study of cultural theory and forms of "social theology."

Finally, I have avoided the use of footnotes throughout the text, in order to maintain the flow and pace of chapters. References, where needed, have been deployed sparingly as endnotes. Readers on either side of The Pond (i.e., Atlantic Ocean) will also note that I have used the terms "Anglican" and "Episcopal" interchangeably. As we shall see, these are essentially two sides of the same coin. While Episcopalians became unavoidably committed to democratic polity and a theological rationale for that, and Anglicans remain inclined to benevolent-reformed models of monarchy (also with a theological rationale), there is but one faith. It just happens to have been practised in two different worlds for 250 years.

Much of what the future holds for churches and mainstream Protestant denominations, of which Anglicanism is a major example, depends on whether democratic accountability is allowed to function and flourish in common ownership, and the churches of Old World theocratic autocracy are finally rescinded. I contend that it is not Anglican faith that is falling apart. Rather, this is a story of two worlds slowly drifting apart following the split between the world of monarchy and the emerging world of democracy. In this, the Old World has passed through its phase of empire, become postcolonial, and is ceding its last residual powers to the new normal of democratic liberalism. In this, the New World continues to ascend.

The Revd. Prof. Martyn Percy
Aberdeen, Epiphany 2026

Introduction

Church, Communion, and Cultural Theory

THE CONSECRATION OF SAMUEL Seabury marked the beginning and end of the Worldwide Anglican Communion. He was the first American bishop, and the second presiding bishop of the American Protestant Episcopal Church (from hereon, TEC). In what follows, we shall be exploring and explaining how Anglican—or Episcopal—faith, belief, and practice is still one single entity. What split the Anglican Communion before it started was the separation of the Old World (Europe, and specifically Britain and the Church of England) and the New World—that of Continental America. We argue that an eighteenth-century climate crisis, English imperialism, slavery, and political revolutions played a primary role in the formation of the Anglican Communion, which only really came about a century later. In many respects, this book is an entirely new account of the cultural origins of global Anglicanism.

These days we rather take for granted the integrity of any program embarking on the "decolonialization" of our educational syllabi, curricula, libraries, museums, and art galleries. This book is not intended as an exercise in decolonizing Anglican/Episcopal identity. Others have already embarked upon that journey, and the burden and focus of this volume is rather different. That said, I have no intention of glossing over the difficulties that Anglican/Episcopal churches have to face when confronting their past, present, and future.

The threefold concerns of class, race, and gender/sexuality are sometimes referred to by conservative critics of Anglican churches as the real Holy Trinity of Episcopalian mission. While this kind of snide comment is commonplace in what passes for ecclesial dialogue these days, the proper and real concerns of churches do, as I have consistently argued, have roots in history and culture, and they should not be suppressed. So as this book unfolds, readers will appreciate that what is being offered here is a new cultural theory of Anglican polity, and of the Worldwide Anglican Communion, which now requires a different kind of reckoning with.

The kind of ecclesiology I have tried to pioneer in more than thirty-five years of academic endeavor does not skip over small details. I hold that the study of a congregation or denomination and the reification of their theology, must include *both* the explicit *and* the implicit (sometimes referred to as the "official" and the "operant") beliefs or traits of a church. Thus, what a church says it believes—in articles of faith, credal statements, and such like—is always vital for understanding its spiritual life.

But no less significant will be the small adverts in a denominational newspaper or the folksy letter from the rector in the parish magazine to the community. These are gold mines of information on expectations, understandings of mission and ministry, and how churches anticipate the life of God is made manifest in their midst. They also represent informal and unpretentious theological texts.

The study of ecclesial polity, from this vantage point, does not presume that churches are merely repositories for agreed doctrines and religious articles. Rather, I favor an approach that takes a far richer account of the web of meanings that individuals and groups are suspended within, by attending to the patterning of polity that is not obviously directly shaped or dictated by overt theological principles.

To be sure, social explorations of ecclesial polity may well take account of formal theological propositions that might purport to shape and delimit churches. But churches are more than that. Always.

For example, I recall some years ago preaching in a beautiful historic Episcopalian church that would have sided with the Confederate forces during the American Civil War (1861–1865). The church still contained an upper gallery with benched seating that was inferior to the pews on the floor of the nave. The seating arrangements clearly indicated a slave gallery.

Lest British readers feel a twinge of smugness at this point, many parish churches had similar seating arrangements based on servitude or class, or on pew rents. Enclosed pews were reserved for the gentry, and were often equipped with heating and could even provide alcoholic refreshment during services. Inferior benches were for the servants and the working class.

Decolonizing the Church

An approach to ecclesial polity through concerns that currently consume us does carry some risk. Decolonizing a museum or degree course is not straightforward, and sometimes more can be lost than apparently gained. The key is to pay attention to the seemingly marginal material. A former colleague of mine focused on the roles taken by missionary wives in the colonies. She noted how the legacy of those women—unable to preach or perform as clergy—consigned them to taking on other roles and responsibilities for setting up schools, colleges, and health clinics. This was what missionary wives were left with, while the apparently important labor of trying to convert the heathen was left to their missionary husbands.

The result? In many countries where Christianity has not succeeded in becoming firmly established as the majority faith, some of the very best schools, universities, colleges, and hospitals were founded by the wives of missionaries who found they had time on their hands. Their legacy is far greater, by some margin, than that of the congregations their husbands sought to plant and grow—many of which have not endured, and waned long ago.

Similar observations could be made about the worldwide fellowship of the Mothers' Union, founded by Mary Sumner (1828–1921). As a woman, she was educated at home but nonetheless learned to speak three foreign languages. Sumner's vision was undoubtedly radical for its day, since it involved calling together women of all social classes in order to support one another, and to help others. Even before the twentieth century, the organization had close to a million members in England, and the movement spread to most other parts of the Anglican Communion through the British Empire and Commonwealth.

Today, Mothers' Union branches in Africa, Asia, and beyond will be at the forefront of AIDS-HIV education in some of the world's poorest countries, and educating communities on sexual health, domestic violence, and campaigning against female genital mutilation. None of this work emerged from a diocese or bishop devising some Mission Action Plan. Arguably, because it has always lain outside male episcopal control, it belongs to the world of the pastoral, operant, and implicit.

As such it is often neglected in study. That Mary Sumner's life and work only figures as a "lesser commemoration" in the Anglican liturgical calendar probably tells us more about the gender of those making decisions regarding whom makes the cut onto such an elite list than it does of the merits of world-changing women such as Sumner.

Clergy wives and daughters, it turns out, are responsible for founding some of the world's most famous soccer teams, Rugby League clubs, and other sports and leisure clubs, as well as theatre and arts associations. As is so often the case with eighteenth- and nineteenth-century denominations, gender or class discrimination have in fact produced lasting legacies, and these include significant aspects of ecclesial identity (e.g., Methodism), conduct (e.g., lay preaching), and artefacts (e.g., parish magazines and other publications). It is therefore important that socio-cultural accounts of churches engage with the textured, grounded, and lived experience of ecclesial life. In all of this, the actors—people—who form and shape the church carry with them the normative social, economic, moral, and political baggage that every citizen of their time will have also carried.

While we might invest determined and directed energies in deconstructing the colonial lens we have inherited for viewing the Anglican/Episcopal world, it is worth noting that critical deconstruction of privileged, normative, White, male heterogeneity is not always identical to an agenda of "decolonization." The former should lean heavily into liberation theologies, liberationist pedagogies, and be rooted in an authentic philosophy of self-aware, self-critical, liberal education. Sometimes—and here there is a risk of caricature—"decolonization" either ignores such foundations, or barely touches upon them, before embarking upon a radical redaction of history and tradition, before finally re-narrating it.

The risk is, plainly, that history is then only subjected to a kind of re-toning: "White-wash," "rainbow-wash," "green-wash," or even "Black-wash" may be cosmetically appealing, but without the deep work of historiography, a change of décor is all we might gain from such exercises. While re-narrating history in this manner can be tempting, the result can be a kind of "history-net-deficit": we only glean from the past what we want to project on to it from the present. I think history, theology, and cultural theory must delve deeper, and be unafraid of peeling back the layers of meaning, taking down walls, and even removing some unsafe foundations.

Indeed, the very ground (i.e., social, economic, cultural, etc.) upon which churches come to be built must be considered if we are to understand how denominations evolve. What I have called the "ecclesial terroir" of church life pays attention the cultural elements that have interacted with beliefs and theology over time. Farmers use the same word for the soil, climate, and other conditions that make coffee beans or tea leaves different from place to place. Vignerons use the same word for grapes and wine.

The factors at work in church identity include history, ethos, practice, custom, culture, local subtleties, and regional distinctives, which make each denomination unique and distinctive.[7] In this approach, I draw on H. Richard Niebuhr's *The Social Sources of Denominationalism* (1929), which asks us to attend to how churches and denominations are shaped by the social, economic, and political forces, including class and ethnicity, always at work in countries and communities.

Anglicanism: An Accidental Communion

Church, Communion, and Culture is, therefore, a brief essay on how the Anglican Communion unfolded—somewhat by accident. The Communion has its origins in seventeenth-century Bermuda, which was wholly unintended; and later in eighteenth-century Aberdeen, which simply vindicates the saying that "necessity is the mother of invention." All of this was in place long before the first Lambeth Conference was even suggested by the then bishop of Vermont (Henry Hopkins) to the Archbishop of Canterbury in 1851. It was to take another sixteen years to gestate into the first gathering of 1867. Here, I hold that by stressing the social, political, and cultural origins of the Communion, we can better understand how individual provinces came to possess their distinctives, and reassess the landscape of contemporary schism.

For example, and as we shall explore in greater depth towards the end of this essay, the Archdiocese of Sydney has been deeply supportive of the Reformed Evangelical Anglican Church of South Africa (REACH). Previously known as the Church of England in South Africa (CESA), it originally separated from the province over High-Church practices (from 1847–1870). But in the twentieth century it evolved an anti-liberation-theological stance on a range of issues. The apolitical stance of CESA, and its previous pro-apartheid stance (including archbishop—Stephen Bradley, in office 1965–1984—who backed the apartheid government) have placed CESA outside the Anglican Communion, although curiously, its ordinations are recognized by the Archbishop of Canterbury. (So, a somewhat similar stance to that of the Episcopal Church towards the single Confederate bishop consecrated during the American Civil War.)

In *Church, Communion, and Culture* we will be contrasting the model of the "Old World" Church of England (post-revolution and a reformed monarchical establishment) with that of the "New World" democratic entity that quickly evolved in early America, thereby giving us two complementary but quite different forms of polity. In so doing, we will follow the life and work of Bishop Samuel Seabury in order to demonstrate that global Anglicanism is indeed one faith, but one that split into two worlds.

Put more sharply, readers might like to ask themselves if they believe in the pre-eminence of a God-willed authoritarianism? Or, an inalienable right to equality? The first model—that of the Old World—offers monarchy, and even if one that is benign, kind, and good, its citizens are "*subjects* in a realm." "Subject" here means deference: there are those who are born or made to rule over you. By way of contrast, the second model—that of the New World—is democratic, and governance and government can be changed by the consent and will of the people. You, the citizen, are their equal.

Modern European democracies that have retained monarchies have recalibrated the role of the ruler into sacred-symbolic and other functional duties. This creates the space and conditions for the democratic processes to work without the intervention of arbitrary and unaccountable power. Of course, democracy is by no means perfect, and even in the early years of the twenty-first century we have witnessed democratically elected leaders trying to reform the very processes that placed them in power, so that they will become (Caesar-like?, or King-like?) no longer subject to the will of the people. Democracy is not immune from despotic and autocratic threats.

It is here that both the Old World and New World orders depend on the rule of law: judges and courts to keep those in power in-check. Threats to fair and just social order occur when courts and judges are persecuted or manipulated by politicians or rulers. Or the politicians and the rulers are the possessors, implementers, and arbiters of the law—as still happens in Old World state churches under its leaders (ecclesiastical law). Much as the story of ancient Israel unfolds in the Old Testament, monarchy carries risks. Not least because monarchy, and certain models of episcopacy, always carries theocracy within its DNA. Any religion or church of the state that has the power to anoint and proclaim the monarch will play a significant part in the ecology of unaccountable power.

When Richard Hooker (1554–1600), one of the finest Anglican theologians ever, was writing *Of the Lawes of Ecclesiastical Polity*, his magnum opus, at the end of the sixteenth century, he was seeking to outline a form of social order that was fair, just, and tolerant. His work subtly crafts arguments for loyal dissent, liberty of conscience, and a form of thinking and acting that does not capitulate to the forces of totalitarian religious or political rule. Over several volumes, Hooker's *Lawes* offer a kindly and critical vision for order that remains keenly alive to the threats posed by theocratic power, whether by monarch or church leadership.

As time has gone on, the Old World order has declined in power and value, and the New World order has become the more globally accepted norm. In some respects, this might also help us understand why Americans insist on the separation of church and state (unlike Europe), but are at the same time much keener on religion mixing in politics (unlike Europe). Once you understand what the state represents (e.g., monarchy, unaccountable power, etc.) and what politics can be (e.g., democratic, not autocratic, etc.), then faith in public life evolves differently.

But to be clear, Anglicanism is still one faith, albeit in two different worlds. The parallels with "two nations divided by one common language"—a dictum often attributed to Oscar Wilde, George Bernard Shaw, and others—will be striking. How can it be that one faith is responsible for the origin and authenticity of two quite different worlds?

Expansion and Retraction

All empires ultimately turn to dust, and most religious systems of belief either unravel, or evolve in order to adapt to the demands of their environment. Empires are frequently proactive and on the offensive, albeit any expansionism is likely to be rooted in fear. Churches and denominations are generally reactive subsets within this cultural chemistry, though normally reluctant to concede that they are rarely proactive. At the very least we need to understand the role fear plays in nationhood, wars, pogroms. Fear needs hate to breathe.

Fear not only has a history; it also drives history. In terms of nationhood, that drive can stem from the fear of existential annihilation, and so is likely to cultivate preemptive atrocities. It can also, at the same time, find space within a dominant and oppressive regime that fears accountability. Each major fear in every generation has a life of its own. We no longer fear the Black Death, or experience the paranoia of the Cold War. But fears appear in new guises all the time—Covid-19, AIDS-HIV, terrorism, and the climate crises, for example, all point to fear being some kind of major key to understanding how societies degenerate if they fail to address their fears, and instead seek to evade them through displaced violence and oppression.

My claim that a single representative event in 1784 decisively split Anglicanism and signaled its end might seem strange, and certainly controversial. After all, there was no Anglican Communion in 1784, and there was not to be such a thing for almost another hundred years. So how could an ecclesiastical body be aborted before it was even conceived? The answer, to a large extent, is rooted in unarticulated fears.

In 1784, the Church of England feared many things it could not identify or discern, let alone control. These included republics that might divest themselves of monarchies, or had already done so. There was still the fear of a Catholic (Jacobite) coup, and the consequences for clergy, which could have been violent and murderous. And bishops feared losing control of episcopacy, oversight, and governance.

So Seabury was not consecrated, as he would have wished, within the Church of England. This was not for his lack of will or desire, but rather because of the unresolved fears of his would-be consecrators. In abdicating responsibility and postponing a decision (a trait present to this day amongst the episcopacy in England), the English bishops were in the end left with no choice save to accept a fait-accompli and face the fact that while Anglicanism was still one faith, it was now operating in two quite different worlds.

The beginning of the end—the downfall of global Anglicanism—can be precisely dated to Seabury's consecration. That said, even without it, the postcolonial era would have delivered the same fate in any case, only later. Global Anglican polity was always heavily dependent on the strength of English imperialism through the British Empire. As this has dissolved, so it has left the Church of England marooned with an identity—and responsibilities—it is unable to bear the burden of. Put plainly, it cannot carry its own weight, let alone the other freight it is often tasked with bearing. So degeneration and collapse are therefore inevitable, until such time as the body comes to some more reasoned mind as to what it can shoulder.

History as we know it is a relatively modern discipline. Although historians have existed since ancient times, modern historiography is, indeed, modern. It is Janus-like, insofar as it faces both backward and forward. The work of the historian lies in recognizing the face of the past in the present, and perhaps casting an eye towards the future. The critical task is to name and set aside the deceptive portrayals we have inherited in the present, for fear of repeated caricatures in the future. Any arrangement of dates and events cannot be comprehensive, ever, so even the most open-minded histories can risk being colorblind, or exercises in gender or ethnic editing and redaction. The past is ultimately as complex as the present, and all the historian can do is chart a path through the past to the present. I wager that the best explanations for what happened before will also be the best guides to what might happen next.

Church, Communion, and Culture is a story of expansion and retraction. It is also a story of degeneration and eventual implosion. It charts the relationship between the British Empire and the Church of England, especially their respective decline and deterioration. Degradation and degeneration describe acts or processes that reduce something to a lower state or condition, or where its quality is spoiled or even destroyed. Societies, soil, and social bodies can all degenerate as a result of external affliction or inner processes, such as ageing, the depletion of disease, and eventually death itself.

Degeneration or degeneracy may also describe what happens to those people who are made to feel they have no value or matter less than others in society. It can refer to national or ethnic attitudes to other peoples, just as much as it refers to the decline of a person's dignity or standing. Degeneration results in a loss of place, status, respect, and reputation. The term implies a depreciation in value, and the deprecation of others. In human anatomy, "senescence" describes the gradual collapse of the body—inwardly—as it yields to age and infirmity. Just as this comes to all of us individually, it also applies to empires and nations. Nothing is forever.

Church, Communion, and Culture explores the expansion, gradual retraction, decline, and fall of the British Empire. Or, more specifically, it seeks to flush out the English interests concealed in appeals to Britishness, and especially the role played by the Church of England as the spiritual arm of the British Empire. This book aims to show how attitudes to slavery, class, and racism played a part in the English bolstering their empire and church in the adoption of their hierarchical worldviews and practices. Yet at the same time, by regarding the rest of the world as somehow lesser than themselves, both the British Empire and Church of England slowly moved from domination and expansion into a state of degeneration. This is a story of national and spiritual hubris in their shared desire for preeminence across the global stage.

The process of degeneration is cyclical, natural, and normal. It is also something that individuals or societies can bring upon themselves. *Church, Communion, and Culture* is concerned with how an empire and a national church breaks down and falls apart. In the post-war era, which is also the postcolonial era, that degeneration has been rapid. So fast, in fact, that those still inclined to succumb to the mystique of the British Empire have found the speed of British decline to be traumatic. In this book, we seek to explain how the fortunes of the British Empire and the Church of England were always in lock-step, and show how the decline of one leads to the deterioration and decline of the other.

Telling the story of an empire and church degenerating and waning in tandem is a challenging task at the best of times. However, I have endeavored to ensure the rich complexity of this saga will engage the curiosity, memory, and inquisitiveness of the reader. To that end, there are three parts to the book, broadly themed around the past, present, and future.

Church, Communion, and Culture inevitably makes some accommodating use of the template set out by the sweeping narrative of Edward Gibbon (1737–1794) and his *History of the Decline and Fall of the Roman Empire*,[8] which sketches the ascendancy of the English, manifest in church and empire, but also indicates where the seeds of eventual collapse were to be found. While Gibbon's work has its critics—anti-Semitism, Islamophobia, Orientalism, and the like are standard charges—the sheer scope of this epic narrative remains substantial and reputable.

Gibbon challenged established church history and proposed that the estimated numbers of Christian martyrs had been hugely exaggerated. Given that many early accounts of martyrdom are hagiographic and idealized, if not mythologized, as is now widely known and accepted, Gibbon's thesis on the estimated number of martyrs is reasonable. Yet at the time, Christianity's adopted version of its early history had rarely been questioned. Gibbon's critique was sound, but also shocking for its day.

In *The Decline and Fall of the British Empire, 1781–1997*, Piers Brendon claims that Gibbon "became the essential guide for Britons anxious to plot their own imperial trajectory. . . . They found the key to understanding the British Empire in the ruins of Rome."[9] Like Gibbon, an important aspect of our concern in this book is not just why the British Empire and the Church of England have been in steady decline in the post-war years, but to try to explain why it has taken so long and appeared to be so slow (and then suddenly very rapid).

Gibbon broadly held to a framework that he believed accounted for the decline and eventual disintegration of Rome. First, the very forces that made Rome great—its legions and armed forces—turned on the emperors and their degenerate regimes. Second, the emperors, out of concern for their survival, and needing to appease both the armed forces and the public, unavoidably reduced their authority and mystique with ever-more expedient political compromises that weakened social organization, governmental structures, law, and order. Third, the enemies of Rome—natural disasters and their consequential harm; stretched economic and resource-related crises; revolts and invasions from hostile forces; and internal strife or civil war—broke the fabric of the Empire apart.

At first sight, and certainly to most English citizens today, the rapid disintegration of the British Empire seems to be most unlike that which befell Rome. Yet while it is true that the armed forces have not revolted against their government, the history of the colonies—rebellion, revolt, emerging nationalism and eventual independence—is arguably just a different and less cataclysmic road to the same end-point. Natural, economic, and social crises have also played their part.

While few English elites cling to the myth of a dangerous memory—that much of the rest of the world was better off under British sovereignty and rule—the reality is quite different. During the Cold War and in the post-war era, Britain was reduced to the role of a missile base for America, and in terms of trade, overtaken by Japan, the European Union, and slowly but surely, China and India. The Empire is no more, and Britain no longer great.

Similarly, Gibbon's work can be applied to the fortunes of the Church of England, which served, to a large extent, as the spiritual arm of the British Empire. The Anglican Communion is a kind of quasi-ecclesial "commonwealth" that has been riven apart by factionalism between wings representing liberals and conservatives, progressives and traditionalists, Anglo-Catholics and Evangelicals. The disputes on gender, sexuality, authority, order, and autonomy are baked into the postcolonial life and legacy of the Church of England, and it has hardly begun to take account of its history and responsibility for the era of empire.

The structure of the Anglican Communion itself has been reduced to an opt-in body on issues and policies, but with few mechanisms to exclude others, discipline, or censure for dissent. Whereas a bishop in some far-flung overseas colony defying the Archbishop of Canterbury a century ago would have seemed inconceivable, it is now so routine as to not even merit so much as a comment in the media, nor indeed a word from Lambeth Palace.

However, *Church, Communion, and Culture* is not concerned with the long-term palliative care of the Church of England and triaging the self-inflicted wounds of wider global Anglicanism. This book is more concerned with sketching an account of the Church of England's effective endorsement of slavery and the financial benefits derived from the trade. The Church of England has until recently evaded scrutiny and transparency in these actions through its pre-eminent position as the established church. In so doing, it has been long opposed, historically, to democratic accountability and open governance, preferring instead to stay within a privileged monarchical pattern of control over clergy and laity that merely pays lip service to egalitarian and elected assemblies.

Approach and Method

Critical history, in contrast, refuses to revere the past. In fact, it rejects such constructions of reality and valorizations of the past, precisely in order to inaugurate those processes that can create something wholly new. Plainly, the danger is that one will be unfair to the past.

As a way forward, I have adopted my usual approach to such enterprises, and drawn on the groundbreaking work of George Lindbeck, who approached and interpreted theology and religion as a cultural-linguistic phenomenon. Lindbeck viewed theology and religion as "regulative" for culture, devising rules and codes that enabled religious institutions to navigate or avoid, and resist or adopt cultural norms.[10] Taken as a whole, the approach and method adopted in the book is one of critical-cultural theory.

As readers will therefore appreciate, this book takes a critical-cultural approach to the favored (historical) story of worldwide Anglicanism and the Church of England, and to the story it tells itself ("serious fiction") and the wider world. This is done in order to challenge the antiquarian and monumental narratives, and likewise the current information-led scientific approaches, that are primarily interested in replicating missional growth through the elevation of training and techniques at the expense of knowledge and wisdom.

Church, Communion, and Culture also shows how external threats to the body-politic have been handled. Revolutions—political, social, and economic—have all caused the Church of England to adjust, adapt, and evolve. Likewise, climate-related crises and natural disasters have also had a powerful impact on the identity of global Anglicanism, which have also fed into the economic, social, and ecclesiastical evolution of denominations.

There is a natural process of degeneration. Not least since the term "degenerate" assumes a normativity, and implies a deterioration in character that departs from basic standards of living or the simplest ideals for normal human life. There is some irony here, since at the height of the powers of an empire, or for that matter the global command enjoyed by the Church of England through the British Empire, the rest of the world would be understood as degenerate, and the dominating sovereign power as pristine.

Even at the beginning of the twentieth century, church and empire regarded (so-called) "degenerates" as covering those with disabilities, "the heathen," "the poor," prostitutes and criminals, certain nationalities (e.g., the Irish) and peoples (i.e., notably Jews and Arabs), and, of course, most other non-Caucasian ethnic groups.

All such groups were held to be inherently weak, and more likely to have hereditary diseases, to capitulate to the temptations of crime, and to be unrestrained in animal-like urges and reproductive capacities. As such, degenerates were deemed to be a threat to civilization itself, and unless weeded out, properly controlled, or educated, would likely swamp the intellectual and moral middle classes. In the meantime, degenerates were to be pitied.

Empire, Degeneration, and Disintegration

What became known as "degeneration theory" was a corruption of Darwinian evolutionary theories—yet it found a welcome host in the British Empire and the Church of England well into the mid- to late twentieth century. However, as this book argues, the actual state of degeneration is far better applied to church and empire. It is the steady deterioration, implosion, and collapse in power and authority that has rendered these vehicles as rusting hulks or slowly rotting husks. Key to this is some understating of what the degeneration consists of, if there is to be any regeneration.

Downfalls are a normal part of the cycle of life in the history of regimes. While regimes may remain at some peak for centuries, they do in the end reach a phase where they are staving off decay and decline. The teleology of denominations (i.e., their long-term projected lifespan and development) is more complex, as we shall see. Yet even here, the vast majority—at least in the Protestant orbit—rise and fall. Revivals will come and go, but the temporal is not eternal.[11]

The middle ground between rise and fall is the hope of revival or regeneration. Yet such hopes, if realized, are not without cost. In the film *Regeneration*, from the novel of the same name by Pat Barker,[12] we encounter traumatized and shell-shocked English officers from the First World War. Doctor William Rivers at the Craiglockhart war hospital (actually a converted stately home in the Highlands of Scotland) is tasked with restoring the sanity of the officers.

When Siegfried Sassoon publishes his declaration of protest against the war, the authorities decide to have him admitted to Craiglockhart and declared insane. Other patients, unable to function as soldiers, are only partially rehabilitated. The methods for dealing with their trauma are themselves alarming. But more alarming still is the knowledge that upon any signs of recovery, they will be repatriated to their regiment and returned to the front line, once again to face further trauma and injury—and almost certain death.

Barker's tragically bleak *Regeneration* is not some positive narrative charting a trajectory of progressive transformation. It is a bitterly ironic saga—even a parable—of ultimately hopeless and wasteful repetition, and it enables the reader to descend the depths of an era bound to a downward-spiraling of inevitable degeneration. In *Regeneration*, young men are made to follow in the footsteps of their fallen or wounded comrades, and can only prove their future worth to their peers by further acts of pointless sacrifice or heroism. Their suffering (but not their demonstrative failure) is actually *valued* as an ideal.

Barker's parable is a story of a "civilization" that upholds its normativity and superiority over others without ever being able to comprehend its utter degeneracy. Furthermore, the degeneration the novel criticizes is not on the Western Front, but rather in the jingoistic political and social attitudes overlaid with church-sponsored sacralization that laud such pointless acts of sacrifice and waste.[13] The birth, rise, decline, and fall of a denomination can lead to new life. But as I argue, only after a death, usually precipitated by a crisis, catastrophe, or revolution. Endless reform can only postpone the inevitable. Death can be delayed, but it cannot be denied. Denominations are mortal creatures.

In today's more sensitive climes, we might say that many of those who suffer most in *Regeneration* are also the victims of significant moral injury.[14] For the most part, they cannot perceive that their wider social realm has no concept of what is taking place—in France and Belgium, or in Scotland, where they are in theory being cared for and rehabilitated—in what is still one of the most costly and catastrophic conflicts in human history. Yet so-called moral injury would be a fair diagnosis, accounting for some of the suffering—a mental, spiritual, and physical collapse resulting from a trauma such as betrayal (by a body or persons hitherto trusted) or being made to witness or participate in an extremely serious moral transgression, such as the killing of innocent civilians or prisoners of war.

Moral injury can produce harmful and long-term dissonance. Symptoms in individuals and groups can include alienation, deep-seated mental and physical reactions to trauma (as remembered, or new) that then trigger shock, anger, guilt, shame, depression, and despair, and can even lead to suicide. Common to these symptoms is the underlying sense of betrayal that will attack ethical, existential, and spiritual identity. Societies that seek to compensate for this by investing the fallen with romantic-sacralized heroism only risk deeper forms of alienation. That said, it may take generations for justice and reparation to crystallize into a more holistic framework. Anger and bitterness, meanwhile, will take their toll.[15]

To counter this, movements like Black Lives Matter have sought to help themselves and others through their enduring suffering in the communalization of their trauma. Naturally, this is not an end in itself. Most of those who suffer serious moral injury seek to be empowered, valued as equals, respected, and ultimately to become at home with the culture that inflicted degradation, trauma, and degeneration upon their people and places.

It is precisely this kind of elegiac "soul repair" with a vision for spiritual, social, and political integration that one finds in the speeches of Martin Luther King Jnr., Desmond Tutu, Nelson Mandela, and Mahatma Gandhi. Their answer to deep moral injury is not repay in kind. Rather, it is to shine nothing less than the light of truth on the degeneration that led to and still perpetuates the multiple betrayals of inequality. Perhaps, therefore, the role of churches in communion with each other and the world, and with God, is to shine a light on the cultures that divide us and denigrate others. Perhaps the vision for a communion lies in engaging with culture, but also learning to transcend those elements that make us all somehow less.

Illustrations

Bishop Samuel Seabury's Life and Times

Courtesy of the General Theological Seminary Archives, Bishop Payne Library

Engraving of The General Theological Seminary at New York (courtesy Bishop Payne Library, VTS Alexandria, VA).

FOR Sale by *David & Nathaniel Ledyard*, 400 Buſhels OATS,—300 Buſhels White BEANS.—100 Barrels CIDER, (of an excellent Quality,)—and a few Kegs of LARD. *Groton, April* 22, 1795.

TEN DOLLARS REWARD.

RAN away on the night of the 11th inſtant, a negro man named JACK, about four feet 6 or 8 inches high, very black, talks broken, walks with his toes out: had on when he went away, a green coatee, patched with blue, red veſt, old blue trowſers, a checked woolen ſhirt, a black hat with a low crown, an old pair of ſhoes; he ſtole and carried away with him ſundry articles of clothing, among which were, a blue broad cloth ſailors jacket, ſix holland ſhirts, a pair of grey elaſtic trowſers, all almoſt new. Said negro is a very ſlow moulded fellow, carried away a ſmall red and white dog, with a bobtail; he is about 25 or 26 years old:—Whoever will take up ſaid runaway, and return him, or ſecure him, ſo that the ſubſcriber may have him, ſhall be entitled to the above reward, and all neceſſary charges paid by

New-London, April 21, 1795. JOSEPH SISTARE.

A Stallion, Jack & Jill, and two three year old Mules well broke for gears or riding, one young pacing horſe, one likely cow, to be ſold by the ſubſcriber in Preſton: The Stallion is CINCINNATI, five years old, 15 1-2 hands high, well made, blood bay colour, beautifully marked in his face and feet, trots and canters genteely; if not ſold will cover at my ſtable, the enſuing ſeaſon, at a moderate price. The Jack was imported, is a good ſire, will be ſold for young mules, delivered within 18 months from the date hereof. The Jill has brought me a Jack, ſired by the Royal Standard, three years old this ſpring, and will cover at my ſtable the enſuing ſeaſon; the young Jack would have ſold for ſixty pounds when four months old; I have a yearling Jill from the ſame ſtock, worth half the money. Who would not wiſh to raiſe ſtock ſo valuable.

Preſton, April 8, 1795. THOMAS BRANCH.

***Connecticut Gazette*, April 23, 1795. Note that the reward offered for the slave Jack and his return is sandwiched between advertisements for sacks of oats and the sale of horses. Slaves were commodified, and described as one might personal lost or stolen property.**

JOHN I. GLOVER,

INFORMS his friends, that on the firſt Day o[f] May next, he purpoſes to remove his reſidenc[e] to No. 190, Pearl-Street, three doors below th[e] Fly-Market; the ſame ſtreet in which he now re ſides. New-York, April 13, 1795.

INFORMATION is hereby given, to all who hav[e] ſubſcribed for the Chriſtian Herald, or Unio[n] Magazine,—deſigned as an aid to a concert o[f] prayer, now in the United States; that the pub lication of ſaid Magazine is *deferred* till the fi[rſt] of May next—and will then appear without fur ther delay, under the title of—The United State[s] Chriſtian Magazine. The reaſons of this delay and the ſmall variation in the title of the work, it is hoped will be fully ſatisfactory to ſubſcribers, when laid before them.

TEN DOLLARS REWARD.

RAN away on the night of the 11th inſtant, a negro man named JACK, about four feet 6 or 8 inches high, very black, talks broken, walks with his toes out: had on when he went away, a green coatee, patched with blue, red veſt, old blue trowſers, a checked woolen ſhirt, a black hat with a low crown, an old pair of ſhoes; he ſtole and carried away with him ſundry articles of clothing, among which were, a blue broad cloth ſailors jacket, ſix holland ſhirts, a pair of grey elaſtic trowſers, all almoſt new. Said negro is a very ſlow moulded fellow, carried away a ſmall red and white dog, with a bobtail; he is about 25 or 26 years old:— Whoever will take up ſaid runaway, and return him, or ſecure him, ſo that the ſubſcriber may have him, ſhall be entitled to the above reward, and all neceſſary charges paid by

New-London, April 21, 1795. JOSEPH SISTARE.

TAKEN *up 8th April, in Connecticut River, near Saybrook Ferry, a ſlightly built two maſt* BOAT; *her foremaſt gone, her mainmaſt, mainſail and boom on board, her top timbers chiefly ſaſſafras, her deck partly pine boards;—ſaid boat now lyes at Saybrook Ferry.— The owner is deſired to prove property, pay charges, and take her away.* SAMUEL SANFORD.

April 20, 1795.

The advertisement is repeated on April 30, 1795, and this time underneath an advertisement for *The United States Christian Magazine.*

MANY of the Creditors of Joſeph and Richardſon Cornwall, having neglected to bring in their Accounts, they are once more earneſtly requeſted thereto; as it is impoſſible to adjuſt the Dividend due to each Creditor, until that is done; and it is hoped that all Perſons who are ſtill in any Shape indebted to ſaid Creditors, will make immediate Payment, without further Trouble to themſelves, or to

JACOB WATSON,
ISAAC LOW, } Truſtees.
WILLIAM TONGUE,

31 34
Sept. 5, 1764.

RUN-AWAY the 12th of laſt Month, Auguſt, from the Subſcriber, living in Roxbury, in the County of Morris, Two Negro Men; one about 20 Years of Age, a ſpritely well-ſet Fellow, underſtands all Sorts of farming Work, and pretends to be a Fiddler; the other about 30 Years of Age, underſtands Houſe Work, Baking, Waſhing, and Cooking; he knows but little about farming: He is a thick clumſy Fellow, with a Scar near the Corner of his Eye: They had on when they went away, Tow Shirts, and Trowſers; the young Fellow had a half worn Wool Hat, & a Soldier's Red Coat, and was barefooted; the other had on an old light blue Kerſy Veſt, with a thick grey Kearſy Lining, half worn Shoes, and no Hat, tho' they may have changed their Clothes. Whoever will take up the above ſaid Negroes, ſo that I may have them again, ſhall have Three Pounds Reward, or Thirty Shillings for either, and all reaſonable Charges, paid them by me,

AUGUSTINE REID.

September 3, 1764. 31 34

The New York Gazette, September 3, 1764, offers a reward for the return of two slaves. The sum of £3 for both or 30 shillings for either is advertised. One of the slaves is described as "clumsy" who "pretends to be a fiddler." The slaves are said to understand housework and some farming. The older slave has a "sear" (i.e., scar) over one eye.

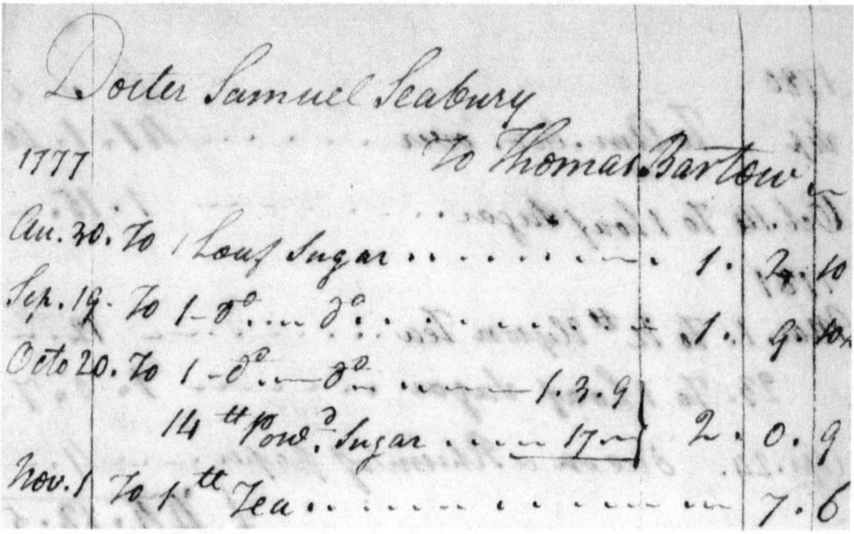

Docter Samuel Seabury
1777 To Thomas Bartow Dr

Au. 20.	To 1 Loaf Sugar	1.	2. 10
Sep. 19.	To 1 — do. ... do.	1.	9. 10
Octo 20.	To 1 — do. — do. — 1. 3. 9		
	14 lb Powd. Sugar — 17	2.	0. 9
Nov. 1	To 1 lb Tea		7. 6

Samuel Seabury's household accounts show that, in common with many others living in America before the War of Independence, vast quantities of tea and sugar were bought and consumed, despite their heavy cost.

Sir, New York, March 28, 1783.

The Opinion I have of Your Candour, & of Your Inclination to preserve & Support the Church of which We are both Members, induces me to write this Letter. There was a Time when the Interests of that Church could not be in better or safer Hands than Yours; I flatter myself that Your Attachment to it still continues, & on this Principle I address You.

The Independency of America, in all probability, will soon effectually take Place. As this Event will remove all Ground of Contest, so should it extinguish all Animosity between the Inhabitants — this is at once the Dictate of Religion, common Interest & sound Policy. You are sensible that this Event will also very much affect our Church, not only in this City, but through all the Continent. This Subject is very near my Heart; & on this, I wish to confer with You. Perhaps Business, or some other Occasion may call You to pass between Philadelphia & the Manor of Livingston this Spring; in that Case, I should be glad to have an Interview with You either at Staten Island, Elizabeth Town, Dobbs' Ferry, or any other Place You would appoint.

But if an Interview be impracticable, I should be much obliged to You if You would favour me with Your Sentiments by a Letter, & let me know what You think of the present State of the Episcopal Churches & Clergy in America. You would also oblige me by giving me Your Opinion about my Continuance here. My Wish is to remain in New York, if I can live in Peace; & such is my Idea of Your Candour & Judgment, that I would be determined by Your Opinion.

Whe-

Whether I have any personal Enemies, is a Matter of which I am totally ignorant. I am conscious that I have not injured any Individual in his Character, Property or Person; & have done good Offices to many. The general Part I took in the late Contest was the Result of Principle & Conscience; to their Dictates I honestly adhered, & conceived I was thereby promoting the best Interests & Welfare of America. But the Views of Divine Providence, respecting this Country, were different; & it is my indispensible Duty to acquiesce in the Decisions of Providence. By recognizing the Independency of America, the King gives up his Claim to my Allegiance; I am thenceforth at full Liberty to transfer it to that State where Providence may place me; & I need not tell you that the same Principles, the same Sense of the Sacredness of an Oath, & the same Dictates of Conscience, will lead me in future, as they have done hitherto, to observe inviolably my Oath of Allegiance.

I could say much more on this & other Subjects; but the present is not the proper Time or Place; & therefore shall only add, that in no Stage of the Contest has my Regard for you been altered or abated; & that whether I remain here or go elsewhere, you shall always have the best Wishes of,

Sir,

Your affectionate & humble Servt

Charles Inglis

P.S. A speedy Answer to this will be very acceptable

Honble. James Duane Esqr

Charles Inglis's declaration of American allegiance, 1783—after the British were defeated and mostly expelled. Samuel Seabury signed a comparable declaration.

A Form of Consecrating Churches, Chapels, and Church-Yards, or Places of Burial.

¶ When the Bishop & Clergy (two at least being present) have entered the Church in their habits, as they walk up to the Altar, they shall repeat the 24th Psalm, the Bishop beginning, & the Clergy answering, Verse by Verse.

The earth is the Lords and all that therein is: the compass of the world, and they that dwell therein.

For he hath founded it upon the seas: and prepared it upon the floods.

Who shall ascend into the hill of the Lord: or who shall rise up in his holy place?

Even

Samuel Seabury's handwritten prayers for the consecration of chapels, churches and places of burial. Seabury writes in a style that mimics *Book of Common Prayer* collects and prayers, and the tone of such intercessions would have been familiar and resonant to those in his episcopal care who only knew the English Prayer Book at this time.

Occasional Prayers to be used in Churches

The following Prayer was used at New London during the prevalence of the Dysentery in the year 87.

O Almighty Lord God, the Creator of all things, the Lord of life & death, of sickness & health; Regard our supplications, we humbly beseech Thee: And, as Thou hast thought proper to visit our sins by great sickness & mortality, in the midst of thy judgment, O Lord, remember thy mercy: Have pity upon us miserable sinners, & withdraw from us the grievous sickness with which we are afflicted. May this thy fatherly correction have its due influence upon us, by leading us to consider how frail & uncertain our life is; That so we may apply our hearts

As the Diocese of Connecticut began to acquire some identity apart from the Church of England liturgy, more prayers were improvised by Seabury. This prayer is for a time of hardship, dated 1787—Britain was still blockading America, preventing imports and exports, and harvests were also affected by adverse weather.

Occasional Prayers

hearts unto that heavenly wisdom which in the end will bring us to everlasting life, through Jesus Christ our Lord. Amen.

¶ For a ſick perſon who deſires the Prayers of the Church.

O Lord, look down from heaven, we humbly beſeech Thee, behold, visit, & relieve thy sick ſervant for whom our prayers are desired: Look upon him in mercy; comfort him with the ſense of thy goodneſs; preserve him from the temptations of the enemy; give him patience under his affliction, &, in thy good time restore him ~~him~~ to health, & enable him, by thy grace, to lead the residue of his life in thy fear & to thy glory: Or else

Seabury's prayer for "a sick person who desires the prayers of the church."

to be used in Churches.

else give *him* grace so to take thy visitation, that, after this painful life ended, *he* may
dwell with Thee in life everlasting, through
Jesus Christ our Lord. Amen.

¶ For a sick Child.

Almighty God, & merciful Father, to whom
alone belong the issues of life & death: Look
down from heaven, we humbly beseech Thee,
with the eyes of mercy, upon the sick Child
for whom our prayers are desired: Visit *him*,
O Lord, with thy salvation; deliver *him* in
thy good appointed time from *his* bodily pain,
& save *his* soul for thy mercies sake; that if it
shall be thy good pleasure to prolong *his* days
here on earth, *he* may live to Thee, & be an
instrumen of thy glory, by serving Thee faithfully

Seabury's beautiful and exquisite prayer for a sick child.

Occasional Prayers

fully, & doing good in his generation: Or else receive him into those heavenly habitations, where the souls of them that sleep in the Lord Jesus enjoy perpetual rest & felicity. Grant this, O Lord, for thy mercies sake, in the same thy Son our Lord Jesus Christ. Amen.

¶. For a person bound to Sea.

O Eternal God, who alone spreadest out the heavens, & rulest the raging of the sea; who hast compassed the waters with bounds untill day & night come to an end: Be pleased to receive into thy almighty & most gracious protection, the Person of thy servant for whom our prayers are desired; Preserve him from the dangers of the sea, &

The journey from America to Europe was perilous, resulting in regular loss of life due to storms, piracy, or disease. The early Church of England missionary clergy despatched to America might expect to suffer a 25 percent casualty rate. A sea-bound voyage was therefore fraught with risk as Seabury's handwritten prayer reflects.

to be used in Churches.

& from the violence of enemies; & grant that he may return in health & safety to enjoy the blessings of the land, with the fruits of his labours; &, with a thankful remembrance of thy mercies, to praise & glorify thy holy name, through Jesus Christ our Lord. Amen.

¶ For a person under Affliction.

O merciful God, & heavenly Father, who hast taught us in thy Holy Word, that thou dost not willingly afflict, or grieve the children of men: Look with pity, we beseech Thee, upon the sorrows of thy servant for whom our prayers are desired: In thy goodness thou hast thought best to visit him with

Occasional Prayers,

with trouble, & to bring distress upon him. Remember him, O Lord, in mercy; sanctify thy fatherly correction to him; endue his soul with patience under his affliction, & with resignation to thy blessed will; comfort him with a sense of thy goodness; lift up the light of thy countenance upon him, & give him peace, through Jesus Christ our Lord. Amen.

A general prayer penned by Seabury for a person "under affliction." In truth, the reality for many Americans in the late eighteenth century was to know nothing other than affliction in their day-to-day life. Times were hard.

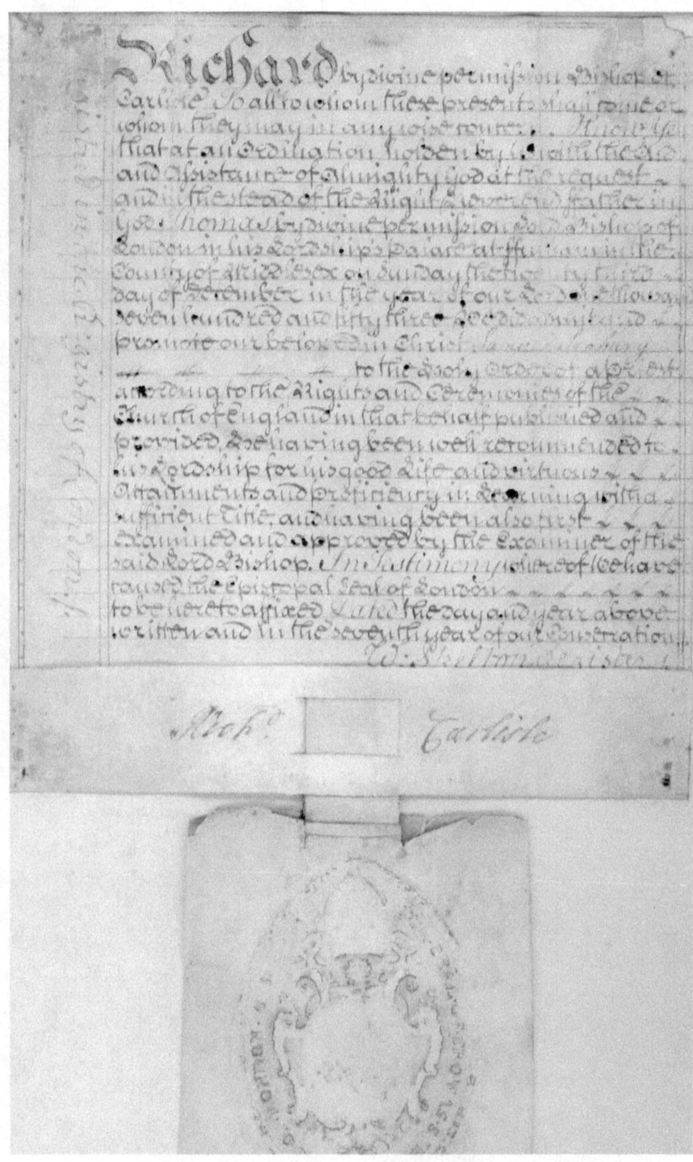

Richard by divine permission Bishop of Carlisle To all to whom these presents shall come or whom they may in any wise concern. Know Ye that at an Ordination holden by us with the aid and assistance of Almighty God at the request and in the stead of the Right Reverend Father in God Thomas by divine permission Lord Bishop of London in his Lordship's Palace at Fulham in the County of Middlesex on Sunday the [illegible] third day of December in the year of our Lord one thousand seven hundred and fifty three We did admit and promote our beloved in Christ [illegible] Seabury to the holy Order of a Priest according to the Rights and Ceremonies of the Church of England in that behalf published and provided, He having been well recommended to his Lordship for his good Life and virtuous Attainments and proficiency in Learning with a sufficient Title, and having been also first examined and approved by the Examiner of the said Lord Bishop. In Testimony whereof We have caused the Episcopal Seal of London to be hereto affixed Dated the day and year above written and in the seventh year of our Consecration.

W. Skelton [illegible]

Richd. Carlisle

Seabury's License confirming his ordination as priest by the bishop of Carlisle in the Church of England. Until the USA acquired its own bishops, ordinations could only be conducted by the Church of England.

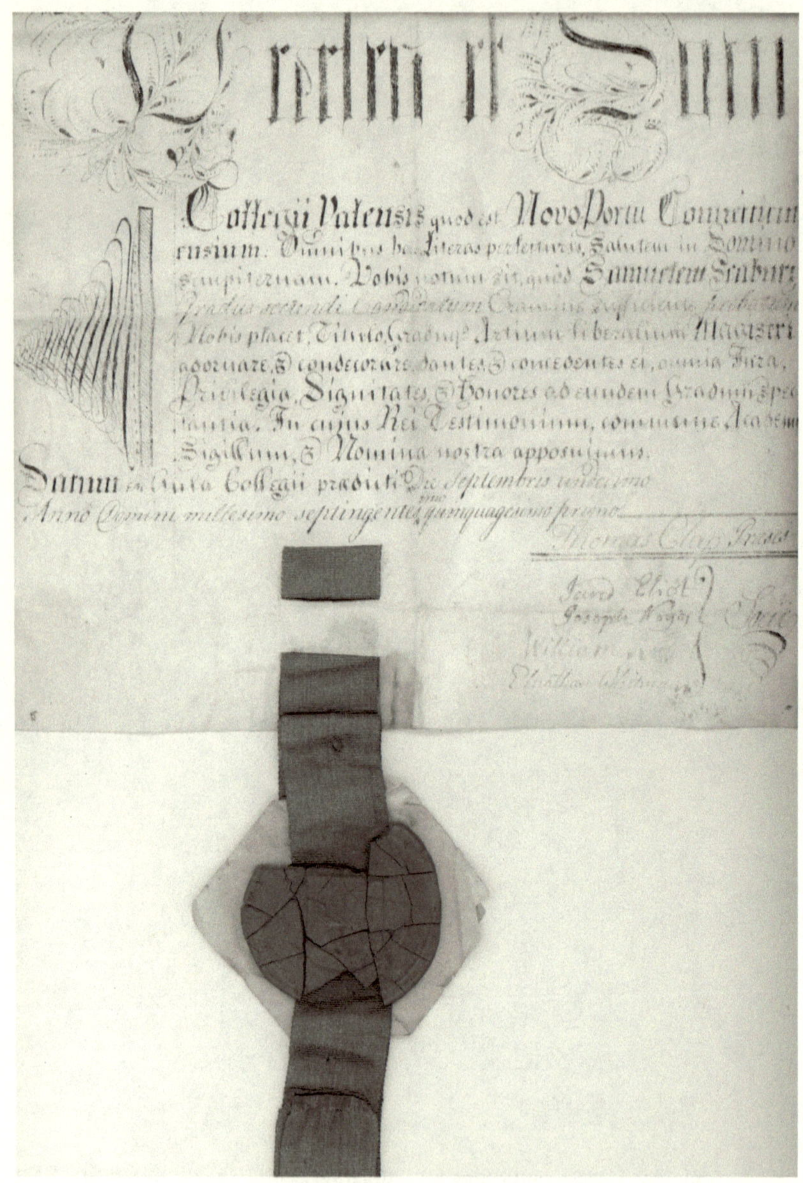

Collegii Yalensis quod est Novo Portu Connecticut-
ensium. Omnibus has Literas perlecturis, Salutem in Domino
sempiternam. Vobis notum sit, quod Samuelem Seabury
Gradus ascendi Candidatum Examine [illegible] probatum
Nobis placet, Titulo, Graduque Artium liberalium Magistri
adornare, & condecorare, dantes & concedentes ei, omnia Jura,
Privilegia, Dignitates, & Honores ad eundem Gradum spec-
tantia. In cujus Rei Testimonium, commune Academ-
Sigillum, & Nomina nostra apposuimus.
Datum in Aula Collegii prædicti Die Septembris undecimo
Anno Domini millesimo septingentesimo quinquagesimo primo

Thomas Clap Præses

Jared Eliot
Joseph Noyes
William [illegible]
Elnathan Whitman

Seabury's Diploma from Yale.

PART ONE

Samuel Seabury's Social World

Life is a seemingly endless stream of ironies. For the most part, when Roman Catholic, Orthodox, or Anglican churches commemorate a person—a saint, martyr, teacher, bishop, or other exemplar—the day that marks their celebration will be their date of birth or death. The churches have few dates set aside in the liturgical calendar for events. (Indeed, I am writing this sentence on one such date—the Feast of the Transfiguration of Jesus, which is August 6.)

When British Prime Minister Harold Macmillan was once asked what was the greatest challenge for a political leader, he replied, "Events, dear boy, events." The same is true for most leaders and organizations. Even church leaders. Events happen. And when they occur, many things are at stake: countries, communities, lives, livelihoods, and entire futures.

The date that the Episcopal Church has set aside to commemorate Samuel Seabury is another event—that of his consecration on November 14, 1784. As events go, it had fewer witnesses than the Transfiguration. But as I seek to show in this book, while this may be a happy theological coincidence, Seabury's consecration was an event of the most enormous portent. (Incidentally, Seabury's date of birth was November 30, St. Andrew's Day, the patron saint of Scotland. The Scottish flag features in a corner of the Episcopal coat of arms to remind American Anglicans of their Scottish ancestry.)

It is also a high irony that the center of the Jacobite Revolts between 1715 and 1745 should be Aberdeen. It was the first Scottish city to proclaim the Stuarts as rightful monarchs, and therefore the hub of rebellion against the Hanoverian monarchs. That Aberdeen should also be the city in which Samuel Seabury was consecrated chimes with the revolutionary tone of the age. English bishops declined to consecrate Seabury as he could not swear an oath of allegiance to George III. The consecration was thus in Aberdeen—the city at the center of the Jacobite Revolt, which is an accident, to be sure, but also a rich irony.

Our purpose here is to throw some light on how events shaped the life of global Anglicanism (or worldwide Episcopalian ecclesial polity), giving it a rich diversity yet also sowing the seeds of its own fissures and fractures. Furthermore, the events that most Anglicans and others might nominate as significant have surprisingly little to do with what has since emerged in the Worldwide Anglican Communion. In fact, most of the events that gave birth to global Anglicanism had very little to do with the church, and certainly not with contentious debates on sexuality, gender, and the like. By retracing the routes that led to such manifest ecclesial diversity, we will gain a different understanding of what it is that keeps Anglicans together, and what it was that set them apart.

The Legacy of Empire

The legacy of empire and church has played a major causal role in inflicting moral injury that has resulted in a long-standing and near-fatal soul-wound on large segments of humanity. Christianity and civilization ought to be two forces for the benefit of all humanity. The church and empire, while laying claim to that mantle, in actual fact did the very opposite. Their combined legacy left communities and nations in tatters, and peoples in despair, with millions of souls left in anguish—yet with a torment that still finds no kind of recognition or rapprochement from the perpetrators. Racism continues, with slavery treated as some unfortunate oversight in an otherwise distant past. The present work of reform and redress, moreover, has simply not reckoned with the pain of the past. Just as postcolonial Britain has collective amnesia about an age of empire, so likewise does the Church of England fail to reckon with its role in the export of its nascent cultural values and outlooks.[16] These include classism, racism, sexism, homophobia, and views on society and politics that are essentially counter-democratic.[17]

As William Faulkner famously notes in *Requiem for a Nun*, the past is never dead—it is not even past.[18] The past is always with us. Likewise,

George Orwell observed in his dystopian novel *1984*, whoever controls the past controls the future, and those who control the present control the past.[19] If English history is in the hands of those who valorize and edit the past, the present and future are unavoidably corrupted. Neat distinctions between the past, present, and future are often illusory, and their separation only serves to support and protect vested interests. To authentically engage with the present, however, would require the agents and conduits of degeneration to face up to their past, and its consequences in the present. That must mean humility, repentance, contrition, respect for all, and courageous compassion are to the fore.

At the same time, *Church, Communion, and Culture* traces the beginning of the end for the British Empire, and the Worldwide Anglican Communion, to a single innocuous act with far-reaching consequences. It is contended that the Worldwide Anglican Communion was irreparably broken on a single day: November 14, 1784. All of the schisms, spats, rows, divisions, and gradual collapses that have taken place since are mere aftershocks following a barely noted earthquake in a backstreet of Aberdeen, Scotland. That first fissure leads to all the later fractures that now herald the break-up of the Worldwide Anglican Communion.[20]

The consecration of Samuel Seabury marked both the beginning and end of the Worldwide Anglican Communion, a century before it could even be said to have properly begun. What split the Anglican Communion before it started was the separation of the Old World (Britain and the Church of England) and the New World (Continental America).

This also helps to re-balance the legacy and culpability for the slave ownership and slave trading, arguing that while much of the blame and guilt has fallen on America, it is the policies and practices of the *English* that now need far greater scrutiny, and whose responsibility in this unprecedented crime against humanity dwarfs American actions. History is not a neat balance-sheet or ledger. English masculinity from the seventeenth to the nineteenth centuries produced heroics and horrors in equal measure, and across India and Africa, to say nothing of the Caribbean, conquest often brought their brand of Western "civilization." The uncomfortable truth, however, is that little of what the English Empire produced was founded on consent. As Sathnam Sanghera notes in his study, great evil and great good were often perpetrated by the same organization, agent, or individual. The postcolonial era is an era of deeper historical enquiry and proper moral reckoning.[21]

Furthermore, the English, with the fulsome complicity of the Church of England, went to extensive lengths to camouflage this uncomfortable truth beneath the umbrella of the *British* Empire. The fact that few English or Britons ever encountered a slave in person, let alone their transporting or working conditions, meant that social and moral awareness of the harm being perpetrated was not engaged with by most members of the public. Moreover, as so many English were financially invested in slavery or its derivatives, any moral issues were subject to the dissonant "out of sight, out of mind."

Critiques of Empire

One critic, Anna Grzymała-Busse,[22] brings together a wealth of historical evidence about papal conflict, excommunications, and ecclesiastical institutions. She reveals how the challenge and example of powerful religious authorities gave rise to secular state institutions and galvanized state capacity. The implications for politics and religion in the USA would become highly significant. In her earlier work, she argues that where churches and national identities have historically fused, churches gain enormous moral authority—and covert, privileged institutional access. These churches then shape policy in back rooms and secret meetings instead of through open democratic channels such as political parties or the ballot box.[23] The Church of England provides a classic paradigm of this, especially through its unique arrangements with government in the House of Lords.

John W. Compton[24] presents a nuanced portrait of the changing values of evangelical voters over the course of the last century. To explain the rise of White Protestant social concern in the latter part of the nineteenth century and its sudden demise at the end of the twentieth century, Compton argued that religious conviction alone was insufficient to motivate empathetic political actions. To understand present tensions, one must pay attention to power, wealth, and culture—and White evangelicals' perception of losses of such things through so-called "liberal" agendas of equality, diversity, social inclusion, and political action.

The eighteenth century was similarly challenged, and it is important to recognize just how "baked in" the social, moral, financial, religious, political, and economic forces of a (largely) English-sponsored imperialism and empire actually were. In turn, this led to such profound and seismic changes across the world, the subsequent developments within Christian denominations were consequential, not causal.[25] To some extent, the melancholy so noticeable in the Church of England and wider Anglican Communion is a condition brought on by the loss of empire and the uncertainty, nascent fears, and uneasiness that the English sense.

As a people, the English face innumerable challenges from within, and yet persist in struggling—vainly and hopelessly—to retain the sovereign position they once held in the world. Just as Stuart Ward's[26] work attempts to do, it is possible to chart the gradual unravelling and disunity of the Anglican Communion. The origin of this malaise arises out of a modern, fundamentally "English condition" (to be discussed later), but one invested in muted cheeriness, passive grumbling, and mild melancholy, enveloped in a culture that valorizes classism, manners, and elitism. It also stems from fear. However, these factors are seldom named. As we shall see, what the English feared from the territories and peoples that they subjugated under the covering mantle of the British Empire—the possibility of their vengeful rebellion and outright revolt—was as awful as the fears of any other empire in history.[27]

The spiritual wing (or arm) of the British Empire—the Church of England for the most part—has adopted a kind of spiritual and historical amnesia here, and instead prefers to speak of mission and a global Communion as its legacy. There is little discussion of its historic complicity in imperial oppression. What the Church of England leadership most fears is its postcolonial irrelevance in a global religious and spiritual marketplace. It fears failure and rebellion—so clings to the remnants of degenerating unity as a means of maintaining some pre-eminence. But fear is the key.

It would be reasonable to conclude that academics are making significant advances in helping us understand how commercial and state interests combined to create empires founded on racism and exploitation yet camouflaged under the protective guise of bringing civilization and Christianity to allegedly inferior peoples. But such endeavor is hardly new. In 1787 an Anglican clergyman, Thomas Clarkson (1760–1846), founded the Society for Effecting the Abolition of the Slave Trade. He had form on the subject. In 1785 Clarkson entered a Latin essay competition at the University of Cambridge. The essay set by the vice chancellor was "Is It Lawful to Make Slaves of Others Against Their Will?" Clarkson had read everything he could, including first-hand accounts and Quaker

Abolitionists making theological arguments against the trade. Clarkson won the prize.

Clarkson's interest might have shifted to new topics in the wake of his win, but he then had, as he later claimed, an intense spiritual experience—a kind of Damascus Road moment—which would lead him to devote the remainder of his life to the abolitionist cause. His Latin essay was translated into English, and in 1786 as *An Essay on the Slavery and Commerce of the Human Species, Particularly the African, Translated from a Latin Dissertation.* Clarkson saw that terrorization, if properly recounted and then fed back to an audience, would produce a different kind of horror and terror—one that resulted in moral action. Put another way, if this is how the (so-called) "civilized" behave towards the allegedly "uncivilized," do the labels themselves not need reversing?

Abolitionists were therefore able to drive even sharper wedges between the advocates of a slave-based economy and the wider public. That fuelled more doubts over the alleged necessity of slavery for civilization, leaving abolitionists freer to argue for the urgency of Christianity over and against the expediency of capitalism.[28] While liberal democratic societies are always work in progress, the Old World order was regressive by comparison. The New World and its (White) regimes looked to liberal values and democratic processes to ensure the freedoms of civic society. However, oppression of the native inhabitants continued. The explanation for the domination of imperialism, irrespective of its coming through a monarchy or some republican democracy, probably lies with capitalism itself, as John Hobson argued in his magisterial study in 1902. Hobson maintained that nationalism did not drive imperialism, but rather it was capitalism and economic exploitation, which were identified as the "taproot" that accounted for the immoral aspects of imperialism.[29]

To be sure, democracy is far from perfect, and nor is it a simple matter in the twenty-first century. Where we have seen the rise of electoral autocracies powered up and turbocharged by populism, we have witnessed the elevation of the strong-armed ruler who suppresses the media, flouts the rule of law, and drives out opposition.[30] Typically, societies where such regimes come to power—electoral authoritarianism ruling through the ballot box or some simulacra of democracy—are ones already deeply scarred by civic trauma, moral turmoil, social injustice, and political breakdown.[31]

All empires ultimately turn to dust, and most religious systems of belief either unravel or evolve in order to adapt to the demands of their environment. Empires are frequently proactive and on the offensive, even though such expansionism is likely to be rooted in fear. Churches and denominations, by contrast, are generally reactive subsets within this cultural chemistry, though normally reluctant to concede that they are rarely proactive.[32]

As we have previously noted, there was no Anglican Communion before 1784. Yet this date marks the terminus of the Communion before it even began. In view of this, we now turn to a consideration of Samuel Seabury himself, and the events surrounding him that led to the birth and eventual fate of worldwide Anglicanism.

Seabury and the Birth of Non-British Anglicanism

Samuel Seabury (1729–1796) was born into a moderately prosperous slave-owning family from Connecticut. Seabury's father was originally a Congregationalist minister, but had become a priest of the Church of England in 1730. Samuel Seabury was raised as an Anglican, and went on to study theology at Yale College before studying for medicine at Edinburgh University from 1752–1753. During this time, he was ordained a deacon in the Church of England by the bishop of Lincoln, and some months later a priest by the bishop of Carlisle. Seabury thus returned to America in 1754 as a qualified medical doctor (after just a year of study) and an ordained Church of England minister (following three years of study).

In common with many Church of England clergy in America when the war of 1776 broke out, Seabury was loyal to the British and had fled to the city of New York, eventually enrolling as chaplain for the King's American Regiment in 1778. For much of the war, he was a noted opponent of Alexander Hamilton. When the War of Independence finally ended in 1783, he opted to stay in America and was loyal to the new government. So, on the face of it, travelling to England to seek consecration must have seemed straightforward. The almost newly independent colonies needed clergy, and for that they needed bishops who would ordain them. After being elected as bishop in Connecticut, albeit as second choice, with the preferred candidate declining due to reasons of health and infirmity, Seabury travelled to England in genuine hope and serious expectation. But the reception he met with from the Church of England bishops was, to put it kindly, cool—bordering on cold disinterest. He spent the better part of a year trying to negotiate for American episcopal orders, but found himself being passed from pillar to post, and treated with a mixture of bemusement and studied indifference. Exasperated, he contemplated taking episcopal orders from the Danish Lutheran Church. Was it to be, or not to be?

It was the intervention of Dr. Martin Routh, a very young president of Magdalen College, Oxford, who dissuaded Seabury from this path. Instead, Routh suggested, why not look north—to the Episcopal bishops of Scotland? He had been persuaded that Danish bishops were not of the "apostolic succession" kind, and that if the ontological lineage was to be maintained in the New World from the Old World, then continuity of episcopacy in the Church of England, which had remained intact despite the Reformation, was the only option. The stage was therefore set. American Episcopalians, in 1784, might have turned east and claimed Lutheran orders. But they turned north, and to Scotland.

So Seabury was not consecrated, as he might have wished, within the Church of England. This was not for his lack of desire or effort. It was due to the unresolved fears of his would-be consecrators. In abdicating responsibility and postponing a decision, the English bishops were in the end left with no choice. They had to accept that Anglicanism was now one faith, but operating in two quite separate worlds.

American States Before Being United

How often, I wonder, is it the case that, when one speaks of the "United States of America," one takes for granted the first word of that title? How easy it is, indeed, to forget the powerful statement being made in this name. For, in speaking of these states as "united," one speaks not only to the present state of unification, but also to the former state of division. It is, perhaps ironically, to matters of unity and disunity alike that one points when making the statement "the United States of America." For, only out of the latter has the former come. And, indeed, it is about just such matters of division, diversity, and autonomy that this first chapter is concerned, because it is with these characteristics that the formative decades of the eighteenth-century colonies come to be seen. In such matters does the church, as much as the state, experience its fair share.

A cursory glance at the ecclesial landscape of early-eighteenth-century America reveals a division of denominational affiliation roughly along the lines of colonial geographical subsets. Up in the New England colonies, for example—comprising Massachusetts, New Hampshire, and Connecticut—it is the Congregational Church, formed from the Puritan tradition of the early pilgrims, that dominated the religious scene. In these colonies, the Congregational Church received legal establishment, rendering the full enjoyment of civil liberties dependent upon membership in this church. (Contrary to some popular belief, there was indeed a time in American history in which the relationship between church and state imitated far more closely an English model; the formal separation of the two did not occur until Independence.) Rhode Island, another in this Northern subset, occupied a unique position, evolving into a *de facto* refuge for Nonconformists expelled from other communities. In distinction to the New England colonies, however, ecclesial establishment was not to be found in the Middle colonies, where two traditions took root: New York became the home of the Dutch Reformed and Presbyterians; New Jersey, Pennsylvania, and Delaware the Quakers. Down south, in the Chesapeake and Southern colonies, Anglicanism held sway, receiving legal establishment in Virginia, Maryland (originally, a Roman Catholic settlement), the Carolinas, Georgia, and six small colonies of rural New York. In tracing the evolution of a distinctly American Anglicanism, however, it is to the New England stage that one must first look for the precursory acts of the drama.

By the early eighteenth century, New England boasted two learned academies for the training and formation of young men for the ordained ministry. Harvard College, established in 1636 on a strict Puritan foundation, had become—by the late seventeenth century—a battleground between liberal and conservative factions within the Congregational Church. By the turn of the century, a small group of Connecticut Congregationalists had become so disillusioned with perceived liberal tendencies in the existing college that they moved to break away; settling in New Haven, they founded Yale College in 1701. Chartered by the Connecticut General Assembly and governed by a board of Congregationalist ministers, Yale quickly became a haven for conservative factions across the Northern colonies, a concrete hope for the restoration of orthodoxy across the region.

To the disappointment of such factions, however, it would not be long until this bastion of Nonconformist conservatism likewise became the subject of ecclesial scandal. In 1722, Yale's president, Timothy Cutler, and tutor Daniel Brown—the sum total of Yale's faculty—gave the college and board the startling announcement that they had converted to Anglicanism. Almost immediately thereafter, they set off for England and received episcopal ordination. To the further bewilderment of the Yale establishment, several other Connecticut Congregational clergymen—influenced, through their study, by Cutler and Brown—likewise departed in quick succession for the distant shores of Anglicanism's home.

This group, soon to be known as the "Yale Converts," had been attracted to a growing and enthusiastic community of Anglicans who, for some years, had gathered not far from the college campus. In 1722, this small worshipping community received its first priest; commissioned by the Society for the Propagation of the Gospel (SPG), the Reverend George Pigot became the first episcopally ordained minister in Connecticut. It is likely that the arrival of the Reverend Pigot proved the tipping point for Cutler and Brown's conversion. These years of interaction between the burgeoning Anglican parish of New Haven and the leadership of its Congregationalist academy left a lasting impact on not only the two members of faculty, but also on the students under their instruction. In something of a "trickle-down" effect, the growing influence of an Anglican theological outlook in Cutler and Brown came, bit by bit, to imprint upon the students of Yale College.

Amongst these was a young Congregationalist minister-in-training, one Samuel Seabury of Groton, the father of this book's focus. Following the tumult of 1722, Samuel's father, John Seabury, withdrew his son from the New Haven academy and transferred his studies to the comparative safety of Harvard. But, despite the senior Seabury's best efforts, the damage had been done; Samuel had been "tainted" with the Anglican views of his Yale instructors and, in 1729, after several years as a licensed Congregationalist preacher, formally converted to Anglicanism.

In May of the following year, he departed for England to receive Anglican orders, carrying with him letters testimonial from Drs. Cutler and Brown. Shortly after his return in December 1730, the Reverend Mr. Seabury was commissioned by the SPG as missionary priest to the parish of New London, Connecticut, where he remained until 1742. As something of an aside, it is worth noting that the credit for Seabury's conversion cannot go to the Yale Converts alone. Alongside the influence exercised over the young Connecticuter through his educational life was that imparted through his marital life. Abigail Seabury (née Mumford), wife of Samuel (Snr.) and mother of Samuel (Jnr.), hailed from a family of loyal New England Anglicans. Her father, James Mumford, was the first warden of the parish of New London, where the Reverend Seabury would later minister.

A close relative of Abigail's, by marriage, was the Reverend James MacSparran, an early SPG missionary responsible for the parish of St. Paul's, Narragansett, on Rhode Island. It is highly likely that the staunchly Episcopalian Mumfords played a not insignificant part in Samuel's 1729 conversion. Tragically for the newly ordained Seabury, however, Abigail died six months after his return from England, leaving behind an eighteen-month-old son: Samuel Seabury Jnr. Having established the context into which he was born, it is his story that we pick up, now.

Samuel Seabury and Early American Church Culture

The early life of the junior Samuel Seabury is little known. From what is known, however, it is clear that the influence of the senior Seabury upon his younger son cannot be underestimated. In contrast to his older brother, Caleb, whose attraction to the nearby merchant port—at the expense of a formal education—led him into a career as a seaman, the studious and bookish young Samuel became the apple of his father's eye; until his move to New Haven to commence studies at Yale in 1744, the Samuels proved virtually inseparable. The young Samuel's time was divided between studies at his father's parish grammar school and travels with his father around the parish and its neighboring communities.

The life and itinerant duty of an SPG missionary was one in which the future bishop was thoroughly immersed from a young age. Although New London was geographically isolated from the centers of Anglicanism in both Connecticut and Massachusetts (Stratford and Boston, respectively), the Seaburys nevertheless maintained frequent connection with the scattered Episcopalian community. This was seen most clearly in the spring of 1740, as the parish of New London prepared to host the annual Convention of the New England Anglican clergy. Chaired by the commissary of the bishop of London, the Reverend Roger Price, and attended by a further nine ministers (including, of course, the senior Seabury), the Convention focused its discussion on a proposed new mission in rural Massachusetts.

While this remained the sole recorded item of business, it is assumed that the "hot-button" issue of a resident American bishop could not have gone unmentioned. (The presence of one Reverend Samuel Johnson, a leading figure and dominant personality amongst the Anglicans of Connecticut, whose leadership of the cause for a local episcopate continued into the 1770s, makes the discussion of this matter at the 1740 Convention practically an inevitability. He will be discussed in more detail later in the book.) It is sure that none of the assembled clergy could have had any idea that the ten-year-old boy who greeted them at the door on May 4, 1740 would go on to become the very bishop for whom they had so earnestly longed.

After nearly ten years of stable and fruitful ministry in New London, 1740 saw in the Reverend Seabury the start of a period of pastoral destabilization, as the turn of the decade brought to the Northern colonies the beginnings of a dramatic change in the ecclesial landscape. On September 14, the famed English Evangelical preacher and a father of Methodism, George Whitefield, landed in Newport. With his arrival, New England plunged into the throes of the Great Awakening in earnest.

Across denominational boundaries and theological divides, the revival movement swept through the Northern colonies, bringing its message of personal conversion and piety to mass gatherings across the region. Styled the "New Lights"—as opposed to the "Old Lights" who maintained the traditional modes of religious expression—the revivalists drew through the port town of New London a tumultuous and near constant stream of itinerant preachers. Following Whitefield, and amongst the notable names, came philosopher and Congregationalist minister Jonathan Edwards and, later, ("Crazy") James Davenport, who held a public burning of "Wicked Books" (i.e., tracts and prayer books of the Church of England).

Scandalized and confused by the intense and abrupt surge of religious radicalism, the Reverend Seabury—a man who, with his son, sat strictly in the camp of the "Old Lights"—petitioned the SPG for a new posting and, in August 1743, moved the family to Western Long Island to assume responsibilities for the parish of Hempstead. Through the heady and emotional years of the early New England revival, the teenage Samuel had remained by his father's side, as the senior Seabury responded to the movement with a combination of disparaging cynicism, impassioned censure, and calm and consistent recourse to the traditional doctrines and liturgies of the Church of England. As will become apparent in his later life, a dogmatic insistence on established conformist teaching and a reactionary response to perceived innovation, demonstrated so keenly by his father in these formative years of childhood, came to characterize the future bishop too.

Shortly after the Reverend Seabury commenced as rector of Hempstead, Samuel left his father's immediate oversight to begin studies at Yale College. Between the senior Seabury's departure from New Haven in 1722 and the junior Seabury's matriculation in 1744, Yale had proven unable to entirely shake off the Anglican influence of Drs. Cutler and Brown. Accordingly, though it remained decidedly Congregationalist in outlook, teaching, and worship, Samuel found a space for his Episcopalian sensibilities to be somewhat indulged. (He was, for example, granted permission to return home once a month to attend an Anglican service of Holy Communion.) Furthermore, given New Haven's location, Samuel and the other resident Episcopalians would have frequently encountered visiting priests from the nearby Anglican strongholds of Stratford, Fairfield, Newtown, and Redding.

Although little is known of his personal life at college, Samuel's educational life will have looked virtually the same as his father's. Essentially medieval in structure, his curriculum consisted of Latin, Greek, and Hebrew, together with logic, rhetoric, geometry, geography, ethics, and metaphysics. (And, in later years, following reforms by Rector Thomas Clap, natural philosophy and mathematics.) Perhaps amongst the most important outcomes of Samuel's years at Yale, however, were the friendships and connections made, several of which would become of great importance in later years.

Of these, the close friendships with William Johnson (son of the renowned Stratford priest), Thomas Bradbury Chandler (an Anglican convert during his college years and convinced High Churchman), and Jeremiah Leaming (an avid writer and later leader among Connecticut Anglicans), came to rank of greatest significance. Though thoroughly immersed in the Congregationalist patterns of prayer and thought that characterized the New Haven academy during these years at Yale, Samuel found space, through geographical circumstance and social networks alike, to not only preserve but grow yet further into the distinct New England churchmanship with which he had been raised. It is this churchmanship—High Church in its doctrine, Evangelical in its preaching, and molded by the response of a convert community from a Puritan background—that shaped Samuel's theological and ecclesiological outlook through his earliest years.

Following his graduation from Yale in 1748, the junior Seabury accepted a post as lay reader and catechist at the new parish of Huntington, a growing mission chapel connected to his father's parish at Hempstead. Samuel held this position for three years, officiating Sunday services of Morning and Evening Prayer, reading printed sermons from approved collections, and catechizing and teaching at the local SPG school in Oyster Bay. In order to supplement his modest reader's income, the young Seabury was able to draw in a considerable amount of money from the practice of medicine. It had long been the senior Seabury's plan that his son should follow him not only into the clerical profession, but into the medical profession too.

This was not an uncommon combination of careers throughout the eighteenth century. The Reverend Seabury is known to have practiced as a physician from 1753 to 1759, though it is almost certain his medical work extended well before this, with apprenticeships perhaps going as far back as his return from England. It is, likewise, almost certain that the young Samuel apprenticed his father in this field, too, learning from him in equal measure the cure of souls and the cure of bodies. While details are scant, it appears that the junior Seabury excelled similarly in this medical work, boasting a thriving practice in Huntington by the early 1750s. Unlike his father, however, and perhaps as some attempt by the rector of Hempstead to live vicariously through his son, Samuel's medical training would go beyond that grasped in an apprenticeship.

Samuel Seabury: Scotland and Ordination

In 1752, the young lay reader sailed for Scotland to commence a year of medical study at the University of Edinburgh, then regarded as the premier faculty of medicine in the world. This time abroad would number Seabury among a small elite who had the ability, inclination, and means to carry out such a costly venture. At a practical level, it would also occupy the remaining year before he reached the canonical age for ordination at twenty-four. Very little is known about Samuel's time in Edinburgh. In fact, more recent scholarship has questioned whether he went at all. (It is curious, for example, that across all his surviving letters and writings, he never mentions his time in Scotland, a country that would come to inhabit a position of supreme importance in his later life. Furthermore, no records exist at the university to confirm his enrolment as a student.

On the other hand, there is nothing to indicate that he remained at Huntington.) In keeping, however, with the historical assumption that indeed Samuel *did* pursue a course of studies in Edinburgh, it is doubtful that he had much interaction with the Scottish Episcopal Church.

The early 1750s still bore witness to the penal laws enforced by the Crown upon Scottish Episcopalians, following the unsuccessful Jacobite uprisings of the 1740s, which prohibited Episcopalian clergy from holding services in anything but a private house and for any more than four people. Despite legendary stories of the young Samuel sneaking through the streets in the dead of night to gather for clandestine Episcopalian services at Old St. Paul's Church, there is no proof of such a tale. What's more, given the staunch Loyalist sentiments of the New England Anglicans—more of which will be discussed, below—it seems highly questionable that a Seabury should be found colluding with such open anti-English sentiment.

Though no records or diaries exist of his time in Scotland, it is most likely that Samuel's ecclesial involvement in Edinburgh centered on the Qualified Chapels—Episcopalian congregations that had accepted the Hanoverian monarchy, the English *Book of Common Prayer* of 1662, and an English episcopate, and were thus exempt from the penal laws. It is probable that, of these, the famous Cowgate Chapel in the Old Town became Seabury's spiritual home during his sojourn in Scotland. By the close of 1753, Samuel's studies in Edinburgh had drawn to an end and he had reached the canonical age for ordination.

Equipped with supporting letters from his father to Thomas Sherlock, bishop of London, and the Committee of the SPG, he made his way south to receive Anglican orders. (As an aside, it is interesting to note that, among the several letters addressed by the senior Seabury to the London prelate, one comprises an earnest note on "the great Obstacle to the Growth of the Church of England in the plantations," which concludes with a detailed plea for a resident American episcopate. It is sure that the young messenger could scarcely have guessed, when handing this letter to Bishop Sherlock, that he would go on to become the very same bishop so desired in it.) Following a positive recommendation by SPG secretary, Philip Bearcroft, and a successful examination by the bishop of London (comprising Greek and Latin translations and a Latin exposition of the Thirty-Nine Articles), Samuel Seabury was ordained to the diaconate on December 21, 1753 in the chapel at Fulham Palace by John Thomas, bishop of Lincoln.

Though he attended the ordination, Bishop Sherlock's declining health prevented him from officiating the rite himself. Interestingly, it is unknown whether the young Seabury had been confirmed prior to his ordination; in the absence of a bishop in the New World, he—together with the vast majority of early-eighteenth-century American Anglicans—had not the opportunity to do so. While there is some precedent for colonial ordinands arranging for the rite to be performed prior to ordination, it is unknown whether Samuel made such arrangements.

Nevertheless, having received deacon's orders on December 21, the young American was elevated to the priesthood a mere two days later. Again, in the surrounds of the chapel at Fulham Palace, and in the presence of the bishops of London and Carlisle (the latter of whom officiated the service), the new priest vowed to conform to the liturgy and doctrine of the Church of England, serving as a priest in the colonies under the license and at the pleasure of the prelate of London. After remaining in England for the winter, the Reverend Mr. Seabury (Jnr.) departed for home shores, arriving in Philadelphia on May 22, 1754.

Despite having been away for nearly two years, the newly ordained Seabury remained with his family for less than a fortnight before travelling west to commence his first ministerial role as SPG missionary to the parish of New Brunswick, New Jersey. Fewer than sixty-five miles from the family base at Hempstead, this factor of proximity was perhaps the main attraction of the New Brunswick posting. With neither glebe nor parsonage to support the missionary, and an unfinished church building to boot, the beginning of Seabury's first pastorate must have come as a rude awakening. With time, the young priest may have been able to turn things around. But, he was never given the opportunity to do so.

Having been the dominant force in Samuel's earliest education and formation across theological and medical studies, and having determined and secured his places at Yale, Huntington, and Edinburgh, and then facilitated his ordination in London, the senior Seabury stepped in yet again, exerting his influence in petitioning the SPG to transfer his son from New Brunswick to the parish of Jamaica, Long Island. The request was soon met, and within less than three years of taking up the post in New Jersey, the younger Seabury was made rector of Jamaica on January 13, 1757. Despite there appearing to be no particular advantage of the one parish over the other—beyond the geographical proximity so important to the rector of Hempstead—Samuel complied with his father's wishes without any recorded protest. It is interesting to note the young man's submissiveness; if he harbored any resentment towards such a domineering influence, it is certainly not apparent up to this stage of his life.

From the time of this move to Jamaica, however, a shift becomes apparent in the young Reverend Seabury's behavior, exhibited in the first instance in a marked antagonism toward several key authority figures who now appear on the scene. The first of such figures is Edward Hicks, Samuel's father-in-law. While the origins of the disagreement are unknown, it is clear that the two men disliked one another intensely from the beginning. Despite Hicks's opposition to the marriage between his daughter, Mary, and the young priest, the ceremony nevertheless went ahead on October 12, 1756. Perhaps unsurprisingly, the senior Reverend Seabury officiated the service.

The feud between Hicks and his son-in-law came to a head in 1759. At the start of the marriage, Hicks had promised the young couple a gift of £400 towards a farm, and provided the Jamaica parsonage with furniture and silverware. Three years later, the promised gift had still to materialize. Far from dropping the matter, Seabury persisted in pressing his father-in-law for the "overdue" funds. Exasperated, Hicks began to claim that his son-in-law owed *him* money, to the amount of £250. Upon Seabury's refusal to pay, Hicks had the furniture and silverware he had gifted three years prior forcibly removed from the parsonage and the young priest arrested. Though Seabury was soon released, once the facts of the situation had been ascertained, the relationship between father-in-law and son-in-law had soured to a point of no return.

Sadly for the rector of Jamaica, the troubles of his domestic life were soon to be matched by those of his parish life. At the same time as the dispute with Hicks was reaching its climax, Seabury had found in the person of John Aspinwall—a wealthy New York City financier and active parishioner—the target of his next campaign. This newly arrived businessman had quickly became a major benefactor at St. George's Church in Flushing—which, together with St. James's, Newtown and Grace Church, Jamaica, comprised the three-center parish of Jamaica—dedicating significant financial resources to the completion of the Flushing church building. Though his arrival should have proven a much-needed blessing to the young rector, burdened with three financially struggling congregations, Aspinwall's enthusiastic and possibly domineering personality may have been the first step in setting him and Seabury off on the wrong foot.

Within months, the New York businessman had invited and paid for Augur Treadwell, a young Yale graduate, to move to the parish and establish a Latin school in Flushing. Shortly after, and with Seabury's permission, Treadwell was made lay reader for the congregation at St. George's. Objectively, this was an excellent appointment; within a very short time, the young reader had succeeded in building up the Flushing mission to the point that it became the largest of Seabury's three churches. The parish rector, however, did not take this turn of events well, reading it—perhaps with some degree of accuracy—as a commentary on the success of his own ministry.

Seabury's resentment only grew with the proposition soon made by the congregations at Flushing and Newtown to formally sever ties with Grace Church, Jamaica, and appoint Treadwell their leader. Against Seabury's wishes, and with Aspinwall's support, the young Yale graduate made the journey to England for ordination in 1762. Though unsuccessful in preventing Treadwell's ordination, the Jamaica rector did succeed in blocking his appointment as minister at Flushing and Newtown; the newly ordained priest moved, instead, to New Jersey, to commence work as SPG missionary to the parish of Trenton. With the Reverend Mr. Treadwell gone, the contentious chapter between Seabury and Aspinwall should have been closed. Within less than a year, however, tensions bubbled over once more.

In a naïve act of pastoral insensitivity, the young Trenton missionary arrived on an unannounced visitation to his former parish in February 1763. With neither Seabury's knowledge nor permission, the Reverend Treadwell preached in Flushing and Newtown and baptized a child in Jamaica. Infuriated by the intrusion, the Long Island rector blamed the whole course of events on Aspinwall, convinced that it had transpired at his encouragement. In the mind of the Reverend Seabury, the New York businessman had become the mastermind of a covert operation to undermine and destabilize his ministry. Paranoid, demoralized, and sensing a profound isolation, the rector of Jamaica turned to the press, desperately seeking from the public mind the affirmation not felt from his flock.

Writing in to the *New York Gazette* on at least three occasions, Seabury openly challenged Aspinwall, airing his private animosities in great detail. The Flushing philanthropist's cool responses must have infuriated the increasingly hot-headed priest no end. After several months, and perhaps unsurprisingly, this public letter-writing campaign had amounted to little more than Seabury's further humiliation, the scope of which had now extended beyond the confines of the parish and well into the greater

New York community. Come the beginning of 1764, Seabury had become a pathetic and mistrusted figure amongst parishioners and local community alike.

The final blow to his confidence, and the tipping point in what had long been an untenable position, came several months later with the death of his father on June 15. With his public and private lives thoroughly shaken, Samuel resigned as rector of Jamaica on December 1, 1766, to take what would be the first position of his own choosing. On March 1, 1767, the Reverend Seabury was inducted as rector of Westchester, New York.

If the Samuel Seabury of the Jamaica years cuts a decidedly unappealing and immature figure, then it is in the years at Westchester that we see a marked change begin, and the seeds of what would become a life of effective and powerful leadership start to flower. Removed from the troubled domestic and ecclesial landscape that characterized the pastorate on Long Island, and with the end of his father's controlling influence, the Reverend and Mrs. Seabury's life north of the city proved (initially) both uneventful and generally happy. Together with the four children born in Jamaica, a fifth came three years after the move. (This youngest child, Charles, would later be ordained deacon and priest by his father, and succeed his father as rector of St. James's, New London.)

Of the comparatively few documented parochial issues encountered by the new rector of Westchester, the most significant appears to have been the discrepancy between high levels of church attendance and low levels of communicant participation. Within a year of his arrival, Samuel reported his disappointment that, of the normally two hundred attendees on a given Sunday morning, no more than twenty-two had ever communicated at a service of Holy Communion. At least for the time being, however, this was not an issue that the Reverend Seabury could do much about. In the absence of a colonial bishop to perform confirmations, numbers of communicant parishioners across the New World were limited to those who had received the rite in England. In such a context, a 10 percent communicant membership in a single parish becomes proportionally quite significant. Nevertheless, for the New England High Churchman, this was far too few, proving yet again the desperate need for a resident episcopate. It is precisely to this matter that Seabury begins to direct his focus during the years at Westchester.

Pastoral Ministry and Precarious Politics

The period of Samuel's third pastorate (1767–1783) bore witness to some of the most dramatic social and political upheaval yet experienced in the New World. Following the Treaty of Paris in 1763, and subsequent forfeiture of all remaining French-held territories in America to the Crown, England had cemented its position as the dominant colonial power and shored up its control of the great Western Frontier. In order to repay the considerable debt incurred by the preceding years of war, several significant levies were introduced to the colonist communities. Amongst the most consequential of these numbered: the Sugar Act of 1764, increasing duties on non-British goods shipped to the colonies; the Stamp Act of 1765, introducing the first direct tax on the American colonies, targeting newspapers, pamphlets, legal documents, and playing cards; the Quartering Act of 1765, requiring the colonies to provide barracks and supplies to British troops; the Declaratory Act of 1766, authorizing Parliament to make binding laws on the American colonies "in all cases whatsoever"; and, the Townshend Acts of 1767, introducing further taxes on glass, lead, paint, paper, and tea.

Across the thirteen colonies, this harsh suite of legislation was widely met with protest and unrest, perceived by the growing Patriot cause as a sinister threat to personal and corporate freedoms. By the early 1770s, sociopolitical divisions had cut a deep rift through the nascent American society; as the clamor for revolution grew, so too did the Loyalist and Patriot camps become yet more entrenched. The Loyalist camp found its stronghold amongst the landed gentry of New York. Conversely, the Patriot cause fared better in the older colonies with a longer established tradition of self-governance—namely, Connecticut, Massachusetts, and Virginia.

As a conservative Church of England priest, Seabury found himself in largely friendly territory in Westchester. While the country rector tried, initially, to stay out of the debate and press on with the normal routine of parish life, he soon found that such an attitude was unsustainable, recording in 1771 that it had become difficult to draw his parishioners' attention to the subject of religion or even persuade them of its importance. It appears, however, that the congregation's focus on the political well-being of the colonial state soon began to influence its rector. Before long, the Reverend Seabury would be found throwing himself headlong and with passion into the world of politics.

In the tumultuous political scene of the pre-Revolutionary period, the Church of England in America encountered perhaps the most severe existential anxiety of any colonial church. Torn between loyalty to the church and loyalty to the nation, American Anglicans were viewed with suspicion from both camps. Initially, Seabury's Loyalist sympathies did not prove a particular stumbling block. Having decided to involve himself in the political sphere, the Westchester rector took to defending the recently imposed English legislation with vigor; to have spoken out against it would have been, for him, akin to denouncing his beloved Church of England, for in concert acted the Parliament and church to which he was subject.

The Reverend Seabury quickly became a high-profile voice in the New York community, using pulpit and pen alike to condemn the Sons of Liberty and attempt to impede elections to the Provincial and Continental Congresses. Shortly after the Boston Tea Party of December 1773, a series of anonymous essays began to appear, defending the Crown and promoting the Loyalist cause. Authored under the pseudonym A. W. Farmer, these widely circulated pamphlets sought to convince the undecided masses that true freedom and social well-being lay in submission to the British Empire, and that any political change desired was best voiced through orderly appeal. Crucially, however, the essays would go on to advocate that such liberties and welfare were most powerfully to be found in the spiritual arm of English governmental control: the bishops of the Church of England.

To those in the Patriot camp, the majority of whom hailed from the Nonconformist traditions, the writings of A. W. Farmer confirmed even the most caricatured impressions of the Loyalist cause—"not only do they want *more* English oversight, but they also want bishops!" Unsurprisingly, it did not take long for the revolutionary agitators to hit back. Principal amongst these counter-assailants was the seventeen-year-old rising star from King's College, New York, Alexander Hamilton. Despite the pushback, however, A. W. Farmer continued. Across the colony, people wondered who this anonymous author was, and—although he would leave it unconfirmed for many years to come—suspicion of the Reverend Seabury ("A Westchester Farmer") grew rapidly.

Misgivings about the country cleric escalated in 1775 when the Westchester church remained pointedly closed on a day declared by the Continental Congress as a national fast in protest against the closure of the Port of Boston. Now convinced of Seabury's guilt, a company of the Sons of Liberty raided the Seabury parsonage on November 22; upon finding no trace of incriminating evidence, they kidnapped the Westchester rector and placed him under house arrest in New Haven. Eventually released on December 23, after insufficient evidence was found to convict, the Reverend Seabury had spent his month of captivity preparing sermons to condemn the next planned Continental Fast. Samuel was now a "marked man," carefully watched by the Patriot camp, so the Seaburys began to search for an opportunity to flee the Westchester region.

The British conquest of Long Island, shortly thereafter, provided the perfect opportunity for such an escape and, on August 22, 1776, the family moved to New York City, seeking refuge behind English lines. There Samuel remained for the next seven years, working primarily as a physician. (It is worth noting that, during this period of quasi-exile, the priest's Loyalist allegiance would take him beyond the publication of written apologetics to service as a guide for British troops through Westchester County, his familiarity with the local terrain proving invaluable to the soldiers. In recognition of his assistance with the New York campaign, he would later be made chaplain to a Loyalist regiment in 1778.)

The Coming Revolution

As the social and political upheaval of the emerging nation, witnessed during Seabury's ten years in Westchester, leaned ever further in favor of the Patriot cause, the Church of England in America was forced to consider the increasingly likely possibility of an Anglican ecclesial establishment *sans* English oversight. Accordingly, and in the absence of a resident bishop to gather the priests in synod, the responsibility fell to the colonial clergy to begin to organize themselves. In 1758, the first Anglican clerical convention (independent of the involvement of the bishop of London's colonial commissary) formed in New Jersey under the leadership of the Reverend Thomas Bradbury Chandler, that close friend and Yale contemporary of the Reverend Seabury.

The clergy of Connecticut followed suit in 1760, gathering behind the Reverend Jeremiah Leaming—another of Seabury's close university colleagues. In 1766, the New York convention was formed, electing the Reverend Samuel Johnson—that early "Yale Convert," elder statesman of the church in Connecticut, and first president of King's College, New York—as president and Seabury as secretary. Within months of its formation, the New York convention joined forces with its neighboring colony, meeting with the New Jersey convention in May.

The following November, this multistate convention would be joined by Leaming's cohort from Connecticut. As something of a "tri-colony Anglican conclave," the massed assembly focused its efforts on petitioning the archbishop of Canterbury and the king to establish a resident American episcopate as a matter of greatest urgency. From this midpoint of the 1760s, these annual state conventions had developed across the colonies; quickly, such meetings came to be regarded as not only normative, but a core element of an embryonic independent American Anglican organization. Significantly, the conventions soon began to look outwards, appointing delegates to attend one another's gatherings and report on local activities.

Such a system would later prove highly beneficial to the Westchester rector, positioned now on the larger scene; by the time of his move to New York City in 1776, Seabury had emerged as a leading voice in the development of Anglicanism across the Northern and Middle colonies. In large part, the credit for such a rise goes to his involvement in what would become known as the Writing Committee. In 1767, under the sage guidance of the Reverend Johnson, the Reverends Seabury, Chandler, Myles Cooper (English-born vice president of King's College, and later priest of a Qualified Chapel in Edinburgh), and Charles Inglis (Irish-born curate, then rector, of Trinity Church, New York, and later first bishop of Nova Scotia) combined to form a writing group of High Church apologists.

Committing their time and energy to the publication of treatises, pamphlets, and open letters, the close band of Northern priests placed the subject of episcopacy at the center of their ecclesial advocacy. Before long, the group—quickly known as the Writing Committee—entered into the world of the press. In response to the emergence of a Presbyterian-led, anti-episcopal column in the *New York Gazette*, the Seabury–Chandler–Cooper–Inglis quartet produced rebuttal after rebuttal in the paper's rival, *The Weekly Mercury*, writing under a pseudonym, "Timothy Tickle, Esquire." This paper war continued until July 1769. Determined that the increasingly influential committee turn its skill to the wider American Anglican scene, the New Jersey convention prevailed on the group—through the Reverend Chandler—to include the Anglicans of the Southern colonies in the quest for an episcopate.

Accordingly, in 1771, the Writing Committee produced "An Address from the Clergy of New York and New Jersey to Episcopalians in Virginia." This is believed to be the first such formal contact on the matter of an independent episcopacy between the churches of the North and the South. Unbeknownst to the Northern conventions, however, the Southerners had not been inattentive to this matter. Indeed, though characterized by a markedly reduced vitriol (and, perhaps, a certain degree of pragmatism), early steps towards the establishment of an independent episcopate were already underway across the Southern churches. It would not be long before the two competing plans met on the political battlefield.

Such a conflict was delayed, however, by the rapidly diminishing capacity of the Writing Committee to continue to spearhead these early dialogues. Beginning with the death of the Reverend Johnson in early 1772, and exacerbated by a political environment increasingly hostile to the Loyalist cause, the members of the group were soon forced to disband. By spring 1775, Chandler and Cooper had fled to England; by early 1776, Patriot troops had taken New York City. Far from impressed by the work of Loyalist apologists, the Patriot forces raided the presses, melting down printers' type to make bullets.

Come the signing of the Declaration of Independence on July 4, 1776, the doors of most Anglican churches across the former Loyalist strongholds had been barred and shut. And, within two months, the Great Fire of New York had razed a quarter of the city to the ground, effecting the flight of half the city's population. With a capital in ruins, a silenced press, an exiled body of priests, and a dead leader of the Loyalist Anglican cause, the quest to secure an independent episcopate had well and truly halted across Northern and Southern colonies, alike. It would be another six years before any significant action was action taken on this front.

Postcolonial America

It is unknown why Samuel Seabury remained in America after the end of the war. The church he had worked so hard to defend had been decimated, the government on whose behalf he had so vigorously campaigned had lost, and many of his closest friends had fled to the safety of England. Perhaps surprisingly, then, it appears that an uncharacteristic pragmatism quickly took root in the middle-aged priest; far from bemoaning the lost world of colonial America, he soon came to not only accept but embrace his newly independent homeland. Had it not been for such an unexpected transfer of allegiance, and had Seabury followed his colleagues to distant shores, the future of American Anglicanism may well have looked remarkably different. His decision to remain, however, would make possible the decisive step taken some seven years post the *annus horribilis* of 1776 by a small company of New England clergy.

On March 25, 1783, ten of the eleven remaining priests in Connecticut gathered in the Woodbury house of the Reverend John Rutgers Marshall. Although no minutes exist recording the proceedings of the meeting, it emerged with a single and (initially) unplanned-for outcome: the election of the Reverend Samuel Seabury as first bishop of the Anglican Church in America. To paraphrase and appropriate that famous line of Ralph Waldo Emerson's "Concord Hymn," this decision "fired the shot heard round the [Anglican] world," forever changing the course of global Anglicanism.

It is likely that this Connecticut clerical convention was called to discuss and respond to the recent publication of William White's ecclesiological treatise, "The Case of the Episcopal Churches in the United States Considered" (1782). It was mentioned, above, that, by the time of the 1771 "Address" from the Writing Committee to the Virginian church, the Southern colonies had already taken initial steps toward realizing some form of local episcopacy. And, indeed, from as early as 1771, such preparatory work had centered around the rising star of the same William White. Though not yet thirty-five, come the time of the Woodbury meeting, the Reverend White boasted already more than a decade of renown across the Anglican churches of the South. Hailed as a leading and vocal Patriot, who would then become a well-received political moderate in the post-war years, White was appointed chaplain to the Continental Congress when still twenty-nine, and devoted himself to the revolutionary cause, from its political epicenter, through the critical years of the war. Together with this political chaplaincy, the young priest served as rector of St. Peter's and Christ Church, Philadelphia, a role he would hold for fifty-seven years.

Though few in number, the Anglicans that remained in the post-war nation continued to disproportionately represent a social, political, and economic elite, particularly in the early colonial Anglican strongholds of the South. Thus well-placed, White became a valued confidant of the newly independent political leadership, several of whom were members of his parish. Of these, three were also signers of the Declaration of

Independence: Robert Morris, English-born financier of the Revolution and White's brother-in-law; Francis Hopkinson, senior jurist and White's rector's warden; and, Benjamin Franklin, polymath drafter of the Declaration and one of White's vestrymen. In short, across the board, White's credentials were impeccable. From at least the early 1770s, the Reverend White had involved himself with Southern responses to the issue of episcopacy. In contrast to the campaigns of the Northern advocates, in which the consideration of such an idea scarcely features, a leading concern in the pre-independent South was the possibility that, should the Patriot cause succeed, the British would refuse to accept American independence. Such a scenario would hand to what had been the Church of England in America nothing less than a death sentence. Without the possibility to raise up an episcopate, the days of Anglicanism in America would be numbered.

Such a concern remained front of mind for the Southerners well past independence in 1776. As such, White's 1782 proposal (henceforth referred to as "The Case") sought to both address the pressing need for a resident episcopate and provide a base-level structure for the formation of an independent American Anglican Church. Confronted with the ongoing situation wherein the imparting of episcopal orders to American clergy continued to be withheld by the English College of Bishops, "The Case" offered an (intentionally temporary) solution to one issue and proposed that presbyteral orders may be conferred to deacons by priests—that is to say, that priests may ordain new priests without the involvement of a bishop.

Despite favoring a resident episcopate, White's approach was pragmatic; new clergy would continue to be needed and, with the advent of a local bishop a remote hope, a change to—ostensibly, now unworkable—tradition and practice was required. In his own words, "a scrupulous adherence to episcopacy is sacrificing substance to the ceremony." It is interesting to observe that such moves in the Southern Anglican colonies parallel almost identical discussions happening among American Methodists. Although it is not known whether "The Case" ever reached the (then-still Anglican) Methodist leadership, it is worth noting that, within two years of White's publication, John Wesley would ordain Richard Whatcoat and Thomas Vasey as presbyters for the new Methodist Episcopal Church of America in the first instance of non-episcopal "Anglican" ordination.

Inasmuch as such a change to historic church order can be argued to have confirmed the separation of Methodism from Anglicanism, so too would the implementation of presbyterian ordination in "The Case" have worked to irreparably divide the emerging Anglicanism of the New World from that of the Old. In addition, and alongside such a (potentially) dangerous proposal, the publication offered a further departure from English custom. Detailing a national model of church governance, White suggests that each ecclesial district—an administrative area mapping, roughly, onto the pre-existing state boundaries of the now long-established clerical conventions—would elect a combination of clerical *and lay* representatives to its national governing body.

Contesting Consecration

It is, perhaps, not at all surprising that such a dramatic proposition set alarm bells ringing across the conservative—and, in many cases, still fundamentally Loyalist—Anglican communities of New England. Significantly, within four days of the publication of "The Case," the Continental Congress received word from England that defeat had been accepted and American independence formally acknowledged. With this, the final barrier to an American episcopate had been removed, and the possibility of local bishops made real.

Despite this, however, White declined to amend his work and issue reprints omitting the call for presbyterian ordination. It is unknown why such a decision was not taken; White's forthcoming advocacy for resident bishops in an English line of succession, and his subsequent reception of just such orders, seems to indicate that, at a personal level, he had no issue with letting go the idea of a "Methodist-like" change to ecclesial polity. Nevertheless, the original document remained unaltered, and circulated in its most radical form. It is this copy that the New England clergy would soon receive, and in the absence of updates to the contrary, take seriously that such was the mind of the South.

As such, the convention of ten Connecticut priests in March 1783, which first met to plan a response to White's proposal, soon became a committee to elect a bishop. In the minds of these ecclesiological conservatives, such a dramatic decision represented the only counter to its equally dramatic Southern opposite. In discerning the right candidate, the committee first voted in favor of the Reverend Jeremiah Leaming.

Long-time leader of Connecticut Anglicans and spiritual successor to the famed Samuel Johnson, Leaming provided a link to the "glory days" of the Yale Converts. His staunch Loyalism and defiant opposition to the Patriot cause—resulting in an extended jail sentence, during which a rheumatic fever left him permanently lame—further succeeding in garnering the ecclesial statesman widespread respect.

For reasons unknown, however, the Reverend Leaming declined the nomination. While later letters make clear that, before long, he came to regret his decision, his determined "no" to the election turned the convention's attention to another candidate. By most metrics, Samuel Seabury did not prove an impressive choice for episcopal preferment. As a parish priest, his record was poor, resigning from his first post almost as soon as he arrived, leaving his second in pastoral disarray, and saying of his third, "My success has not been equal to my first expectations. I find it difficult to convince people that religion is a matter of importance." Furthermore, the New York priest's writings reflect an obstinate, dour man with a dogmatic—perhaps to the point of off-putting—idealism about the life of the church. Even more extraordinarily, however, he had never served a parish in the state, having left Connecticut almost thirty years prior.

As such, it is likely that he had little more than an acquaintance with most of the self-styled electors, sharing close friendship with Leaming alone. To top it off, the Woodbury meeting was a decidedly private affair; it is almost certain that Seabury would have had no knowledge of its occurrence and thus could not have pleaded his case before the convention. Given all of this, the ultimate decision to elect the New York priest as first bishop of Connecticut—and, accordingly, first bishop in the United States—seems almost inconceivable. He was, without a doubt, the darkest of horses. In the absence of records from the electoral synod, the reasoning behind the choice of Samuel Seabury remains unknown. Perhaps his war-time public advocacy for the Loyalist cause, later work on the Writing Committee, and more recent involvement in the broad leadership of the multi-state conventions marked the otherwise unattractive cleric as a politically savvy option.

Perhaps his dogged competitiveness and conservative idealism was seen as an appropriate and timely retort to the radical and pragmatic propositions of the South. Or, perhaps, no such considerations were in the mind of the electors, and Seabury's name emerged out of nowhere as a mysterious work of the Holy Spirit. All of this is, of course, mere speculation. Whatever its reasons may have been, the Connecticut gathering concluded with its attention and hopes fixed on the unsuspecting priest from New York. For, indeed, surely no one was more surprised at this decision than Samuel Seabury himself.

Despite having settled on Seabury's candidature, the convention was under no illusions as to the difficulty of the task that lay before them. Broadly speaking, the obstacles in the path toward securing an American episcopate fell into two categories. First, the Church of England—and, more specifically, the archbishop of Canterbury—remained to be convinced to consecrate an American cleric. This would be no mean feat, requiring the resolution of several complications at political, legal, and ecclesiological levels alike. At a political level, the residual effects of the war had not yet worn off and relationships across the Atlantic remained tense. As Seabury would soon encounter during his unsuccessful journey to London, the provision of such a lifeline to the newly independent church of a newly independent nation, in the aftermath of a sorely humiliating defeat, was low on the English priority list.

At a legal level, the complicating factor persisted that the Anglican rite of episcopal consecration contained a requisite oath of loyalty to the British sovereign; such an oath could not be taken by the citizen of an independent nation. At an ecclesiological level, the very concept of what an American bishop would look like would prove fundamentally alien to the Church of England hierarchy. In the absence of both legal establishment and the subsequent possession of equivalent sociopolitical rank to the English Lords Spiritual, an American episcopate would operate solely within the sphere of pastoral and ecclesiastical authority; unlike his English counterpart, the American bishop would possess no intrinsic political power.

Redefining Episcopacy

A dramatic redefinition of what the episcopal office could look like would, therefore, be required in England before any action could be taken to effect such a transformed episcopal ministry in America. And herein lay a further difficulty. Since the royal suppression of the Convocations of Canterbury and York in 1717, the Church of England had been denied the fora for debate on questions of doctrine and practice. It, therefore, lacked any formal provision to discuss the implications of an American episcopate. Across the board, the obstacles awaiting Seabury in England were manifold. Alongside these, however, ranked the hurdles yet to be overcome on home soil.

Come the 1783 election, American Anglicanism had formed into two opposing camps: those who favored the election and consecration of bishops prior to the formal establishment of ecclesial structures, largely located in the North; and, those who prioritized the development and implementation of church organization before the institution of an episcopate, largely located in the South. Convinced of the former, the Connecticut clergy set about organizing for the bishop-elect's travel and consecration, with little thought to the future implications of such unilateral action. Indeed, as will be seen, this decision would later prove an impediment to the life of the national church. Despite the host of obstacles around which they had yet to navigate, the Connecticuters were not entirely without hope in planning Seabury's voyage.

Though sending the bishop-elect into hostile—or, at the very least, apathetic—territory, the New England electors looked with optimism, and staked much, on the support expected from a select group of friends awaiting the Reverend Seabury's arrival. Since arriving in England in 1775, the Reverends Thomas Bradbury Chandler and Myles Cooper had quietly gained for themselves considerable influence in the nation's ecclesiastical circles. By 1783, Chandler had been in London for nearly eight years. The majority of the expatriate's time appears to have been spent in near constant advocacy for the cause of an American episcopate. His efforts succeeded in securing the formation of a committee of the SPG to consider the cause, and in obtaining (informal) permission from the bishop of London to allow the clergy of Connecticut to omit the prayers for the Royal Family in the Prayer Book rites.

Alongside his politico-ecclesial activism, Chandler also rose quickly in the social circles of the Church of England's elite, becoming a known associate of both the archbishop of Canterbury and the bishop of Oxford. While the Reverend Chandler occupied his time in London, Myles Cooper found a base further north. Upon his return to Britain, Cooper was appointed senior minister of the Cowgate Chapel in Edinburgh, then the senior Qualified Chapel in Scotland. This position of not inconsiderable distinction ranked the English priest amongst the leading representatives of Hanoverian control in Scotland.

Together with Chandler and Cooper, Charles Inglis would likewise make the journey to England, arriving in late 1783. For the first time in nearly ten years, the famed Writing Committee of the pre-Revolutionary years would be reunited, their once-theoretical advocacy now given material shape. With such support awaiting him, and armed with testimonials, letters of introduction, and a certificate of election, bishop-elect Samuel Seabury departed for England in early June 1783.

Seabury's Journey to Consecration

Shortly after his arrival in England on July 7, Seabury secured an audience with the ageing bishop of London, Robert Louth. Until Independence, the prelate at Fulham Palace had exercised episcopal oversight over the Church of England in America, and continued to hold responsibility for the activities of the SPG. This seemed, to the former SPG missionary, an appropriate first port of call. However, despite receiving a warm welcome and a word of support and encouragement in the venture, Louth appeared either unwilling or unable to assist with its implementation.

As Seabury would later record, the bishop of London was "an amiable man, but very infirm, and I think his memory and other faculties are declining; he avoids business as much as possible." Notwithstanding this disappointing start, the American soon made contact with the archbishops of Canterbury and York. To the metropolita, Seabury passed on a letter from the Connecticut convention, laying out the case for an American episcopate. This letter provides a fascinating insight into the intention of the electoral synod, and—perhaps more broadly—into the attitude toward episcopacy held by the conservative factions of the American North:

> This part of America is, at length, dismembered from the British Empire; but, notwithstanding the dissolution of all *civil* connections with the parent state, we still hope to retain the *religious* polity, the primitive and evangelical doctrine and discipline, which, at the Reformation, was restored and established in the Church of England. To render this polity complete, and to provide for its perpetuity in this country, by the establishment of an American episcopate.[33]

The note would go on to reference White's 1782 proposal, offering opposition to the same as a further reason to consecrate the bishop-elect:

> This early and only measure we can devise for this purpose, is effectually to prevent the carrying into execution a plan of a very extraordinary nature which advocated temporary

> presbyterian ordination, lately come to our knowledge and published in Philadelphia.[34]

To Seabury and the Connecticut clergy, the arguments outlined in the letter evidenced an unobjectionable—and, even, commendable—case. And, indeed, such appears to have been the attitude of Archbishops Moore and Markham. As at Fulham, Seabury found at Lambeth and Bishopthorpe Palaces cordial receptions and, in response to the request, earnest expressions of sympathy and support. Nevertheless, the primates remained hesitant to take the lead in championing the cause through such political and legal circles as would be required to make the consecration possible.

Against pushback from the American cleric, they expressed their uncertainty about the propriety of consecrating a bishop for a diocese that was, at the time, non-existent, fearful that without institutional support he would become an object of ecclesial disunity. Likewise, despite testimony from the Connecticut convention that such was unnecessary, the prelates made clear their reservations about proceeding with the consecration in the absence of formal, written sanction concerning the same from the Connecticut government. Evidently, the model of a distinctly American episcopacy remained foreign to the English ecclesiastical mind. Curiously, however, such concerns about the lack of concurrence with the American civil authorities did not originate with the archbishops.

In a well-intentioned attempt to assist in the matter's legal resolution, the archbishop of Canterbury had sent a copy of the Connecticut appeal to then-secretary of state for home and colonial affairs, Lord North. Prime minister of Great Britain from 1770 to 1782, North had become intimately familiar with the New World; indeed, it was on account of the British defeat at the Battle of Yorktown that he had been removed from office a year earlier. North was well aware of the plurality of religious opinion and expression across the former colony, and understood that the desire for episcopacy across the developing nation was, perhaps, not as fulsome as the New Englanders had implied.

Keen to avoid the impression, therefore, of an uninvited English intrusion into another government's sphere of autonomy, particularly in view of the continued state of heightened tensions, the political powerbroker had made clear to the primates that a parliamentary bill to allow for the dispensation of the state oaths in the rite of episcopal consecration would not be passed by the reigning ministry. This complication was communicated to Seabury by the archbishop of Canterbury and appears to have formed the basis of his rejection of the American appeal. Unsatisfied, however, the increasingly frustrated Seabury pushed back with vigor. Despite assurances from the archbishop that the matter was, indeed, being discussed by the episcopal college, the New York priest continued to hound the chief prelate, determined that the consecration should proceed as planned.

It is likely that this dogged persistence played a substantial part in eventually alienating Moore, whose formerly sympathetic stance had deteriorated to a dismissive irritation. Before long, Seabury found himself cut off from access to the archbishop, with the full playbook of bureaucratic stalling techniques and administrative excuses deployed against him. Exasperated, the bishop-elect turned again to his Writing Committee colleagues for strategic advice. Likely thanks to Thomas Chandler, an audience was secured with the bishop of Oxford, in the hopes that the cochair of the SPG committee on American episcopacy may prove an ally.

In another blow to Seabury, however, this too proved a fruitless venture. Shortly thereafter, a meeting was arranged with Lord North himself, to seek to negotiate the legal impediments to the plan. Not only did this, likewise, prove futile, but it also resulted in a material loss to the Connecticut cause; at some point while in his possession, the secretary of state managed to lose—or, possibly, discard—the copies of Seabury's letters testimonial. To make matters worse, the news of the bishop-elect's journey to England had spread quickly back in America. Infuriated by the move, then-president of Yale College and leader of the Connecticut Congregationalists, Ezra Stiles, set to work rallying opposition to the episcopal cause across New England.

Central to Stiles's campaign was the support of his close friend, Richard Price, English Nonconformist minister and philosopher, whose vocal support of the Revolution had won him critique and acclaim in equal measure. A confidant of Prime Minister William Pitt, Price exercised his political influence to ensure the continued opposition to any such legal changes as would permit Seabury's consecration. Faced with a set of obstacles remarkably larger than those originally envisaged, the final straw came for the New York priest by way of an enormous blow to morale and confidence from amongst the company of his electors. Of the eleven Anglican clergymen in Connecticut, four had decided to move north to Nova Scotia, bringing the majority of their congregations with them. Far from family and home, with the support of allies near and far appearing to dwindle, and facing hostility to his consecration by forces on either side of the Atlantic, it appeared that Seabury had nowhere left to turn.

On August 31, 1784, after more than a year of unsuccessful campaigning, the bishop-elect of Connecticut took what would become one of the most decisive steps in the history of global Anglicanism. Writing to his long-term friend in Edinburgh, Myles Cooper, Seabury made known his decision to seek episcopal orders at the hands of the Scottish bishops. On October 24, he departed London for Aberdeen. Consecration into the line of the Scottish Episcopal Church was not an entirely unanticipated option. While, indeed, "English orders" were the preferred choice, there is some evidence to suggest that the idea of a Scottish consecration was loosely floated as a "Plan B" even before Seabury departed from New York.

That such a suggestion would be made is, perhaps, not entirely surprising. Come the early 1780s, the episcopally ordered churches of New England and Scotland (particularly as found in its heartland of the north-east) bore striking similarities. Both existed as minority communities within strongly Congregationalist and Presbyterian territories, respectively, and appealed frequently to the early Christian image of being a "faithful remnant." Both were characterized by a preference for High Church doctrine, a theological slant reflected most keenly in attitudes towards the sacraments and the episcopate. (This will prove significant, later on, come the development of the first American Prayer Book.) And, both had encountered the consequences of the English Church's displeasure. Nevertheless, with less than half the number of laity across Episcopalian Scotland than found in Connecticut, alone, it is likely that the thought of a Scottish consecration for the first bishop in America had received little attention.

As such, no formal plans had yet been considered as to how this alternative might be achieved. Unbeknownst to the Seabury campaign, however, the groundwork for such a plan had already begun. Back in November 1783, the bishop-elect recorded a chance meeting with one George Bisset, a former colleague from New England. Aberdeenshire-native and sometime rector of Newport, Rhode Island, the Reverend Bisset had numbered among the Loyalist refugees who had sought the safety of London at the height of the war.

No doubt, Seabury had made known to his Scottish colleague the reason for his being in the capital and the difficulties he had encountered while there. Via a fellow Scot, James Elphinstone, Bisset then made contact with one John Allan, an Episcopalian priest in the Diocese of Edinburgh. Of Allan, he asked that a question be put to the bishops of the Scottish Episcopal Church. The question read, "Whether consecration can be obtained in Scotland, by an already dignified, and well-vouched American clergyman, now at London, for the purpose of perpetuating the Episcopal Reformed Church in America, particularly in Connecticut." As it happens, this was not the first time that such a question had been put to the Scottish episcopate.

A year earlier, the Reverend Dr. George Berkeley, son of the philosopher bishop of Cloyne, had approached then-coadjutor bishop of Aberdeen, John Skinner, with a novel proposition. In order to assist the newly independent Anglican Church in America, in which Berkeley had grown up and his father ministered, an itinerant missionary bishop would be consecrated in Scotland and sent, like an eighteenth-century St. Augustine, to the struggling church in the New World. Although Skinner, together with Bishops Robert Kilgour (Aberdeen) and Arthur Petrie (Ross and Moray), deemed such an idea fanciful and inappropriate, its consideration had prompted the coadjutor bishop to remark, "'Tis not to be doubted [that] the Bishops of this Church, on a proper application [from the Church in America], will think it their duty to extend the precious benefit [of episcopal orders] to them."[35]

Accordingly, in response to Bisset's question, the primus (Bishop Kilgour) responded to Bisset in the affirmative on December 13, 1783; together with Bishops Skinner and Petrie, three of the five Scottish bishops had expressed their willingness to consecrate the American priest. Of the two episcopal dissenters, only one expressed a strong opinion on the matter: Bishop William Falconar of Edinburgh—who died before the consecration took place—noted a general objection to the proposal, but would not elaborate further; Bishop Charles Rose of Dunkeld and Dunblane, however, opposed the plan with fervor, later making a point of having nothing to do with the event.

Deeply suspicious of the Loyalist Seabury and his English-sponsored ally, Myles Cooper, the elderly Jacobite champion displayed a paranoia with the conviction that the planned consecration would precipitate a renewed Hanoverian takeover and a tightening of the ongoing penal laws. Despite Bishop Rose's objections, however, Seabury had secured the support of three bishops in Kilgour, Skinner, and Petrie; with the minimum canonical number of consecrators for episcopal ordination thus met, the plan could proceed.

For the first time since his arrival on British soil, it seemed that the long-awaited advent of a bishop for the Church in America may indeed become a reality. Yet, in the face of such a favorable change of circumstances, and despite having received this news in late December, Seabury would persist with trying for an English consecration for a further eight months. By the end of August 1784, however, with the last hopes of receiving episcopal orders in the Church of England dashed, Seabury wrote to Cooper, making known his final decision to accept the offer of the Scottish bishops. Indeed, the bishop-elect's lack of contact with his northern rescuers had prompted the primus to remark to Bishop Petrie, "As Dr. Seabury had been so long silent, I reckoned the affair had been dropped."

Nevertheless, upon receiving confirmation, through the Reverend Cooper, of the New York priest's acceptance of the original offer, Bishop Kilgour reiterated his willingness to proceed with the consecration and invited Seabury to the northeastern see. Receiving the letter on October 11, Seabury quickly responded that he would arrive in Aberdeen by November 10. Shortly thereafter, a date was set for the consecration—Sunday, November 14—and plans for the event began in earnest.

Samuel Seabury arrived in Aberdeen on November 5, 1784, and made the acquaintance of Bishop Skinner the following morning. The bishop-elect appears to have made a good impression on his would-be consecrator, who would shortly thereafter inform his colleague in Moray that, "[Seabury] seems to be truly pious in his sentiments; fair, open and candid in his disposition; and without any of that duplicity which too often marks the characters of those who have much to do with this designing world."[36] Such a promising start would soon prove advantageous to the American candidate.

On November 8, a final attempt to prevent the consecration arrived in the form of a letter from a William Seller of Inverugie and an Alexander Murray of London. Both priests had close connections—the former as cousin, the latter as protégé—to the Reverend Dr. William Smith, first provost of the College of Philadelphia and president of the Maryland clerical convention. Ordained as priests together in December 1753, Smith and Seabury had long been ideological rivals, the former rooted firmly in the camp of William White and the Southern approach to episcopacy and the latter in the camp of Samuel Johnson and Jeremiah

Leaming and the radically different Northern attitudes to the same. Indeed, within five months of Seabury's election in Connecticut, William Smith had been elected bishop of Maryland.

In keeping with the plan championed by White, however, Smith's consecration was on hold until an institutional ecclesiastical structure had first developed. Whether the decision to protest Seabury's Scottish ordination came directly from White or from the initiative of his British supporters is unknown. Nevertheless, determined that the bishop-elect of Maryland should be the first bishop in America, and that the consecration should take place in England and occur only after the establishment of appropriate institutional structures, the Reverends Seller and Murray petitioned the primus to change his mind, arguing that a bishop in the Scottish line of succession would prove a schismatic stumbling block in the yet delicate context of the emerging American Church. Perhaps Kilgour may have taken heed of this warning, were it not for the letter's excess of personal slights to Seabury's character. Subsequently convinced by Skinner that such attacks were not warranted, the primus discounted the protest and decided to proceed.

Accordingly, on November 12, the three prelates convened with the American candidate in the co-adjutor's house. Following two days of interview and examination, through which Seabury appears to have performed with distinction, the date for the consecration arrived. Nearly eighteen months after his arrival from New York, Samuel Seabury was about to be made bishop. On the morning of November 14, 1784, the Reverend Seabury, Bishops Kilgour, Petrie, and Skinner, and some nearly five hundred Episcopalian laity—together with a sizeable cohort of the forty-five Scottish presbyters—gathered in the large private chapel of Bishop Skinner's Aberdeen city residence. In keeping with stipulations of the 1662 English and 1764 Scottish Prayer Books, alike, the service began with Morning Prayer and then followed into the Lord's Supper.

Bishop Skinner preached the sermon, taking the apostolic commission of Matthew 28 as his text, and used the opportunity to both expound a High Church doctrine of episcopal (apostolic) succession and attack the Erastianism of the English Church. This (apparently characteristic) sermon by the co-adjutor bishop prefaced the consecration proper, which took place according to the rites of the English Ordinal. (It is important to note, here, that the rite of consecration Seabury received in Scotland was almost exactly the same as he would have received had he been consecrated in England, the oath of loyalty to the sovereign being the only omission.)

Despite even significant differences between the liturgies of the English and Scottish Prayer Books, the Ordinal—that is, the collection of liturgies for the ordinations of deacons, priests, and bishops—remained the same. Indeed, it would be the middle of the twentieth century before any significant changes were made to it by any Anglican Church. A distinctly Anglican ecclesiological principle can be seen here: degrees of diversity in virtually every other liturgy notwithstanding, a shared and uniform rite of ordination has been deemed indispensable to the common church order by which Anglican ecclesial communities have been fundamentally linked. Having thus received the laying on of hands from the assembled bishops, Seabury joined their ranks as a member of the episcopal college. Some 496 days after his arrival in London, and some six hundred days after his election in Woodbury, Samuel Seabury had succeeded in his quest to receive episcopal orders.

An American Bishop

In the episcopal ordination of Bishop Seabury, the Anglican world bore witness to the first consecration of a bishop whose ministry would be exercised on "foreign" soil. The bishop's service would be to an Anglican Church neither British nor colonial, but entirely independent. This was, as yet, uncharted ecclesiological territory, the implications of which could only be guessed at. The magnitude of the decision to consecrate the American priest was not lost on the Scottish bishops; in extending this benevolent gesture to the emerging church of the New World, an opportunity for a degree of self-advantage was found.

In something of an "exchange" for having received episcopal orders, Bishop Seabury was to sign a seven-point concordat, sealing the "bond of union" between the "now rising Church in Connecticut" and the "Catholic remainder of the ancient Church of Scotland." Devised by Bishop Skinner, the document lays out over seven confessional articles a range of ecclesiological affirmations, paraphrased as follows:

1. That the two Churches wholly affirm the doctrine contained within Holy Scripture, and commit to maintaining the common faith ("once delivered") in unity

2. That the Church is the mystical Body of Christ, who is its sole head; that Christ has appointed bishops to manage the affairs of this spiritual society; and, that the exercise of ecclesiastical government belongs strictly to the jurisdiction of the bishops, independent of lay involvement
3. That the Churches of Connecticut and Scotland are, and commit to remaining, in full communion with one another
4. That, slight discrepancies arising from contextual circumstance notwithstanding, the two Churches shall remain in unity of worship, doctrine, and discipline
5. That the Holy Eucharist is the principal bond of union among Christians and the most solemn act of worship in the Christian church; and, that the Church of Connecticut will commit to celebrating the eucharistic rite according to the liturgies of the Scottish Episcopal Church
6. That brotherly fellowship and mutual correspondence between the two Churches shall be maintained, for the purposes of support and edification
7. That this concordat is declared only for the glory of God and the good of his church, and reflects an attempt to promote the cause of truth and the common salvation; and, that it is signed in a spirit of mutual love for, and confidence in, one another and each other's successors in office

Signed the day after the consecration (November 15, 1784), the agreement appears to have received Seabury's wholehearted support, with no amendments recorded. From the perspective of the new bishop of Connecticut, such a document must only have sweetened the deal. Not only had episcopal orders been imparted to the young American Church, but so too had an early and strong ally been made, whose High Church roots—and commitment to help foster the same in the West—reflected closely the flavor of Anglicanism characteristic of the New England churches.

Furthermore, the confirmation that the spiritual government of the American Church is to be independent of "lay powers" will have affirmed the (by then, almost thirty-year-old) decision of the Anglican communities of the American North to exclude the laity from its embryonic bodies of ecclesial governance. (A stark contrast to the "laity-inclusive" attitudes of the American South, this second article of the concordat would come to prove a further point of tension upon the new bishop's return.)

From the perspective of the Scottish bishops, on the other hand, this "alliance" with the emerging American Church would prove beneficial. Already far larger, wealthier, and freer than the Episcopal Church in Scotland, and with the full expectation of substantial growth on the horizon, the Anglican Church in America would—through the implementation of this concordat—bear responsibility for both supporting and carrying on the legacy of the Scottish tradition through which its episcopate began. Still choked by the effects of the penal laws, and thus limited in its capacity for growth and local expression alike, and with no sight of forthcoming relief, it is not surprising that the Scottish bishops should find personified in Samuel Seabury a lifeline by which the proud Episcopalian tradition may be continued. Thus sealing in the concordat the optimistic hopes of both Churches, the bishop of Connecticut marked the completion of the task issued him so long before by a small company of proactive priests in Woodbury.

Following his consecration, Seabury remained in Aberdeen for less than a week before beginning the slow return south. After a fortnight in Edinburgh, spent mostly with John Allan—George Bisset's colleague through whom the question of the Connecticut consecration was first put to the Scottish episcopate—the new bishop departed for London on December 7. Based in the capital for the next two and a half months, the winter of 1784–1785 saw a rapid end to the "honeymoon" period enjoyed in the North. After a long—and, ultimately, unsuccessful—campaign to convince the SPG to continue the stipends of (now independent) American Anglican missionaries, Bishop Seabury closed the chapter of his British sojourn with a degree of pessimism.

Despite his having secured the seeds of a "New World episcopate," the financial future of his beloved home Church remained unsure. On such a mixed note did the new bishop depart from London in late February 1785, arriving in Nova Scotia on April 23 and Newport on June 20. After an absence of more than two years, Samuel Seabury had returned to New England. Writing almost immediately to secretary of the Connecticut Convention, Abraham Jarvis, the bishop's first concern was to call a meeting of (what were now) "his" clergy. Accordingly, on August 2, 1785, America's first episcopally led clerical convention was held.

PART TWO

Culture and Context

THE STORY OF THE Anglican Communion is, to a large extent, one of trading wedded to military-imperialist expansion, the building of an empire, and the role played by state religion—the Church of England—in affirming the trinity of commerce, civilization, and culture (Christian) imposed on peoples who, with rare exception, neither invited nor welcomed these English exports. There is a kind of English cultural amnesia about this history. The imposition of colonial rule—commerce, Christianity, and civilization—required a fourth "C," namely *conquest*. That the Church of England went along with such actions all over the world will barely figure in any history of mission, where the missionaries will invariably be presented as pioneers and heroes. Some were, for sure. But this sanitization of the past risks not being able to see the darker depths at work. At the same time, there are some postcolonial theorists who have turned missionaries into little more than pantomime villains, which rather trivializes the motivations of many, and the hardships that most endured for what they believed to be a higher purpose.[37]

That said, the slave trade was effectively a "White plague" that wiped out much of West Africa. The colonial rule imposed on native populations across India and Africa was often a barely concealed form of "enlightened despotism," in which self-determination and democracy were brutally repressed as "rebellion." Of course, in an ecclesial polity that has consistently invested its episcopacy with a mystique that harbors a high degree of enlightened despotism, which still persists to this day, the synergy between the Church of England and the British Empire is rarely uncomfortable for either party.[38]

Politics reacts to culture. It rarely drives change, but rather responds to it. Religious organizations, such as churches and denominations, invariably take much longer to react to change, and are also far, far slower to bring about such change. The worldviews and outlooks that we are raised with can always be questioned and sometimes set aside. But the culture in which we are born, raised, taught, and cultivated conditions how we think, act, and imagine.

The word for "slave" is drawn from the same Latin root as the "Slavic" peoples. For many European and Near Eastern languages, slave and Slav were synonymous. For centuries, the Slavic peoples had been the most readily available source of slave labor. To some extent, the Slavs only had themselves to blame. During their own period of substantial expansion and conquests, and following the collapse of the Roman Empire, Slavs had expanded into the Iberian peninsula, North Africa, spread across the whole of Europe, and had reached Asia Minor and parts of Syria and the Near East. Galatia, a province of Turkey, is derived from the Slavic Gaul tribes that migrated there. (Note: St. Paul's Epistle to the Galatians was written to the churches of central Asia Minor, and therefore addressed to the direct descendants of Gaul's Celts and Slavs.) The Balkans, Albania, and other territories saw significant Slavic penetration, and traces of this can still be seen in certain languages (e.g., Finnish and Turkish).

Indeed, in eleventh-century Spain, which following Muslim invasions had fragmented into almost three dozen mini-states, some were ruled by the direct descendants of Slavs. These states were known as taifas, and several of them—notably Jaifa, Almeria, Denia, the Balearic Islands, Murcia, Tortosa, and Valencia—were ruled by Muslim Arab-Slavs, who were blond-haired and blue-eyed in appearance. Slavs had got themselves into these important positions through their military service to the ruling caliphs in previous centuries, where their conquest had resulted in the Slavs becoming slaves. They had been made to suffer and toil to work their way up the social and political ladder. For centuries, Slavs were sold as sex-slaves, made into eunuchs, and enslaved in harems.

By the eleventh century, slavery was endemic across the Arab world, and the market for captured Slavs extended from the sub-Sahara to Central Asia, and across all Europe. African Barbary slave traders worked with European traders in this, with Slavs the main ethnic group bought and sold. The Arab world was the undisputed leader in this global market, and although we can never know the precise numbers involved from medieval times, the volume of human trafficking was in the millions, and on a scale never seen before.

In England, the population at the time of the Norman Conquest consisted of no more than two million. It is estimated that in 1066 one in every ten English people was a slave bonded to a manor, lord, or religious house such as a monastery or convent. Yet by 1120, England had no slaves. However, a much higher percentage of the population had opted into being bonded, or forms of serfdom. The English Church was a stakeholder in this economy, and remained so until the agricultural land reforms and industrial revolution of the eighteenth century began to transform the labor market. Diets changed too. Agricultural workers were fed with pints of weak beer and bread to keep them active—but not especially nourished. The mills and factories of the Industrial Revolution required a different kind of stamina, and the staple diet quickly became tea and sugar. This was of course produced through slave labor abroad to enable productive working-class serfdom at home.

Sometimes, to understand the evolution of empire and church, it pays to follow the money. Scottish Angus beef owes its quality and proliferation to the English clearances of the Highlands and enclosures to create substantial pastures. Between 1710 and 1790, the average weight of cattle doubled, and selling price and profits tripled. In 1600, the weight of oxen, at best, was 500 pounds (or 230 kilograms). Today, a modern Angus beef cow is 1,800 pounds, or 815 kilograms. The greater the productivity of the land for the Church of England, the greater the tithes. This continued well into the nineteenth century. Furthermore, in England, Wales, and Ireland, higher productivity and an ever-depleting workforce (due to the Industrial Revolution) incentivized clergy to have fewer laborers, thereby further enhancing their tithe-based profits. As English colonies multiplied, imported food became cheaper and cheaper. As long as slavery continued to be productive abroad, church and government in England continued to benefit.[39]

Mechanization in food production would, however, eventually have political and economic consequences. English ports built vast factories and warehouses for refining raw sugar. The advent of tinned food—a French invention much admired by Napoleon, and quickly developed and adopted by military forces across Europe—transformed consumption. The railways also changed the economic landscape for food production and consumption. By the end of the eighteenth century, many slave plantations were increasingly uneconomic to run. With social pressure building to end slave trading—tea and sugar boycotts such as that led by William Fox in 1791, for example—it was only a matter of time before slave trading was abolished in 1807.[40]

Yet none of this quite explains the continued trade in slavery conducted by the British and other European countries *prior* to the New World being exploited and settled, and the beginnings of Dutch, Spanish, Portuguese, French, and British Empires. The missing piece in this jigsaw is the relatively small Baltic state of Lithuania. It wasn't until the end of the fourteenth century that this nation adopted Christianity as the state religion (the result of dynastic union with Poland). Primarily Slavic, Lithuania was therefore the last "local supply" of slaves, since Christianity, under Roman Catholic teaching and canon law, had consistently outlawed Christians making slaves of other Christians.

Put more bluntly, by the turn of the fifteenth century, Europe was officially a pagan-free zone. Or rather, the pagans were now baptized. Again, history and etymology is important. "Pagan" only meant "villager, peasant, country person, rural, provincial" and the like. The association with pagans as non-Christians was to come later. To the medieval and ancient world, a pagan (from the Latin, *pangere*), was simply someone fixed to a particular location, and not mobile. A pagan might still be a bonded serf in feudal, early medieval England. But they would still be a Christian and not a slave.

Yet even during the seventeenth century, slavery was something of an occupational hazard. Christians were not immune from enslavement. John Knox (c. 1505–1572), the leader of the Scottish Reformation, spent two years chained up as a galley slave with other Scottish lairds, following a French raid on St. Andrew's, Fife. In 1554 the Elizabethan privateer and seafarer Sir John Hawkins formed a syndicate of merchants specifically to engage in slave trading. Hawkins's main modus operandi was to steal slaves off the Portuguese by hijacking their ships and selling them on at considerable profit to Spanish colonies. Famously, in 1564, his crew captured four hundred Africans being transported by the Portuguese and sold them to a Spanish settlement in what is now modern-day Colombia. Even in the nineteenth century, the fudgy boundaries between indentured laborer, serfdom, and slavery were blurred. In Assam, India, to quench the British thirst for tea, 95 percent of the crop-pickers were imported from overseas. No medical facilities or care were provided to the workforce, and mortality rates ran as high as 30 percent. Laborers—many were women and children—would be stripped and flogged for trying to escape.

Slave Trading and the Making of National Myths

As many historians and students of politics and law are aware, Great Britain has no written constitution. It is also worth remembering that the Church of England has no written doctrines of its own either. Such absences place great responsibility upon, and vest considerable power within, the judges as interpreters of law. It is no secret that for many in the Church of England, with its own ecclesiastical law that very few comprehend, let alone abide by, this has produced a culture in which episcopacy wields enormous power. Bishops are judges, pastors, executives, priests, . . . and can also be your prosecutor or defender. All in the same day too, moreover. That which is unwritten, yet must also be obeyed and can demand fealty, will always be a potential channel for abuses.

While the ecological consequences of slavery seem hard to fathom, the human cost could be greater. Widespread sexual exploitation of female slaves led to sexual disease, which in turn reduced fertility amongst female slaves. Fewer children meant less profit for slave owners, and infant deaths due to congenital syphilis from venereal disease were commonplace. As Alex Renton notes, some plantation owners realized that the mistreatment of women was uneconomic. To head off the campaigning pleading of the abolitionists, female slaves started to be educated, and their children baptized, from the late eighteenth century, with edicts forbidding the physical punishment of women. The churches bought into this as progress, naturally.[41]

Of course, many plantation owners, including upright Christian exemplars, regarded the low birth-rate amongst enslaved women as indicative of their natural inbred immorality, and their inherent heathen outlook. Even in the last half of the nineteenth century, with slavery outlawed in British colonies, the authorities were trying to reintroduce whippings and the treadmill as punishment for petty crime. In 1865, children caught pilfering were required to work for free on plantations for up to five years, which in effect amounted to the reintroduction of children being placed in slave labor.[42]

The very making of the Third World is a colonial legacy. Mike Davis charts the decline of British agriculture against the backdrop of cheap imported consumable goods from across the British Empire. The mechanization of English agriculture via the Industrial Revolution produced a significant bump or uplift in Church of England income for much of the eighteenth century through the tithe system. Indeed, Charles Darwin's father hoped his son might become a rector or lay rector of a parish, which might have funded his interests in natural science. The Darwin family could have bid, at auction, for a handful of "livings" (i.e., parish) that with a tithe barn and glebe land produced a steady annual income of £300 (about £50,000 or $65,000 in today's money). Darwin himself would not have needed to be ordained, let alone attend the parish church, as poor curates could be hired for as little as £50 a year (£8,000, or $10,000 today). It was not uncommon for landowners to be lay rectors of several parishes. Usually, a vicarage or rectory would only be built if the owner intended to reside there. Most did not.

However, the late eighteenth century and much of the nineteenth century posed challenges in financing the Church of England. Yet those challenges were largely met through many of the new income streams derived from the exploitation of the colonies, which as Davis shows, led to regular periodic famines in Africa, India, and elsewhere in Asia. The creation of subservient client colonies leaves the people and the land at the mercy of economics, politics, and weather, and Davis cites numerous instances where entire populations were left to starve. As with slavery, the Church of England, like other wealthy English corporations, was a beneficiary of the politics and economics of investment risk and returns, and it gained from its early stake in internationalism.

It would be unforgiveable to let the bicentennial of the Demerara Revolt in August 1823 go without mention. John Gladstone was the slave owner at the center of the brutality, and is it happens, the father of William Gladstone, a four-time prime minister of Great Britain. The uprising that occurred in Demerara, British Guiana (now called Guyana) came in the aftermath of the Haitian Revolution of 1791–1804, which had driven out the Spanish and established the first independent Black republic outside Africa. In 1816 some four thousand slaves in Barbados rose up against their British masters. This revolt was brutally crushed. But the stage was set for further revolts, and in Demerara, August 1823, nine thousand slaves rose against the brutal regime presided over by John Gladstone, in which rape, torture, brandings, beatings, and executions were daily occurrences.

The revolt incited around thirteen thousand Africans to rise up on more than sixty plantations across the region. On August 20, 1823, two hundred slaves were shot dead when British troops opened fire on a gathering of two thousand protesting strikers who were refusing to disperse. The leaders of the revolt were tortured and decapitated, and their heads speared on spikes as a warning to others. John Gladstone, at the time of the revolt, owned over 2,500 slaves outright by purchase, or through mortgage loans. Slaves were property, so a mortgage loan was perfectly normal.

The revolt, though unsuccessful, inspired the 1831 Jamaican Uprising. Just two years later the British Parliament passed the Emancipation of Slavery Act in 1833. Even here, please note, the gradualism of change. In 1807, the slave trade in the British Empire was abolished (with Jefferson's American government following suit in 1808). But slave ownership was *not* abolished. That would take another quarter of a century, with slaves in the colonies (excluding these areas still ruled and governed by the East India Company) not being freed until 1838—and only after slave owners, rather than the slaves themselves, received compensation. Many slaves then had to work as unpaid "apprentices" on colonial estates and plantations for several years after 1833, before being finally awarded their emancipation.

The Black Lives Matter movement can trace its origins to these atrocities. These events were and are crimes against humanity. The legacy of such evil lives on, however. Modern Guyana is divided ethnically between the descendants of the enslaved from Africa and from India that John Gladstone began importing (numbering over 230,000 by the end of the nineteenth century), and the Indigenous peoples of the region. European settlers barely accounted for 4 percent of Guyana in 1833, yet were substantially compensated for the loss of all their "property"—slaves. Furthermore, the slaves were forced to continue working—for free, and for a further six years—as their "apprenticeship," which only when completed would result in the actual award of their emancipation and freedom.[43]

Even Niall Fergusson's *Empire* (2004) remarks on the average Englishman's utter incomprehension of Hindu and Islamic faith, which by necessity had to be chalked up as "heathen." For many missionary societies, what began as chaplaincy to the colonial masters expanded into conversionist efforts launched upon Indigenous populations. Slavery was baked into the funding of this missionary work, and often essential to its actual delivery. By the mid-eighteenth century, evangelism was cast as light to those who were languishing in darkness; truth to those perishing in ignorance; civilization to those living in depravity; and salvation to those who would otherwise perish as heathen. There was an invisible trinity at work: commerce, civilization, and Christianity, which went hand-in-hand. Few churches or denominations were prepared to engage in the critical self-reflection that would have acknowledged the fourth "C": conquest. To convert the heathen, they first had to be subdued.[44]

It is easy to overlook the fact that one key modus operandi within the colonialist endeavor was to invest in fostering division between different religious or ethnic groups. In India, Hindu and Muslim alterity and rivalry was exploited, and even the caste system was overly defined, concretized, and weaponized against Indigenous populations.[45] Daniel Defoe (1660–1731) and his infamous hierarchical classification system—which he developed in political, social, and historical works—travelled well across the British Empire. Defoe's taxonomies appealed to those who were keen to impose order on the cultural disorientation they experienced when abroad. It also gave the colonists a rationale for their mandate: divide and conquer; separate and rule.[46] All across the Empire, English exclaves and enclaves boomed. Most had a Church of England chaplain as pillion, providing the spiritual legitimacy for the imperial expansionism.[47]

The legacy of the British Empire has been firmly incorporated into the Church of England polity too, and beyond. It expresses itself in nascent ways for the most part, through cultures of monarchical deference, mannered-ness, class, and social order. In other words, the very "civilization" that the Victorians and Edwardians sought to export to the heathen and the colonies carries with it idealized notions of English identity, conduct, and propriety. Because these rules and codes are not written down, the elite have extensive interests in maintaining a hierarchical social order that is far more dependent on class, hereditary power, and the like. This mostly suits the English. But it is an aspect of culture that has been sacralized over the centuries. The cultural contexts for other expressions of Anglicanism are quite different.

Cultural Divisions

How can we possibly justify dating—and so precisely—such a decisive split and fissure in the Anglican Communion (November 14, 1784) before Anglicanism had even so much as dipped its proverbial toes in foreign seas? The answer lies in understanding the social-cultural history that Samuel Seabury's ministry emerged within. Only when that is understood can we begin to grasp why the fracture in Anglicanism has grown over time.[48]

In 1775, severe grain shortages in France led to bread riots. In 1783, a volcanic eruption in Iceland darkened the skies over Europe, leading to extreme weather fluctuations. This climate crisis, combined with economic collapse, contributed to the French Revolution. The American Revolution, starting in 1775, was influenced by abrupt freezing in the Northern Atlantic, disrupting trade and leading to increased taxes by the British. The Boston Tea Party in 1773 was a response to these taxes. Economic hardships and resentment towards British rule escalated, eventually leading to the revolution.

Frank Snowden's work provides intriguing insight into the role of pandemics in societal reordering.[49] His argument that pandemics have always reordered society is particularly relevant. Plagues and famines don't just happen overnight; they require certain conditions. The devastating intersection of climate disruption and political upheaval is a vivid picture of the human suffering that results from these crises. He gives examples, such as the first Great Awakening in America and events in England, attributing the socioreligious revolutions to extreme weather conditions.

As Jenkins astutely observes, the comparable climate crises afflicting America in the late 1730s and early 1740s were to be repeated in the second Great Awakening, beginning in the 1790s in remoter states, such as Kentucky and Tennessee. Revolutions, like revivals, tend to occur when there is nowhere else to turn.[50] They arise typically out of desperation, long-term alienation, and a sense of powerlessness. The American and French Revolutions were related to the effects of climate crisis, just as Europe was to suffer further revolts and turmoil from 1815. In both cases, Icelandic volcanic eruptions (Laki in 1783 and Tambora in 1815) spewed out so much sulfurous gas as to cause a "fog" over all Europe and America. Extreme cold, crop failures, and food shortages followed, with demand exceeding supply. Some religious sects emerged at this time, fearing the end of the world.[51]

Understanding the geopolitical landscape of the final quarter of the eighteenth century is of fundamental importance in accounting for the shifts in religious identity and institutions too. France lost many of its priests, since they were perceived to be agents of the Crown. Religious persecution is rarely confined to being solely about faith, since the political ordering of society then, as in ancient times and in our present world, is inevitably bound up with loyalties that include faith.[52]

There is a problematic moral geography in relation to the Anglican Communion that needs some serious reckoning. The expansion of Anglican churches on the back of the British Empire requires careful and considered critiques in the twenty-first century. If the wider global Communion is to be an authentic agent of spiritual and ecclesial change in the future, it will have to reckon with the moral, social, political, and religious foundations upon which it was able to expand in the first place.

Consider, for example, the consecrations of Gene Robinson, Barbara Harris, or Jack Spong. It is a matter of record that the presiding bishop of TEC, Frank Griswold, was often asked by other Anglican primates across the Communion, "How could you let these consecrations happen?" The presumption behind the question is revealing. For it assumes a world of backdoor diplomacy, courtiers, and strings that can be pulled in order to stymie such appointments. Think of Jeffrey John as bishop of Reading, Southwark, or Llandaff, or Nicholas Henderson's appointment and withdrawal as a bishop in Africa. All democratic decisions overturned—"on reflection"—by the powers-that-be.[53]

The monarchical establishment works differently from democracy. The Old World order operates through paternalistic implicit means, and has no need of a written constitution. Those who rule reign. The New World order, in contrast, has a constitution, and works through explicit democratic debate, and clarity in governance. So how did Frank Griswold reply to his critics? He explained that there was an election for these episcopal vacancies; the people voted; the diocese approved; and then the General Convention ratified the vote and the appointment. The people had spoken.

But, countered the critics, how was that theologically *proper*? Griswold would explain again that the people had spoken; they had thought, weighed, and prayed through these deliberations. The Holy Spirit can just as easily work through democratic processes as any directive, monarchical or autocratic, concerning the anointing of a candidate. The agency of an autocratic unaccountable elite is not thought to be essential for the good working of the third person of the Trinity, even in the New Testament.

Cultural Roots

The end of the eighteenth century was an extraordinary time to be British. Thomas Paine believed that the world would be a better place if Britain was reduced in stature, and the monarchy abolished. Other radical and revolutionary thinkers pressed for Britain to become a republic in order to rid the world of slavery and economic bondage under the East India Company. Religion was part of the autocracy. The Test and Corporation Acts of 1661, 1673, and 1678 had all placed restrictions on the civil liberties of persons who were not prepared to assent to the doctrines, practices, and teachings of the Church of England. The extension of exclusions and prohibitions placed on Catholics and Nonconformists continued well into the nineteenth century, which affected who could stand for Parliament, study at university, and otherwise live a normal, free life. It is puzzling how the English promoted themselves as pioneers and paragons of freedom across the world, yet all the while invested in severely restricting freedom, even in Britain.[54]

Edmund Burke thought Britain was unsalvageable. The influential writers Edward Gibbon, Catharine Macaulay, and David Hume were deeply uncomfortable—nauseous, even—over the Britain that was emerging at the end of the eighteenth century. This as a country where the exploitation and subjugation of other nations was seen as normal, entitled, fair game, and backed up by military force. In turn, this was overseen by a mercantile class whose greed seemed limitless, and who propagated classism, elitism, and racism. Indeed, the entire social construct of "Western civilization" is something of an oxymoron. It was a code for the imposition of commerce and conquest, endorsed by the spiritual wing of the enterprise, namely the Church of England.[55]

Both America and France in the last quarter of the eighteenth century witnessed regime change after the traumatic economic effects of climate events. Sometimes, dramatic geophysical events spawn intense religious speculation. For example, the devastating earthquake that afflicted Lisbon in 1755, killed twelve thousand people and destroyed nearly every church. The subsequent tsunami accounted for further destruction and casualties, with significant damage and deaths reported in Morocco, Galway (Ireland), Cornwall (ten-foot-high waves), Finland, and reaching as far as Greenland. Brazil also registered damage to property. The earthquake happened on All Saints' Day, prompting speculation amongst theologians and philosophers that the disaster was a sign of divine judgment.

As Brian Fagan notes, such attributions were hardly new. Lutherans viewed an exceptionally deep snowfall on Leipzig in 1562 as a sign of God's displeasure, much in the way that Jonah had hoped God's wrath would fall on Nineveh. In 1563, the German town of Wisensteig burnt sixty-three women suspected of witchcraft to death who were held to be responsible for the freezing weather and the failure of intercessory prayers to reverse the climate change. A small "ice age" from 1588–1620 saw record numbers of women burnt to death in France, England, and across Europe, blamed for witchcraft and God's anger for human sin that caused the weather to change adversely, leading to crop failures, bread riots, and mass starvation. In the Swiss region of Bern, it is estimated that over a thousand women were burnt in this period. Flooding in the Low Countries after heavy rainfall also prompted people to reason that this was God's punishment. On the other hand, the hurricane-force winds of 1588 that blew the Spanish Armada to destruction were regarded by the English as a favorable sign of God's intervention.[56]

To be sure, few today would attribute an earthquake or hurricane to some direct action of divine retribution. But as a metaphor, climate crises and tipping points work well for our current context. In particular, we are invited to contemplate the actions that governments, nations, churches, and denominations might take towards the "cultural climatology" to which they are exposed, as well as take stock of the normative, regulative, or comfortable temperature that exists within their own polity.

In one sense, we could say that religion is a regulative framework for collective moods, amongst other things. Critics of Anglican polity have often mocked Anglicanism for its Goldilocks-Laodicean preferences (see Rev 3:14–22). So neither hot nor cold—just tepid; the classic *via media*—best served at "room temperature." And because Anglicanism is born of England, just like its climate, the polity often struggles to cope with extremities. Anglicanism is a remarkably temperate ecclesial polity: cloudy, with occasional sunny spells and the odd shower. The outlook, in a word, mild. The English love mildness. And Anglicanism—at least in its English forms—has almost apotheosized "mildness" as the ideal spiritual temperature to set the necessary tone and mood.

More seriously, one might surmise that the English proclivity for mildness goes further, and invests niceness with sacred-moral value. Carrie Tirado Bramen's work[57] is alive to how the English export of niceness to the American colonies was eventually refracted, and then diversified. The English proclivity tends towards expectations of civic order guaranteeing niceness in secular and ecclesiastical polity. For Americans, expectations of niceness are primarily located in individualism rather than corporate entities. The differences might look superficial, but they have a bearing on attitudes to empire and imperialism. The English have tended to see their expansive empire as one of benevolent assimilation and mild sway.

As a rule, the English do not like to think of their empire as being grounded in military force, coercion, or exploitation. They mean to be nice, after all.[58] While wishing to avoid national stereotypes, the notion of a national temperament has important consequences for the character and personality of institutions. So notions of niceness, niceties, politeness, manners, and modesty will all play a significant role in farming the inchoate grammar of assent in a denomination, let alone an empire. The obviousness of this can be seen in the export of pastoral, nice, kind, muscular-male images and ideals of Christ to the colonies in everything from stained-glass images in colonial churches to selected hymns and liturgies, and the sermons and teachings.

Unconsciously, the English exported their "Christology of Niceness," which of course they believed that they faithfully followed, and were shaped by. Wholly unaware of the classism and inherent racism of such theology, the English are affronted by challenges to their preferred mode of conduct. With such theological constructions of reality in place, the English will struggle to ever see themselves as the aggressor across their empire, nor comprehend the virtues and cause of the protester and rebel. Christ is no less present in such paradigms. But Jesus will not be portrayed as a disrupter of the status quo, whether civic or religious.

The English-made stained glass in the churches of the colonies upholds English virtues: manliness, strength, kindness—and the safety of a world that is improved by niceness.[59] The English are invested in niceness and mildness. It is only slightly offset by the total authoritarianism of a monarchical God (and his Church of England) that has the right and power to rule and reign, irrespective of the democratic will and consent of the people.[60] Here again, classism and those hierarchies inculcated through elitist education systems that institutionalize rationality and rules, and violence and punishment for their breaches, will all find their way into shaping theological horizons. The hidden rules of English behavior have a lot to answer for.

Cultural Division in Anglicanism—Early Signs

If you were to ask the average Episcopalian churchgoer what Anglican splits and divisions come to mind if the subject is ever raised, the chances are they'd nominate a handful of issues or events. The usual candidates would emerge: sexuality, gender, liturgical reform, and perhaps ethnicity or class. Some would add to this list divorce and remarriage, schismatic ordinations and consecrations, and other contested events and outlooks that have subsequently caused significant rifts. I appreciate that an approach to ecclesial polity through concerns that currently consume us does carry some risk. Decolonizing a museum or degree course is not straightforward, and as previously mentioned, sometimes more can be lost than apparently gained.

The foundations for Anglican (or Episcopal) polity are rooted in fears (of loss of control, and of republican democratic government displacing monarchies), splits, and fractures that were not necessarily terminal, but neither did they have much to do with the church—at least directly. And yet these remain serious and unaddressed challenges. But equally, they are not easily repaired. They are baked into a legacy of empire, and its eventual degeneration.

As Peter Frankopan the historian suggests, Henry VIII's motivation for empire-building was a mixture of envy, fear of being left behind by other nations who had already had a considerable head start on empire-building and colonizing, greed, self-aggrandizement, and concerns about being dominated by the new wealth of older foreign neighbors.[61] The English might have been the epitome of the petite bourgeoisie and a nation of shopkeepers, even in Tudor times, but they were not about to be cut out of the spoils Spain, Portugal, France, and the Dutch were already beginning to enjoy from the late fifteenth and early sixteenth centuries. Slaves, spices, gold and silver, precious metals, and new lands claimed for the monarchs of these countries, including the Holy Roman Emperor, Charles V, drew the English into the hunt for riches beyond their own shores.

As Frankopan astutely observes, Henry VIII was positively embarrassed by the accumulation of wealth and power being enjoyed by Dutch, Spanish, French, and Portuguese monarchs, commissioning "explorations," often under the thinly veiled guise of Christian mission to the heathen, but with boats returning laden with treasures. Henry VIII was green with envy, and as a highly competitive individual, not enjoying the experience of being left trailing in the European wealth league.[62] But is it really fair to claim that aspects of the English Reformation were motivated by financial, political, and territorial rivalries?

To answer that, one must go back to the Anglo-French summit of June 1520—the Field of the Cloth of Gold (*Camp du Drap d'Or*)—which took place on the border of England's last remaining stake abroad, namely Calais. The object of the gathering was to enhance the bond of friendship between Henry VIII and the French monarch, Francis I, and demonstrate parity of wealth in a pageant of exhibits, treasures, and possessions that paraded affluence of the monarchy and nobility. Henry VIII had earlier, in May, held an identical (and equally expansive) summit in the Netherlands with Charles V. The gatherings were carefully choreographed to establish equality of arms and prosperity, so that there was no need for further competition. However, Charles V and Francis I were indisputably superior in terms of wealth, power, authority and the extent of their domains. England was, by any account, the lesser power in both meetings. The meetings were successful, insofar as they enshrined non-aggression pacts across Europe so that resources could be diverted to resisting the growing challenge of Ottoman expansion.

Spanish and Portuguese colonization was already well underway in the fifteenth century, with both nations making forays into North and West Africa, the Caribbean, and the Americas. England was barely at the races, so to speak, and the rapid accrual of treasures, lands, and resources did not escape the attention of the English. So the English break with the Roman Catholic Church that ultimately took place in 1534 was born out of an alloy of issues. Ideologically, some of the groundwork for the English Reformation had been laid by Renaissance humanists. In 1520, an Augustinian monk by the name of Martin Luther had begun a breakaway movement—protestors against papal authority and some Catholic doctrine, who were dubbed Protestants—who likewise drew on the rationality of Renaissance thinkers.

However, the English Reformation began its life as more of a political affair rather than being a straightforward theological movement. In 1527, Henry VIII had requested that Pope Clement VII grant him an annulment of his marriage. The pope refused. In response, Henry VIII effectively weaponized Parliament, and between 1529–1536 it passed a series of laws abolishing papal authority in England, stripping all religious houses and orders of their wealth and lands, and declaring Henry to be head of the Church of England. With Henry VIII's new powers, final authority in doctrinal disputes now also rested with the monarch. Though the English religious reforms should not be conflated with the political reforms that preceded it, these were enacted under the Reformation Parliament of 1529–1536, uniting the secular and religious sources of authority under one single sovereign power. This was a sequestration of religious powers and assets under state control.

The Church of England did not actually make substantial changes to its doctrines until much later.[63] That it did so is undeniable, as the Thirty-Nine Articles affirm. The Church of England is theologically Protestant, but performatively and liturgically Catholic in appearance. In other words, a typical English fudge. It is a hybrid that maintained the quasi-monarchical powers of baron-bishops, but under the banner of "catholicity," so never offering shared power and authority to congregations, thus denying them autonomy and the benefits of subsidiarity. Further confusions obscured English Anglican identity in the centuries that followed. It rarely speaks of itself as a Protestant church, which it is, and the Coronation Oath affirms that. It believes that it has Evangelical and Catholic wings, which it does, though these are influences on styles of worship and churchmanship, and at most are to be regarded as distinctive accents speaking over a common core of doctrines. Confusingly, in the wider Anglican Communion, it is these accents that were inculcated, not the core doctrines. More than half the Anglican provinces in the world don't subscribe to the Thirty-Nine Articles, and even fewer swear any oath of allegiance to the British monarch.

Henry VIII's fight with the pope over his wish to have his marriage to Catherine of Aragon annulled was also mixed up with the relative sense of impoverishment that Henry believed he had to endure. Yes, he needed the pope's annulment. But the pope was not in a position to grant such a thing without the approval of Charles V. It was Charles, ultimately, who had the real power in Europe, and that extended to being able to block a papal decree if desired. In what would now be deemed a conflict of interest, the pope said "no" to Henry VIII's petition. But the decision really lay with Charles, who was (of course) related to Catherine of Aragon—she was his aunt. Catherine did not want divorce. Blood is thicker than water. Charles supported his aunt.

Seen in this light, the ensuing English religious revolution was bound to be something of a ruse to seize the assets and treasures of the monasteries, convents, and priories, which was a far less expensive way of amassing an awful lot of power and wealth, and propelling Henry upwards in the European monarch league-table of wealth. It was nationalization on an epic scale. Lead stripped from church roofs and stone from monasteries, priories, and convents, which were dismantled and resold for their building materials, along with their lands and revenues. Gold, silver, priceless books and paintings were sequestrated, and kept or sold. Henry VIII had, in challenging the pope to grant him an annulment to Catherine, inadvertently picked a fight with Europe's richest man, Charles V. Henry lost. But the Reformation reversed the result, and the rapid program of religious asset-stripping in England gave Henry a triple win. He got his new wife. He got his wealth. And he broke the power of Rome to interfere in England.

To some extent, the Big Four nation states of the sixteenth century—the Netherlands, France, Spain, Portugal (only later to be joined by England to make it the Big Five)—had been groomed and goaded by the tall tales told by the explorers they commissioned and funded. It was the Spanish and Portuguese forays into central and South America that yielded substantial returns on the investment in exploration, which in turn led to such merciless exploitation.

The English, however, were decades behind the curve in acquiring wealth, power, and lands abroad. Henry VIII's organized program of asset-stripping changed that. It was, however, the basis on which the foundations for an empire were to eventually be established. The mix of commerce, politics, and religion was not simply an English vice. The United East India Company of the Netherlands, known as the Dutch East India Company (dating from 1602), was founded within a few years of the English East India Company (dating from 1600), but the Dutch deployment of ships and personnel in the causes of commerce and conquest was greater than the English and the rest of Europe put together.

In all this, the East India Company was frequently able to call upon the Church of England's clergy for chaplaincy duties overseas, and the newly acquired fortunes of English Anglicanism were therefore wholly bound up in the asset-stripping of religious houses under Henry VIII (the head of the English Church), which paved the way for the commercial expansion and exploitation of overseas territory. The entwining of commerce, civilization, Christianity, and conquest over the next few centuries was able to enjoy the services and support of the Church of England as the spiritual arm of an empire. In turn, the Church directly and indirectly benefited in wealth, geographical influence, and reputation.

The costs of such exploitation were reprehensible, and their legacy continues to this day. From 1757, Robert Clive (1725–1774, the first governor general of Bengal, and also a baronet—the first Lord Clive of Plassey) had been able to combine the military and commercial muscle of the East India Company to intervene in local civil wars, and amass enormous wealth and power for his employers and sponsors. By 1770, Clive had become one of the richest men in the world by virtue of taking over the taxation of Bengal. The exploitation that followed was one of ruthless greed. Two million pounds of revenue (which would amount to tens of billions today) was appropriated and redistributed to East India Company officers. The price of food soared, inflation rocketed, and famine followed, with millions dying of starvation—possibly up to one third of the population. This was an entirely English-made disaster.[64]

Then Karma comes. Karma is a form of spiritual irony. Within Indian religion, it refers to the universal causal law by which good or bad actions determine the future of an individual. The Bengal famine caused a huge labor shortage, which led to a rapid decline in productivity. Revenues quickly collapsed, prompting a run on the shares of the East India Company. The English government had to intervene with a banking bail-out, and by 1773, the only way to steady the nerves of investors was the tax on tea imposed on the American colonies. The rest, as they say, is history.

The Church of England and the British Empire

Throughout this period, hundreds and hundreds of English Anglican clergy served the East India Company militia and the colonial administrations as chaplains. The chaplains were overseen by English bishops, and clearly seen as key personnel in the protection of the East India Company's interests. Humphrey Prideaux (1648–1724), who was dean of Norwich, argued that the wealth and success of the Dutch East India Company was entirely down to God's favor, as colonies founded by the Netherlands had been actively furthering Christianity. Prideaux urged the East India Company to adopt Church of England chaplains, so as to establish sound Protestant belief and oppose popish ambitions. Churches and schools were duly set up and run by the Company, with Church of England chaplains presiding over the foundations.

Church of England interests were deeply embedded in the monopoly held by the East India Company. Church of Scotland (Presbyterian) ministers were only reluctantly allowed to minister in India from 1814, when the East India Company was forced to renew its charter. The East India Company had also strongly discouraged evangelists and missionary societies from working in India, on the grounds that Christianizing the Indigenous population would impact the economic interests of the Company, and also interfere with slave labor. In the end, parliamentary legislation had to be brought forward in the early nineteenth century to enable permits and licenses to be issued to missionaries seeking to serve in India. Nonetheless, for more than a century, the Church of England's own interests had been furthered through its collusion with a commercial monopoly, backed by armed militia.[65]

The havoc wreaked upon India was to continue well into the twentieth century, with Winston Churchill, no less, arguing that India had to be held onto at all costs if the British Empire was to remain a serious entity. Churchill's fear of losing India was rooted in his conviction that for Britain to *look* great, it needed substantial imperial domains, and the labor to serve its empire. Even when a cataclysmic famine took hold of Bengal (again) between 1943–1944, British reputation was privileged above political reform and welfare. It is estimated that between one-and-a-half million and three million died.[66]

It is precisely this kind of double-think that kept English slave colonies such as Bunce Island in business (located in Freetown Harbor, Sierra Leone). Bunce Island was settled and fortified by English slave traders from around 1670, who sold captives on the American and Caribbean plantations. The island was run by London-based firms, including the Royal African Company, which again could call upon the Church of England. Slaves on Bunce Island did not benefit from the 1807 Act that banned the slave trade. As they were already the property of their owners, the Act of Parliament did not apply to them, nor to other British slave-owning colonies. Banning the slave trade did not free those who were slaves already.

The English ambition for its own empire and the global aspirations of the Church of England were joined at the hip the moment Henry VIII embarked upon his unique spiritual, political, and fiscal project. Henry VIII feared inferiority in wealth, power, and influence. His desire to have the English at the top table of European dynasties eventually paid off when the others began to decline, which left England presiding at top table. It renamed itself the United Kingdom and Great Britain. But this was still essentially an English-led drive for preeminence.

As we noted in the introduction, micro-studies of denominational histories show that it is the small details—the small advertisements and notices in the newspapers—that remind us that the past is a foreign country.[67] In the local newspapers before and after the American War of Independence, we read advertisements requesting tutors to help with schooling, dancing, and music. There were tutors offering such services, but who lacked the community space to provide their education. Yet modern readers would be shocked by the regular appearance of small ads offering ten-dollar rewards for "runaway slaves" and "missing negroes."[68]

In these old newspapers, one is immediately confronted with this awful and heinous atrocity: the trade in human beings, which was legal and normal. In the 1700s in this New World, before and after becoming independent, people of all ages, and because of the color of their skin, were bought and sold as chattels. They had no rights, and as far as those posting these advertisements were concerned, these people were, quite literally, lost property. If you were to find such lost property, you could return him or her to the owner, and be paid ten dollars for your trouble. Some of the advertisements listed "domestic"—that is to say, female—slaves, and their children too, also as lost property. And some of the slaves who had been bought and were now to be sought were mere juveniles.

Seabury was himself a slave owner, having inherited some slaves from his father. The Seabury family was socially conservative, and not radical. And slavery was intrinsic to the social and economic life of the thirteen Eastern Seaboard colonies that started to break away from Britain in 1775, and formally announce that intention with the Declaration of Independence on July 4, 1776.

Uniting Kingdoms

One of the more persistent myths in British (or English) history, and locked deep into the national psyche, is that unlike most other European countries and America, there has been never been a revolution. The beguiling nature of the assertion is meant to connote England as a land of settled peace and stability since 1066. In fact, nothing could be further from the truth. The Peasant's Revolt of 1381, led by Wat Tyler protesting the imposition of a poll tax and ongoing serfdom, saw widespread violence against wealthy landlords and the wealth of the church. The rebels were inspired by the teachings of the radical preacher John Ball, who taught that all men and women were created equal. This was a revolution, and sufficiently anti-establishment to result in the murder of the archbishop of Canterbury.

The seventeenth century alone saw revolutions in 1640, 1647, 1649, 1653, 1660, and 1689. The Irish Rebellion and Revolution (supported by the French) in 1798 was brutally repressed, and a tipping-point for the Act of Union in 1800 that incorporated Ireland. The Jacobite rebellions in the eighteenth century, and the riots and revolts on working conditions (e.g., culminating in the Peterloo Massacre of 1819, leading to the Reform Act of 1832) were revolutions.

From the perspective of this book, we are primarily concerned with those revolutions that were rooted in eighteenth-century Enlightenment thinking, the emergence of an educated middle class, industrialization, and urbanization, and which led to the breakaway of the American colonies. The American and French Revolutions had inspired a generation that dared to believe in the possibility of a democratic republic. Many of the those arguing for revolution had read John Locke's (1632–1704) *Two Treatises of Government* (1689),[69] arguing against the idea of absolute monarchy. The Old World was no longer fit for purpose, and with the rise of deism, an increasingly well-read laity, the strength of new Nonconformist denominations (e.g., Methodism), the stage was set for a determined political and civic rejection of any single monarchical-orientated established religion. The Church of England's patrimony was regarded as especially hostile.

Here, it is the Irish Revolution of 1798 that is arguably the most problematic for the English. Ireland did have its own Parliament, but the population was split 80:20 between Catholics and Protestants. The Protestants owned 95 percent of the land, and Roman Catholics could not stand for Parliament or go to University without affirming the Thirty-Nine articles of the Church of England (i.e., the "religious test"). Presbyterians in Ulster were therefore also barred from full participation in civic life, and the early calls for an Irish republic comprised a relatively united front of Catholics and disenfranchised Protestants, objecting to English domination. Moreover, as the English were fighting other wars overseas, the proxy militias hired to keep order by the English were bitterly resented.

There were celebrations in Belfast and Dublin when the French invaded (too late, as it turned out) to reinforce the Irish revolt. Revolutionary leaders such as Theobald Wolfe Tone (1763–1798) led a united Irish army that drew from Belfast and Dublin, and Protestant and Catholic. The very first Belfast-based Orange Order lodges were in fact pro-republican.[70] The common enemy was English imperialism and the rule of the many by the (largely absent) English few. Yet the Irish Revolution failed, and in a matter of months had been brutally suppressed.

But not all revolutions are founded upon violence and bloodshed. The Hanoverian monarchs had been parachuted in following the "Glorious Revolution" of 1688, which had seen the removal and exile of James II from the British throne. In England, at least, this was a largely peaceful transition, though this state-sanctioned Protestant coup had dreadful and violent consequences in Ireland. The revolution was the forced removal of a Catholic monarch to make way for the establishment of a new Protestant and united kingdom. Dutch Prince William III of Orange was the only son of William II and Mary—the princess royal and granddaughter of Charles I of England. Thus, William III had some legitimate claim on the British Crown. Britain now had, through the Hanoverian lineage, a firmly established Protestant faith in power. But even here, nothing was straightforward. William and Mary had no heirs. So, on the death of William III in 1702, the crown passed to Anne—daughter of the exiled James II, and so the last of the Stuart line to reign.

However, the British Parliament, anticipating such issues and already fearful of a return to a Catholic monarchy, had passed the Act of Succession in 1701, which specifically excluded any Catholic from becoming king or queen. Anne and her sister Mary had both been raised as devout Anglicans, but such was the climate of fear surrounding Catholic counter-revolution, Parliament still sought to ensure that monarchical lineage remained firmly Protestant. Anne was married to the Lutheran Prince George of Denmark, but her reign was plagued by ill-health. Obesity and seventeen pregnancies ended with no children, and contributed to her early death at the age of forty-nine.

This led to one of the more curious quirks in the history of the British monarchy. Now that there were no direct heirs, Britain turned to more distant relatives of the Protestant monarchy established by law. Specifically, the nearest relative to Anne—George, ruler of the electorate of Hanover. George I ascended to the throne in 1714. The Protestant faith might have seemed secure at this juncture, but an attempted revolution was led by James II's son, Edward Stuart, in 1715 (the first Jacobite rising). A second revolution was attempted in 1745 by his son, Charles Stuart, more usually known as Bonnie Prince Charlie. The Jacobite cause had a more than indirect bearing on the birth of the American Protestant Episcopal Church. Not because Americans preferred one monarch to another in the stand-off between the Stuarts and the Hanoverian lineage, but rather because the Americans rejected monarchy outright.

That both these Catholic rebellions—or attempted revolutions—were to fail, was in no doubt indebted in part to the sea-change taking place in British democracy. Parliament might have had its elected representatives and peers, but it had also evolved an early form of government through the recent development of the office of prime minister, and also cabinet for governance. Robert Walpole (1676–1745) was arguably the first prime minister, and with his ministers Walpole established a stable political foundation for succeeding ministers, and an effective working relationship between Crown and Parliament.

The British monarch, George III (1760–1820) was responsible for the 1808 Act of Union that joined Great Britain (England, Wales, Scotland) and Ireland into the United Kingdom. George II (1727–1760) and George I (1714–1727) were German, and officially Lutheran. So far as George III's reign in Britain was concerned, he was a card-carrying Scottish Presbyterian, with the Church of Scotland established by law. But George III was at the same time supreme governor of the Church of England, despite not being an Anglican. Anglicans in Scotland were regarded as Jacobite sympathizers loyal to the House of Stuart, and therefore James II. As such, Episcopalians in Scotland faced the real possibility of fines, imprisonment, and deportation if more than four of them were to gather in a single room. They were not allowed to use their churches and chapels for worship. Never before has a denomination taken the words of Jesus—"where two or three are gathered in my name, there I am amongst them" (Matt 18:20)—as a set quota that should ideally not be exceeded.

Readers acquainted with the 1991 play by Alan Bennett, *The Madness of George III* and the later film adaptation in 1994 (*The Madness of King George*), will be familiar with the fictionalized biographical study of the second half of the reign of George III, and his lengthy battles with mental illness. The film and the play both focus on the loss of the American colonies and the inability of the Royal Court to manage the erratic and deteriorating mental health condition of their monarch.

To all intents and purposes, Episcopalians in Scotland were akin to some form of underground church. They had devised novel ways of getting around the restrictions imposed on their meetings. For example, it was not unknown for a minister to stand in the hallway of a makeshift "house church" (barely permitted), and preach and teach to all the rooms of the house, none of which could contain more than four people.

This helps to explain why Seabury was consecrated not in a church, but only in an upper room of a hall, off a busy street in the city of Aberdeen, with only three other bishops present to witness this. A fourth had been invited, but cried-off claiming sickness, though he signaled his consent. However, our concern here is to gain a thicker understanding of the geopolitical landscape that gave rise to an independent continental Anglican Church.

Climate, Culture, and Conquest

For sure, the Declaration of American Independence in 1776 was one of the main lines that was crossed in the eventual establishment of the American Protestant Episcopal Church a decade later. However, the evolution of this new church was more gradual than many suppose. True, one can walk the Freedom Trail in Boston, and visit the museum that holds an Anglican Prayer Book, where the name of George III has been scratched out—as Bostonians no longer pray for the British monarchy. Then again, British forces did not finally evacuate New York until early 1784.

But just as George III was in the process of losing the Atlantic colonies and entire continent of America, on the other side of the world at around the same time, he was gaining an entirely new one. Captain James Cook's first voyage of discovery and scientific explorations from 1768–1771 "discovered" (what is now) New Zealand, Tasmania, and Australia, and claimed them for the British Crown. Over the course of the next twenty-five years, new colonies would be established in another New World. This was a revolutionary age.

However, there was something else taking place with the establishment of these early plantations outside Britain. These early experiments in colonization were largely English-led, and exclusively for the furtherance of the Protestant cause. Ireland was already proving to be fertile ground for new waves of English, Crown-sponsored settlers, who were driving ancient Irish landlords from their holdings, and in so doing, establishing the united Crown of Britain as a Protestant bulwark against the continued encroachments of European Catholicism. This was a continuous endeavor throughout the seventeenth century.

Charles I was executed in 1649, charged with tyranny and crimes against his own subjects. Dubbed the "man of blood," Charles I was executed for his exercise in theocratic and despotic monarchical reign, especially his claim to a "divine right" to rule, and therefore not accountable to the people of the land, its parliament or laws. The revolution ushered in by Cromwell was meant to replace an autocratic monarchy with a parliamentary democracy, which in turn would see an end to repressive tyranny. However, Cromwell's subsequent use of the military to enforce his own position as lord protector of the Commonwealth effectively led to Britain being governed by another despotic regime. The later government of Oliver Cromwell became more akin to that of a regime in power by some coercive military coup, with Parliament shut down, and dissenters imprisoned, banished, or forced to flee for their lives.

When Oliver Cromwell died in 1658, less than a decade after the execution of Charles I, his son, Richard Cromwell, succeeded him as the lord protector. Henry, the younger son, would have been a far better choice, as Richard was weak and prone to vacillation. It is an irony—of sorts—that Oliver Cromwell anointed his successor on the basis of primogenitary reasoning rather than meritocracy. The result, predictably, was that a military coup ensured the armed forces were in power. One kind of tyranny under Charles I was now replaced by another kind under Richard Cromwell, who was effectively (albeit briefly) a puppet dictator.[71]

It is against this background that parliamentarians journeyed to the Netherlands to negotiate with the exiled Charles for a return as monarch, provided certain conditions were met. The subsequent Declaration of Breda (April 1660) established Charles II as the lawful king, in return for which he issued general pardon for crimes committed during the English Civil War and Cromwell's protectorate. There were guarantees for religious freedom, compensation paid for losses of land, payments in arrears to members of the army—who would now be in the service of the Crown. The authority and freedoms of Parliament were essentially restored. In effect, the monarchy was now subject to the law and to Parliament. Two reigns of tyranny had been brought to a close.

However, the specter of tyranny never entirely vanished, and it was to recur again with considerable force in the late eighteenth century—notably with revolutions in France and America, and revolts and uprisings in colonies and countries across the world. The era of revolution and revolt saw governance irrevocably altered, as monarchies were swept aside in favor of emerging democracy. The seismic fissure in the Anglican polity is rooted in the politics of eighteenth-century Scotland and the model of church adopted by Scottish Episcopalians. Put simply, Scottish Episcopalians were deemed to be disloyal to the Crown, and treated with the same kinds of suspicion that Roman Catholics were to endure for centuries. The political and military tussles with Roman Catholics, and their suppression by rule of law, has far-reaching consequences for the polity of the American Protestant Episcopal Church. Because despite inheriting Anglican DNA from Scottish Episcopalian polity, it also inherited a spirit of dissent that was against monarchical rule.

The prevailing political culture of eighteenth-century Scotland presumed that Episcopalians were loyal to the House of Stuart and the Jacobite cause.[72] Accordingly, deprived of legitimating monarchical authority for their polity, they became what were known as "non-jurors." The Nonjuring schism will seem like a peculiar episode in the history of ecclesial polity to most modern readers. It refers to the schism (yes, another one) in the churches of Britain following the deposal of James II in 1688. For some clergy—2 percent is the estimate, and it included the saintly Bishop Thomas Ken—James II was God's anointed sovereign. So, these clergy did not support this coup d'état that saw William of Orange imposed on the peoples of Britain. The term "non-juror" comes from the Latin verb *juro*, meaning to "swear an oath." As these clergy would not swear an oath of allegiance, they were dubbed non-jurors.[73]

There were several bishops and a number of clergy in the Church of England who took this course, and they were deprived of their livings as a result. Seabury was therefore treated by the senior bishops of the Church of England with polite indifference when he sought episcopal orders. As he would be unable to swear the oath of allegiance to George III and his successors, no Church of England bishop would contemplate making any American a bishop.

But the result in Scotland was arguably far more interesting. In 1690, the Presbyterians, following the accession of William III, restored the fullness of the earlier Scottish Reformation. So-called High-Church practices were outlawed, bishops were deposed, and the Church of Scotland—the Presbyterian Kirk—became the national church. Episcopalians found themselves hounded and even persecuted. Ministers who refused to accept this abrupt religious revolution were promptly expelled. It was only in 1711 that Scottish Episcopalians, through an Act of Parliament, were able to gain a very small fig-leaf of autonomy and modest respectability. However, the problems for Scottish Episcopalians had barely begun.

Roman Catholicism: An English National Phobia

It is perhaps difficult for many modern readers to comprehend the English fear and horror of Catholicism, what many thought it might represent in terms of political rule, and the extent to which the government would go to suppress Catholicism. The 1701 Act of Settlement was specifically designed to secure Protestant succession to the throne, which in turn supported Parliament and the Church of England, especially its episcopal lineage and finances. The 1689 Bill of Rights had already established the order of succession following the Glorious Revolution of 1688. But William III (of Orange) and Mary had no children. Queen Anne was the sister-in-law of William III, and she had no children either. The closest surviving Protestant relative of the English royal family was Sophia (a granddaughter of James I, and now of the Hanover lineage). However, George I, on accession to the British throne, bypassed fifty-six Catholic nobility who had superior claims to the Crown. With the death of James II in 1701 (in exile), George I succeeded to the throne as fifty-seventh in line! But he was the most senior Protestant with a claim on the Crown.

1701 was year for the English Parliament to take matters in hand. The English government had settled on Sophia, elect of Hanover, as the heir presumptive. However, Queen Anne still reigned, and would do so until 1714. That notwithstanding, George I was inducted into the Order of the Garter in 1701 at the behest of English Parliament. The Scottish Parliament (known as the "Estates") were not aligned with this strategy, and in 1703 passed a bill declaring that Queen Anne's successor need not necessarily become monarch of Scotland—unless the English gave the Scottish full freedom of trade for its merchants across all the English colonies. The English Parliament balked at this, but Queen Anne eventually acceded to the Scottish request, passing the Act of Security in 1704.

The English Parliament retaliated in 1705 with the Alien Act, imposing severe restrictions on Anglo-Scottish trade unless and until the Scottish Parliament agreed to recognize the Hanoverian lineage. The 1707 Treaty of Union was the agreement of both parliaments to acknowledge one monarch, and form a united kingdom—the United Kingdom. This union, incidentally, created the largest free-trade area and collaboration in eighteenth-century Europe. It was largely delivered on English terms, primarily for the protection of English interests, and intended to maintain a Protestant government, church, state, and monarch—and at the same time rule out any continental Catholic challenge. With this in mind, the unhappy history of Whig–Tory relations with the European Union are hardly surprising, with Brexit emerging as an English-led movement that was not endorsed by the Scottish, Northern Irish, or Welsh. As ever, the English prefer their monarchical-endorsed autonomy over and against the benefits of collaborative democratic federalism.

That said, when George I did eventually come to the throne in 1714, the vast majority of Scottish Episcopalians chose to side with Edward Stuart as the rightful monarch, who was the son of James II. By not recognizing the reign of the Hanoverians, the Scottish Episcopalians consigned themselves to decades of marginalization and penalization until the death of Charles ("Bonnie Prince Charlie") Stuart in 1788. It is hard for twenty-first-century readers to grasp the full extent of the difficulties in which Anglicans in Scotland had found themselves from the sixteenth century through to the end of the eighteenth century.

Scottish Episcopalians had retained some support during the turbulence of their Reformation, and then Cromwell's revolution. But the settlements—terms of peace, in effect—after the demise of the short-lived republic and return of the monarchy left Episcopalians in an invidious position. Successive gestures (Acts of Indulgence) in 1693 and 1695 allowed Scottish Episcopal clergy to retain their livings if they accepted the monarchy. If they were unwilling to do so, they were deposed and deprived. Around one hundred Episcopal clergy took advantage of the offer, conditional upon swearing the oath of allegiance to the new Hanoverian lineage. The remainder declined, giving rise to house churches and meeting houses comprising clergy and congregations loyal to the Stuart lineage.

In 1719, however, any Episcopal congregation or church meeting that would not pray for the new king (George I) were closed. Episcopalian bishops dwindled in number—death and the deprivation of livings reducing their number to just one by 1720. To make matters more complicated, so-called "Qualified Chapels" for Episcopalians began to emerge in Scotland. They literally did "qualify," as they adopted the Church of England's *Book of Common Prayer*, and their congregations were led by English or Irish Anglican clergy, loyal to the Hanoverian lineage. There may have been three-dozen such congregations at their height, but the number of deprived Episcopalian congregations would have been far, far greater.

It was only in 1788 that this changed, when the remnant non-juror Episcopalians refused to recognize the claim to the throne lodged by Henry Benedict Stuart on the death of Charles Stuart. The fact that Henry Stuart also happened to be a cardinal of the Roman Catholic Church was a bridge too far, even for Episcopalians. This was the point at which Scottish Episcopalians recognized the Hanoverian claim to the throne, and offered their allegiance to George III. By 1792, Scottish Episcopalians were once again legal and able to function—perhaps for the first time in the two-hundred-and-fifty years since the Scottish Reformation.

The irony is striking for the American Episcopal Church, since it rests on not one rebellion, but two. Both the last Jacobite revolt and claim to the British throne and the American War of Independence with a revolution against the British throne have helped to create an Episcopal Church founded on revolt against monarchy and its claims to legitimacy, and the beginnings of a polity rooted in democracy. Although in noting this, we must bear in mind that the Jacobite's were hardly democrats, since they were championing an alternative rival monarchy with very different theological sympathies.

Seabury was consecrated by three Scottish bishops who were nonjurors (i.e., did not recognize the authority of the reigning British monarch, which was hardly a problem for an American republican). But it would mean that some of the still wavering Americans who thought that British rule might still be restored, and the colonies revert, were not necessarily likely to receive or recognize "foreign" episcopal orders. Politically, there was a fear in both Britain and America that the consecration of a bishop not loyal to the Crown represented an anti-monarchial stance. The monarchical establishment works differently from a democracy. The Old World order operates through paternalistic implicit means, and has no need of a written constitution. Those who rule reign. The New World order, in contrast, has a constitution, working through explicit democratic debate and clarity in governance.

In many respects, we are faced with pitching autocracy against democracy as an Old World versus New World rivalry. The revolutions of France and America were against monarchical governance and tyranny, as those who claimed to be subjects of such regimes could argue that those who reigned over them were unreliable and unaccountable, and somewhat capricious in their care for the citizenry under their rule.

Many have come to believe that an Old World autocracy cannot survive in public life (save as some symbol for the legitimate rule of law, and an elected government), and nor can it survive as a model of governance in ecclesial life. This has led to the current dynamic of one Anglican faith operating in two rather different worlds. That said, monarchical oversight was never entirely expunged from the USA, even after the 1776 Declaration of Independence. In many respects, the terms of the American Constitution looks quite similar to those that Oliver Cromwell sought to rule Britain with before 1660. Perhaps we should not be surprised that this left the door open for power and authority to be wielded by a capricious lord advocate (Cromwell), much like a modern-day despotic American president might.

Conclusion

As noted in the introduction, looking forward to November 14, 2034 may not immediately present as an especially auspicious anniversary to anticipate. But this date will mark, without doubt, the 250th anniversary of the decisive split in the Worldwide Anglican Communion. For the date also marks the beginning of a rather different future for Anglicanism. If we are right, and the Old World order of monarchical power is giving way to a New World of democratic consensus (albeit with challenges from authoritarianism and autocracies), then this is a timely moment for organizing some reasoned and peaceable revolutions.

In an age when nationhood itself is breaking down, denominations across the world have a particular responsibility to model forms of commonwealth and communion that do not depend on protecting some national narrowness or sectarian interests. We do well to remember that there are around two hundred countries in the world, but more than five thousand ethnic groups. Our planet probably does not need more fragmentation into ethnic enclaves. Instead, we need to work harder at peace-building across ideological, class, ethnic, and religious divisions. And increasingly across borders that separate oppressor from oppressed, rich from poor, those who are free to move from those who are restricted and lack liberty.

This may seem like a thankless task or vocation (and frankly, rather a liberal one too, I confess). Yet thankless though it may be, there are plentiful alternatives to top-down monarchical control, or some restrictive iron cage of imperialism and empire. Unity and federalism are not mutually exclusive. In the classic dictum of political philosopher Joseph Nye,[74] the choice may seem to be between hard power and soft power, but the use of force and coercion (i.e., hard power) is rarely an option, and even if so, should only be a last resort.

Most denominations outside the Roman Catholic and Orthodox Churches only have forms of soft power available for their formation, organization, and leadership. They cannot direct members as subjects. Their polity depends on consensus, negotiation, persuasion, patience, and developing communion, even where there is no consensus. Democracies depend on such conditions. The Church of England and Anglican polity needs to do much, much more to find its new theological rationale in such charisms, and find its life in conversations, accommodations, and negotiations—not weakly applied subjugations.

One of the key tests for church leadership in the future must rest with restoring the concept of faithfulness and fruitfulness, which are quite different from the concepts of success and results that the world around us may value. What is needed now is prophetic action, but also strategic patience; resolve and renewal, but also reflection and reformation. One key root in this is humility, and the development of a humble church that understands its core duties and obligations are first and foremost to God and to society, not to loyal paid-up members of some religious supporters' club.[75] Christianity is a faith of conscription, not subscription. Believers do not elect to donate or contribute to the church in order to receive benefits and favors in return.

Degeneration is an entirely natural phenomenon. It can refer to the deterioration of cells, bodies, institutions, and empires over time. Normal wear and tear and ageing take their toll. Sometimes, degeneration is a social, cultural, or personal lifestyle phenomenon. Sometimes, it is disease, viruses, wars, famines, and other crises that cause bodies to collapse and societies to crumble. Sometimes, the seeds of degeneration have lain within the body from the outset, wired into a person's DNA, or its social equivalent in wider society. Some degeneration can be predicted and resisted. But much cannot, and is part of the cycle of life and death.

The consecration of Samuel Seabury preempted the end of the Worldwide Anglican Communion, with the first American bishop marking the ecclesial fracture, but it remains undeniable that Anglican—or Episcopal—faith, belief, and practice remains as one single entity. What split the Anglican Communion before it started was the separation of the

Old World (Europe, and specifically Britain and the Church of England), and the New World (Continental America).

The year 2023 marked the 175th anniversary of the "Springtime of the Peoples (or Nations)"—the revolutions that spread across some fifty countries and states over Europe in 1848. To this day, it is the most widespread wave of revolution across Europe. The triggers for revolt were perhaps predictable.

First, the revolutions were essentially democratic and liberal in character, seeking to remove Old World monarchical structures and oligarchies, and replace them with independent nation states.[76]

Second, growing urbanism, increased technology, economic developments, and other social changes had led to widespread dissatisfaction with the prevailing political leadership.

Third, demands for greater freedom of the press and wider participation in democracy stoked calls for universal suffrage, rather than the power to vote only being vested in property owners.

Fourth, rural-to-city migration was the result of food shortages, potato famine, and an increase in the frequency of instances of mass starvation.

Fifth, popular idealism sought to remove the power of the landed aristocracy and nobility, and replace such vested interests with meritocracy and democracy.

Sixth, emerging liberal, socialist, and romantic ideologies inspired the working class to rise up and challenge prevalent social order, which was widely seen as elitist, self-serving, and out of touch.

Seventh, and finally, the revolutions were initially empowered and effective as coalitions of radicals, liberals, reformers, the middle classes (bourgeoisie), workers, peasants, and serfs.

However, as uncoordinated revolutions, they were comfortably suppressed by military force. Some suppressions were brutal, and tens of thousands were killed, forced into exile, or deported. By 1850, the revolutions had almost all been put down. The Holy Roman Empire had been dissolved under Napoleon's conquests of 1806, but the remnants of power and authority across small states continued to be exercised by the Catholic churches. For many Catholics, the failure of the revolutions was greeted with joyous relief.

But this was to be a pyrrhic victory for Catholicism over democratic republicanism. For failing as they did, the revolutions nonetheless marked an entirely new chapter of change for Europe. Many nations and states threw off the shackles of Old World monarchical power. The New World order that had been quickly maturing in the USA was now, finally, returning to its parental homelands. The Age of Empire was unravelling at home, even as it was being exported to the colonies. Liberal democracy was the future.[77]

Ultimately, the rejection of monarchical authority and power and the embracing of democratic accountability will be the fate of the Anglican Communion. Along the way, the majority of Protestant denominations will be unable to avoid internal civil war on sexuality and gender, and this will set off an unseemly fight over resources and naming rights. American Baptists and Scottish Presbyterians have already sampled such divisiveness in earlier centuries on other issues. This will become the fate of many other Protestant national churches too. Finally, this will mark the end of the Church of England as we know it. The civil war is already well underway. As a national and global church, it simply cannot be reformed any further, nor find the pathways to hold together as one body. Only a decent revolution can save it.

The narrative of a global Communion has then metastasized over time, and become a growth-mass that is beyond the control of the Church of England or any archbishop of Canterbury. The growth-mass inhibits the constituent parts of the body from working together, and like a tumor or sarcoma, presents a localized threat to specific organs. The larger the growth-mass looms, the worse it looks, though in actual fact the condition is unlikely to prove fatal. That said, reduction of the mass through therapies that treat the body cells and target the tumor are likely to be required. Surgery is unlikely to be of long-term help.

The exporting of oppression by a (doubtless well-meaning) White, male, superior, imperial upper-class culture across the Anglican Communion produces a bitter harvest of comparable responses. Whether it is gender, sexuality, marriage and divorce, the victims of sexual abuse, racism, and sexism, we see, time and time again, the same history repeating itself. Those in control presume that their virtue is superior, and that their position and power is inherent by some right not chosen by them. Their authority is, likewise, a gift they hold on to, for fear of losing control.

The Communion then becomes paralyzed, not by division, but by the inability of the originators to perceive that in their own valorizing of power, even in a postcolonial church, they have retained all of their capacity for domination. Genuine inter-dependence and mutuality is lost at this juncture. A denomination that deifies and reifies sovereignty and omnipotence at the expense of humility and service, and essentially can only pity the powerless, is ripe for revolution.[78]

This is a journey for the English as much as it is for the Church of England. In the kind of critical history that we are offering—also a kind of critical ecclesiology—our purpose is to expose some of the foundational myths that have told a story of a worldwide Communion—a postcolonial global denomination that is multilingual and multicultural. Much more work would need to be done if such a body is to break free of its inherent classism, racism, homophobia, sexism, and imperialism. That work would be very deep and far-reaching. Those occupying positions—with powers and privileges—will need to reckon with the past. It is still far too easy to call upon notions of sovereignty to make an apotheosis of episcopal-ecclesial authority, and then rule through domination and subjugation.

The choice before the leadership of the Church of England is now very stark. Does it hang on to the mystique of unaccountable and opaque monarchical power vested in episcopacy? Or, does it embrace accountability and democracy? I would argue that any leadership harboring imperialist outlooks and practices, and using quasi-monarchical patterns for oversight and polity, is destined for extinction. As a model of governance, it has lost the trust, confidence, and respect of the nation, and the church members and clergy barely tolerate the tortured opacity of episcopal modus operandi. Bishops who can't even seem to produce minutes of meetings on issues of huge significance for others, and the impact on them, simply have little place in the modern world. Models of high-handed imperialism and quasi-monarchical leadership in the Church of England will eventually die.

The context that requires this is England itself. It has entered an age of chaotic, unpredictable politics that is as much at home in the Church of England as it is in the Westminster government. The perceived betrayal of values and ideals—often screamed from the both right and left—makes this a hard time to be a minister in government, or a bishop. They seldom appease their own constituencies, let alone those who regard them as unsympathetic to their causes and beliefs. The labels and markers that used to serve as a reasonably reliable guide to the contours of disputes no longer work. British people can be both progressive and conservative. English churchgoers can be both orthodox and open-minded. Social class bubbles have long burst, and relationships across divides are arguably more complex and attenuated due to social media and rapid increases in knowledge exchange.

Against this background, there is a global rise in gloom accompanied by chaotic worldviews. Less social stability now means that individuals and groups can occupy "contradictory class locations" (in the words of social theorist Erik Olin Wright). If there is to be progressive change in England and the Church of England, there needs to be a new understanding of the chaotic complexity that shapes contemporary culture. Views are no longer fixed on a wide range of social and moral issues. Churches, political parties, institutions, and organizations need to rediscover their charism for empathetic listening. They can no longer assume that believing and belonging are aligned, or that historic loyalties can be presumed upon. When we start to peer into the details of what we thought we saw, the picture that emerges can often be startling and unsettling.

PART THREE

Cultural Consequences

LIKE MOST CHURCHES, HOMEGROWN expressions of Christian faith are difficult to really understand unless you spend time on their ground, and immersed in the culture that is partly responsible for the distinctives that make up this or that local version of faith. Yes, every local version of faith likes to think it is catholic and universal. Every local version of faith can treat others not like themselves as foreign, strange, deviant—or worse. Human societies live by labeling. All communities do this too, as must individuals. The human mind is constantly filtering, ordering, screening, reorganizing, and categorizing. What is true, false, dangerous, safe, clean, and unclean are wired into our shared worldviews, social functioning, and mindsets. Humans cannot avoid making a whole variety of judgment calls—every few seconds.

As we noted in the introduction, a critical-cultural approach to ecclesiology rests on the proper analysis of the social sources of churches and congregations to explain the theological character of denominations. Contemporary and "grounded" ecclesiology has now developed into a distinctive and discrete field within the broader arena of theology and religious studies. For more than three decades, I have worked as an ethnographer of contemporary Christianity, drawing on anthropology and sociology alongside theology to provide a richer account of the ecclesial proclivities that mark out churches as distinctive and different from their peers. This work owes something to contextual theology, but it is also more than that, and it includes probing attempts to uncover the latent structures and strategic agencies that underpin a religious tradition, moving away from a purely systematic theological exegesis (of the church) toward a meticulous, close-up ecclesiology. This allows us to explore issues such as the role of class, ethnicity, gender, politics, and economics in the constitutive construction of denominational identity. In this kind of enterprise, ecclesiology emerges as a social or cultural theory, leading to an approach in the study of the church that can be classed as a form of "ecclesiological realism" that explores and explains how churches became what they are.[79]

So, here and at this point, our excursus moves to reflect on what is known as "Sydney Anglicanism." It is a detour, because I am not sure it has much to do with Sydney, being Anglican, or even being Evangelical. As any social anthropologist will tell you, labels are simultaneously relative, subjective, absolute, and objective. At least, that is, to the person deploying the terminology. Very few denominational labels were adopted by the group they now refer to. Anglican, Baptist, Methodist, Episcopalian—these are all nicknames used by others. The subject just gets stuck with the label. But they rarely help you to understand or accurately categorize a group.

In what follows, I want to see if I can look at what we refer to as "Sydney Anglicanism" in a variety of luminosities. By varying the kinds of light-illumination we shed on a subject, it can perhaps help us to see apparently familiar objects quite differently—sometimes much more softly, or equally, sometimes coming into much sharper focus. Sydney Anglicanism is an important subject, since it regards itself as a beacon of light and growth. It speaks of itself as a faithful, virtuous, orthodox, moral, and spiritually invigorated expression of Anglicanism. It promotes itself as the only serious contender for evangelistic endeavor that leads to church growth, despite the official statistics suggesting numerical decline.[80] Hubris is baked in.

Introducing Sydney Anglicanism

There are not many studies of Sydney Anglicanism. There are a handful of critiques that take the kind of approach James Barr took to his studies of fundamentalism, and the best and most accessible of these are by Muriel Porter.[81] They represent one kind of "illumination" of Sydney Anglicanism. As those familiar with my ecclesiological investigations will know, I prefer a blend of social, cultural, and anthropological tools to help us see and comprehend what we encounter. Used carefully, these help to explain the theological priorities of a group, and the language, dialect, and accent with which a group expresses its faith.

In the twenty-first century, the emerging dividing lines that separate society and split communities are different to what they were at the turn of the twentieth century. New alloys of belief can be beguiling. For example, left-wing individualism (which can be doctrine in almost any mainstream political party in the developed world) presumes that all people really need is opportunity, a level playing field, education, and a bit of graft. True, equality should give everyone an equal chance. But it is more complex than that. Factors like wealth, class—social spheres, strata, wealth, poverty, and opportunity—still determine people's lives in the twenty-first century.

As a rule, denominations, congregations, and dioceses are not very good at recognizing their visible and invisible classist assumptions. This is strange when one considers how chapel and church distinctions in the recent past often pivoted on class as much as belief. Or, for that matter, how early Pentecostal churches and their distinctiveness were earthed in class and ethnicity, not just on their emphases on religious experience. As we noted in the Introduction, H. R. Niebuhr's *The Social Sources of Denominationalism* (1929) was keenly aware of how elite Episcopalians were, in contrast, say, to poorer inner-city denominations. Niebuhr thought that the effort to distinguish churches primarily by reference to their doctrine and to approach the problem of church unity from a purely theological point of view was fruitless, so he turned from theology to history, sociology, and ethics for a more satisfactory account of denominational differences. His study of the social character of the Christian churches was intended to be a practical contribution to the ethical problem of denominationalism.

Niebuhr went beyond Max Weber's work in linking particular Protestant denominations to the growth of capitalism. Niebuhr saw that many forms of Protestantism in embracing the development of capitalism had moved to individualistic rather than collective concerns. He was particularly insightful in his discussion of how denominations dealt with the issues of slavery and secession from the Union during the American Civil War (1861–1865). The churches that had begun as "movements of the dispossessed," with the emphasis on equality of God's children (e.g., Baptists, etc.), would have been expected to condemn slavery. But in the

Confederate South, *no* mainstream denomination condemned slavery—it was regarded as an economic necessity.

Christian Indigenous tribes in the Civil War mostly fought for the Confederates, as the taking of slaves—whether from other tribes or captured Europeans—was common practice. All denominations divided in the Civil War, with the Northern churches continuing to condemn slavery (and slave owners) and the Southern churches proclaiming the importance of slavery to protect an "inferior" race. Only when war ended did the denominations patch up their differences—or not, as in the case of Southern Baptists and Confederate Methodists.

Church, Culture, and Classism

More recently, David Morgan (1937–2020) was a sociologist whose first study was on the educational background of Church of England bishops (over sixty years ago when he wrote his doctorate, most were public school and Oxbridge), and whose last book was a study of snobbery. As Morgan pointed out, the ground of our snobbery has shifted in modernity from one of social position to material or cultural possession. We see this at work in religion—high and low church can be snobbish about each other, as can liberals and conservatives. Even religious faith will develop its own "spiritual snobscape," and that can lead to a disavowal of others, or an inverted snobbery (pride) in one's lack, rather than in one's conspicuous consumption, power, and possession.[82]

Snobbery derives from complex micro-cultures, which are often rooted in class, but they can also be glimpsed in ethnicity, gender, and sexuality. Snobbery—when practiced—is permission for one group to gossip about, patronize, and perhaps denigrate another group. In recent times, we have seen this in politics (e.g., pro-Brexit or anti-Brexit), economics (e.g., certain "bargain basement" retail stores and what they are deemed to represent, or fashions and fads), and society (e.g., class, career, possessions, aspirations, etc.).

The first British ships arriving to colonize Australia in the wake of Captain Cook's "discovery" carried soldiers, convicts, chaplains, explorers, scientists, and others. On board Cook's first wave we can count twelve Jewish people, but no Methodist settlers. Methodists convicted of a felony were disfellowshipped, so a Methodist convict was an oxymoron. The same was not true for Roman Catholics, who were overrepresented in the penal colonies. Anglicans would be the presumed default denomination for anyone not declaring an alternate allegiance.

On Cook's first voyage, encounters with Indigenous groups resulted in some hostilities, but for the most part the meetings were marked by curiosity, wariness, and hospitality. Cook's first voyage was scientific, and so collecting plants, animals, and data—especially mapping the stars, oceans, land, and reefs. Some of the Indigenous people saw this as an opportunity to collect samples from the explorers. One member of Cook's crew got so drunk one night while on watch, he had failed to wake up, let alone raise the alarm, when some natives climbed aboard the vessel and removed his ear lobes as trophies. (Cook's diary does not tell us exactly how much rum the sailor had drunk, but it is safe to say any hangover was exceeded by merciless ribbing for the journey home.)

The early Australian settlements relied on forms of social ordering, discipline, and reform that derived their authority and rationales from either military or religious sources. Rather like New Zealand, much later, cities developed social and denominational characteristics that were more apparent than any counterpart left behind in Great Britain—though Belfast, Liverpool, Glasgow, and parts of London provided important indicators of how social and class divisions were rooted in religious identity. Initially, the Anglican churches were both the providers and beneficiaries of their quasi-established position in Australia, with their elite boarding schools. Equally, schools for the disadvantaged and those taken into social care (i.e., Anglicare) have persisted as significant reminders of just how much social, moral, and cultural capital was vested in one dominant denomination by virtue of its colonial legacy and privilege. Today, Anglicare in Sydney has ten thousand clients, with a turnover measured in hundreds of millions of dollars, and a property portfolio (e.g., hostels, charity shops) topping two billion.

The first thing to note about Sydney Anglicanism is that it is very, very wealthy. However, this wealth owes much to the origins of how settlements were established and ordered in Australia. Rather as the Church of England did in the Victorian period, denominations saw it as their duty, calling, and opportunity to establish schools, missions, youth clubs, workhouses, hostels, and alms-houses and to originate social and welfare organizations (e.g., adoption, fostering, midwifery, etc.). Australia was hardly very different, just fewer people to begin with, and even fewer constraints—and a penal workforce put together with extensive amounts of cheap or colonized land that made the later accrual of denominational wealth and asset management virtually inevitable. There were fewer churches built, and none of age or historic significance that required considerable financial upkeep.

Second, in the last quarter of nineteenth-century England, the state had begun to take these institutions over. The Church of England could still be found running missions in deprived areas. It continued to have valued representation in chaplaincy (e.g., hospitals, prisons, schools, etc.), but it was rarely running these institutions. The same trends were taking place in Australia too, as it moved rapidly from being a colony of settlements (from 1788) to a country (January 1, 1901). This rapid process of organization—some might say, wrongly in my view, secularization—left bishops in charge of congregations, churches, their dioceses, and a handful of schools. All the while, however, their asset base had increased in financial value significantly.

Third, differentiated power struggles between classes, ethnic groups, and denominations would emerge in the late Victorian period through to the later part of the twentieth century. Rather, as with Belfast, Glasgow, and Liverpool, Roman Catholics were overrepresented in the working classes and among the laborers. The emigration of workers to Australia carried residual political and cultural assumptions, perhaps most notably those stemming from tensions in Ireland. Australian military recruitment in the Great War produced explicit forms of identity politics that would play out in various forms of denominational rivalry. Irish Catholics in Australia could be perceived as less loyal to the Crown and the Empire.

Fourth, Sydney Anglicanism represents a social, economic, and classist reaction to the large numbers of Irish Catholic laborers and convicts who were being deported to Australia. In the eighteenth century, Catholicism was viewed as the faith followed by degenerates. The exported English Anglicanism stood for law and order, government, ordained social hierarchy, and civic stability. Irish Catholic clergy, when they eventually began to arrive in Australia, were treated with deep suspicion and hostility by the colonial government. To a large extent, Irish liturgical politics have been transplanted into Sydney Diocese. The canons of the (very English, anti-Catholic) Anglican Church of Ireland prohibit priests from wearing certain "Romish" vestments, such as a chasuble. Sydney, likewise, excludes such vestments in canon law.

In Australia, Roman Catholicism has historically been the religion of the poor, convicts, and laborers. Anglicans and other Protestants, by contrast, have generally enjoyed higher social status and far greater wealth. Just as end of the Great War saw renewed tensions in Ireland, civil war, and then cession, the faint ripples of such divisions are replicated in Sydney. It is not possible to understand the "DNA" of Sydney Anglicans without having some grasp of modern Irish history, as the tribal Catholic versus Protestant rivalry is rooted in the distinctive cultures that were exported to Australia from the eighteenth century onwards.

Culture and Christianity

Even today, the legacy of inter-denominational rivalry lives on, regardless of its roots. Most twenty-first-century folk in the developed world will regard religion as a private matter, and faith as something discreet. They do so despite the evidence of conflicts in Northern Ireland, Bosnia, or Rwanda, and presume these to be rarities. But religious divisions in communities that weaken the collective identity and economics of a city or country are actually commonplace. For example, almost every major Scottish town and city was once divided between Protestant and Catholic. Even in a sport such as soccer, that means that a fairly small city like Dundee hosts two football teams—Dundee and Dundee Unity (formerly Dundee Hibernian; it is Catholic, with Hibernia being the ancient name for Ireland, meaning "winter"). The two football grounds are virtually next door to each other.

In Edinburgh, the Hearts-Hibernian derby is another Protestant–Catholic rivalry. Rangers and Celtic (Glasgow), likewise, reflect sectarian division. Class plays a part in all of this too. Notably, Aberdeen remains the largest city in Scotland with only one football team—a direct consequence of its negligible Irish-Catholic population from the seventeenth century onwards. With no religious competition, there is no result. Our point here is that economically, Scottish football is weakened by the legacy of its religious sectarianism. Only Glasgow, Edinburgh, and Aberdeen—due to size and other factors—can sustain their football. The city of Dundee is only fractionally smaller than Aberdeen, but divides its football loyalties, economics, and support due to old and long-forgotten sectarian divisions.

As I previously noted in *Clergy: The Origin of Species* (2008),[83] denominations actually *evolve*. The major mainstream denominations in Australia have a history of enjoying enormous social influence in an emerging country with few formal social structures. However, and in some respects, their evolutionary story of the last two-hundred-and-fifty years is one of slow secularization, marginalization, fragmentation, and disintegration. This is a domino effect. The Anglican Church still clings onto its original monarchical entitlement—especially to speak on social and public matters—and presumes that the wider population will be receptive. But just as Irish Catholicism has struggled with successive scandals on forced adoptions, pedophile clergy, the covering up of sexual abuse, and yet opposition to same-sex unions, divorce and remarriage, so too has Australian Catholicism.

The scandals of Irish Catholicism are similar to those that also consumed the Australian Anglican churches. This has been of the same order, via their historic involvement in education, welfare, the treatment single mothers, fostering and adoption; yet also differently in respect of the treatment of Indigenous peoples and other groups. As such, Australia inherited and incubated similar problematic behavior patterns that have some commonality with Canadian Anglicanism. Colonization in lands where the distances between settlements are simply vast meant that the long arm of the law could be thousands of miles away from addressing abuse of any kind. Religiously motivated social control can be highly oppressive, and extremely abusive. Only recently, in an age of inexpensive and fast social networking and communication, does the history of these abuses emerge.

The Protestant–Catholic religious divisions in today's Sydney, however, go some considerable way to explaining the spiritual DNA of its distinctive brand of Anglicanism. But it is not possible to gain a more comprehensive grasp of the dynamics at work in Sydney Anglicanism until the early history of the Plymouth (or "Exclusive") Brethren is engaged. Plymouth Brethren are a low church and Nonconformist Christian movement whose history can be traced back to Dublin, Ireland, in the mid- to late 1820s, and in their separatism from established Anglicanism (Church of Ireland). John Nelson Darby (1800–1882) was their founder, but they can also trace their origins to the proto-Pentecostal Catholic preacher Edward Irving and his followers (Irvingites).[84] The group emphasizes *sola scriptura*, the belief that the Bible is the supreme authority for church doctrine and practice, over and above any other source of authority.

The Brethren–Anglican links in Sydney are partly a matter of convergence as a progeny by descent from Ulster. But the convergence goes deeper and is grounded in a visceral antipathy towards Roman Catholicism and what it is deemed to represent. The Conservative Evangelicalism and Ulster-ultra-Protestantism of the likes of T. C. Hammond were received as "mainstream" Anglicanism upon disembarkation in Sydney, which also explains aspects of the emerging polity. The Brethren's roots partly function as a simulacrum of the communitarian and sectarian attitudes, whereby the tribal and kraal-like loyalty reinforces the identity of the church as an enclave of the pure, redeemed, and sanctified, who must resist anything worldly or secular. Our attention to the morphology of Brethren polity is quite proper here, since this explains why Sydney Anglicanism feels so different from other parts of the Australian Anglican Church and the wider Anglican Communion. The Brethren-like feel is communitarian and sectarian. Thus, we might speak of Sydney Anglicanism as having a kind of "Brethren style," but without adopting its theological substance. That said, there is plenty of theological convergence between Sydney Anglicanism and Brethren congregations.

The late eighteenth and first half of the nineteenth century were febrile and fevered times, with many fearing the end of the world itself. It is hardly surprising that "end-time" sects emerged, such as Joanna Southcott's Panacea Society. Raised in the recent wake of the American and French Revolutions, and contemporaneous with the threats of Napoleonic conquest and tyranny, the British upper classes and aristocracy were living in fear of their way of life being annihilated, and their lives ended too. Democracy and political accountability were demands from the masses, not initiatives sponsored by the ruling elites. Few will appreciate that Darby was an Anglo-Irish Anglican, and from the wealthy landed class. Protestant and anti-Catholic, the early Plymouth Brethren had wealthy sponsors. Darby himself was able to visit America five times between 1862–1877, and was a Confederate supporter during the Civil War, which he witnessed first-hand. Darby was also able to visit Sydney, where his biblical literalism and strict Calvinism took root in the Ulster Anglicanism already present.

Plymouth Brethren generally see themselves as a network of like-minded free churches, not as a Christian denomination. They will usually refer to themselves as "Christian," rather than as Brethren. Meeting informally to celebrate the Lord's Supper from 1825, central figures were Anthony Norris Groves (a dentist studying theology at Trinity College, Dublin), Edward Cronin (studying medicine), John Nelson Darby (an Anglican curate in County Wicklow), and John Gifford Bellett (a lawyer who brought them together). They used no liturgy, nor did they recognize ordained ministers. For the early Brethren, all were ministers of the

Lord. In their view, their guide was "the Bible alone," and so they sought to follow it according to their own interpretation of the biblical text.

The first meeting in England was held in December 1831 in Plymouth, Devon. Those meeting were soon simply referred to as "Plymouth Brethren," although the term "Darbyite" was also used, especially when describing the "Exclusive" Brethren (as distinct from the "Open" Brethren). The movement spread rapidly throughout the United Kingdom (including Oxford, London, Yorkshire, etc.). By 1845 the assembly in Plymouth had more than a thousand people meeting in fellowship. Overseas missions took place very early on in Brethren history, with the successful establishment of "meetings" in Switzerland and parts of France. Attempts to plant meetings in Baghdad, Madras, and other cities were failures. Darby made trips to the USA and to Australia (the latter as early as 1852), where these missions enjoyed considerable success.

Today in Australia, the Brethren have almost forty independent schools, and well over fifty thousand followers. As classic Weberian Protestants, their businesses are estimated to be worth twenty-two billion Australian dollars to the Australian economy. The church encourages participation at meetings by all adult males (i.e., "brothers"), but with women (i.e., "sisters") only choosing and announcing the hymns. Apart from joining in with group singing, women are otherwise required to be silent in church meetings in line with the Brethren's interpretation of 1 Corinthians 14:34. Exclusive Brethren do not recruit to their churches, and have strict codes of separatism from the wider world, a world that is regarded as degenerate and a source of defilement. Members must remain pure and undefiled; those leaving the movement are regarded as "lost" and apostate.

Over the years, the Brethren have suffered schism (e.g., between "Open" and "Exclusive"), and also struggled with some of the issues familiar to new religious movements, sects, schisms, and cults. These have centered on money, sex, and power, order and control, and also included charismatic leadership (e.g., from James Taylor, 1899–1970, and his sexual infidelity as a test of members' faith and fidelity, and the "Aberdeen Incident" of 1970, to the more recent leadership of John Stephen Hales, and his son Bruce Hales, with their expensive taste in private jets). However, to this day, Brethren membership confounds sociologists and skeptics by continuing to hold its own across the world.

To some extent, their growth (organic, with negligible external recruitment) turns on the tight compacts formed between locality, separatism, business, and faith. For example, Plymouth Brethren in south-west England were prominent in local fishing industries, as they were in Aberdeen. The businesses were small, family owned, and autonomy was easily maintained. Agriculture and farming business in Australia offered the same ideal commercial conditions for sustaining separatist community life, while also guaranteeing income.

While the impact of nineteenth-century Evangelical revivals in Scotland faded in the twentieth century, there were spontaneous outbreaks, including Jock Troup's mission among fishermen of the northeast in 1921. We note this here because it produced an unforeseen legacy that persists into the twenty-first century, namely the extraordinary proliferation of ice-cream parlors and confectionery shops in most Scottish coastal towns. As the revivalism spread, so did temperance, and with that, the sale and consumption of alcohol declined, as did the number of bars. But as the Americans later discovered under their own prohibition era, banning alcohol drives up sugar consumption. From the late nineteenth century, Scotland had already seen a steady-but-modest increase in Italian immigrants after the Republic had been declared. In the aftermath of the First World War, many Italians experienced extreme poverty and famine in their home country, with some walking across Europe to find new work and homes, mainly from the provinces of Lucca and Frosinone. The numbers emigrating to Scotland increased significantly, plying their trade in confectionery and catering.

Theology and Culture

The church–world dichotomies and synergies that run through all denominations are also present in every fiber of being in Sydney Anglicanism. The polity and practice of Sydney Anglicans is a reaction to their cultural cosmopolis, and generates something like a latter-day version of *Pilgrim's Progress*. The city will be narrated as a kind of playground, tempting the unwary into the portals of hell. For those who have the eyes to see, there is a narrow, winding path to salvation. Few will be saved. The road to perdition is well-paved with good intentions. John Bunyan's allegory has made him the poster-boy for extremely conservative approaches to soteriology. Heaven is for a tiny remnant. Hell is for everyone else. If you are not on the right path, you are destined for annihilation. Therefore, it is imperative you be separated from the world in order to be pure. If you leave the Brethren, for instance, it would be normal for any remaining family to have little if any contact with you from thereon.

To understand Sydney Anglicanism, one needs to appreciate its similarities to the Exclusive Brethren. These are not accidental, and resemblances with conservative university Christian Unions, which also have Brethren roots, are apparent. Brethren promote what they regard as a "traditional" marriage and family life. Children typically live at the family home until they marry, and are required to marry within the fellowship. Physical contact between young men and women before marriage is not tolerated, and courting between couples may be chaperoned. In theory there is nothing to prohibit a young Brethren adult attending a university for education, although this will be frowned upon—mixed halls of residence and unpoliced free time being seen as likely portals for "backsliding" or "falling away."

The Brethren paradoxes on gender are intriguing. Brethren women can succeed in business and in education on their own terms. Public relations pamphlets will reassure readers their women can take part in all aspects of worship, but in their churches they will be subservient to men, sitting behind them in meetings. Recent debates in certain Sydney Anglican churches have asked if women should be allowed to read the Bible out loud during church services, or teach at Sunday School to a mixed group of teenagers.

But the importing of such attitudes into Sydney Anglicanism only make sense when one realizes that a woman's place at a Brethren meeting only permits her to select and announce the hymns, and she is expressly forbidden to pray out loud or teach. The Brethren women wear a scarf or ribbon in their hair to signify that the man is head of the woman. Brethren men will be expected to provide for their families while the women manage the household. Very few people not born into the Brethren will ever become members, and relatively few of those born into the group will eventually decide to leave.

Sydney Anglican women do not wear such attire, but their recent diocesan report on domestic abuse makes it clear that even in such situations, the man remains the head of the woman, and divorce is probably a greater evil than remaining within an abusive marital relationship. The report argues that wives remain bound to submission in their marriages to their husbands. The report states,

> In many instances . . . physical distance between the abuser and any victims [may be necessary, including children, but] . . . the desired goal of living separately is the healing and restoration of . . . the marriage [so that] repentance and reconciliation, and a healthy relationship free from [violence, abuse, etc, so that] . . . the abuser gets professional and spiritual help to repent of, unlearn and change their . . . destructive ways of behaving. . . . [True, freedom and] threats and control may never be attained. If not, the couple will, of necessity, continue to live separately. But this is not an argument for divorce in and of itself—just because it does not happen every time, it doesn't mean God can't make it happen.[85]

It is impossible to read the report cited above without one's blood beginning to chill. But where do such attitudes stem from? It is more than likely that it operates from a culture invested in entitlement. Sydney Anglicans are passionate believers in the eternal subordination (i.e., submission) of Jesus to his Father. To suggest otherwise—and many theological outlooks would take issue with Sydney's theology here—risks a potentially more exhaustive interrogation of Sydney's preferred construction of the hierarchical relationship within the Godhead, in which the necessity of violence (i.e., the Father against the Son) is sacralized as essential for our salvation.

The culture that Sydney Diocese cleaves to is therefore one of God-willed entitlement. Men, ministers and husbands, occupy their hierarchical position by divine appointment. Moreover, their position depends on women being subordinate, and confessing their eternal submission. Any threatened breach of this pattern can be subjected to discipline, and the venting of anger (as God's wrath). So, while violence is still denounced, it is also the case that from such a position, the legitimacy of violence, as a tool of discipline and even salvation, is potentially within reach to those who perceive that their God-given male power and control is facing some threat.[86]

The peculiar culture of Sydney Anglicanism has taken more than 175 years to gestate, and is the result of tribal intermarriage (almost literally) between various Brethren and Anglican families, and a general if inchoate understanding that the interests and outlooks of these two tribes are near-identical. Both groups are socially and politically conservative, and anti-progressive-liberal. On some battlefronts, therefore, Sydney Anglicans will join forces with their Roman Catholic counterparts (e.g., on opposing the legalization of same-sex-equal marriage). Doctrinally, however, the Brethren–Anglican alliance will decisively reject Roman Catholicism, and vice-versa. These mutual doctrinal denigrations can be quite vehement.

Here again, Sydney has more in common with Glasgow, Liverpool, and Belfast than it does with any other modern city in the twenty-first century. Religious divisions run deep, and are hard-wired into the DNA of the culture. Unlike their British counterparts, Sydney's divisions have seldom required any kind of close physical proximity to the "othered" neighbor who is deemed to be following an entirely different faith. Those who puzzle over how Sydney manages to be multi-faith, multi-cultural, rainbow-tribal, and highly diverse—and yet also host a version of Anglicanism that has more in common with the Exclusive Brethren than any other expression of Christianity—need only develop a cultural-spatial understanding of the city. It isn't really a city in the way many Europeans use the term. It is more like a series of connected districts, with quite local-tribal loyalties, which in turn have detectable social, political, religious, ethnic, and demographic aspects.

Culture, opined Peter Drucker, will consume strategy for breakfast. To really understand Sydney Anglicanism, one needs to grasp the separatist DNA-coding that makes this body of ecclesial polity quite so distinctive. For example, Thomas Chatterton Hammond (born in Cork 1877; and died in Sydney 1961) was one of the first modern principals of Moore (Theological) College in Sydney. T. C. Hammond was an Irish Anglican cleric whose work on reformed theology and Protestant apologetics has been influential among Evangelicals across the Commonwealth. He was also grand master of the Grand Orange Lodge of New South Wales, and a fierce critic of Roman Catholicism.

Hammond's *In Understanding Be Men*[87] was still required reading for members of Christian Unions when I was an undergraduate. The book has been around for almost a century, and it speaks from the heart of White evangelical maleness. As Kristin Kobes Du Mez notes of American counterparts,

> While dominant, the evangelical cult of masculinity does not define the whole of American evangelicalism. It is largely the creation of white evangelicals. The vast majority of books on evangelical masculinity have been written by white men primarily for white men; to a significant degree, the markets for literature on black and white Christian manhood remain distinct.[88]

Sydney's ecclesiology fits within the same pattern: the church as God's people meeting around God's word, overseen by the adult White male gaze, and one that is easily riled to righteous anger, or sacralized fury.

This leads to church meetings being centered around the public reading, explanation, and response to God's word—cerebral and reasoned. Anglicans in Sydney generally identify themselves primarily with their local congregation rather than a denomination or institution. In other words, their ecclesiology and theology is more akin to that of the Exclusive Brethren than anything else. It is not Anglican, or even especially Evangelical. It is descended from Ulster Protestantism, which is tribally anti-Catholic, with some Evangelical publications even classing Roman Catholicism as a "cult" alongside Mormons, Jehovah's Witnesses, Christian Scientists, and Christadelphians.

Tribally, this brand of Ulster Protestantism is also committed to monarchical patterns of polity, and despite the congregationalist nature of the ecclesiology, churches are in fact subjected to high degrees of centralized control and authority in the hands of an elite. In terms of their overall identity, Sydney Anglicans will narrate themselves and their mission in much the same way as English Protestants did in seventeenth-century Ulster. Sydney Anglicans are settlers in a heathen land, bringing the pure truth and light of the Protestant faith (and rule) to those who are in darkness.

This is a masculine and muscular mission, and the perceived hostility of the environment that might resist such a gospel only confirms that this ministry is mainly for men. The men expect their will to prevail, and to be obeyed. As Kristin Kobes Du Mez notes, this explains why the outcome of this ecclesial outlook is expressed in American or Australian nationalism:

> Christian nationalism—the belief that America is God's chosen nation and must be defended as such—serves as a powerful predictor of intolerance toward immigrants, racial minorities, and non-Christians. It is linked to opposition to gay rights and gun control, to support for harsher punishments for criminals, to justifications for the use of excessive force against black Americans in law enforcement situations, and to traditionalist gender ideology.[89]

As with church, so with nation.

Muscular Christianity and Necrosis

If aspects of White, upper-class, idealized Victorian–Edwardian missionary religion were examples of "muscular Christianity," then the present state of churches promoting such faith is best described as necrotic. It was the nineteenth-century German pathologist and anthropologist Rudolf Virchow (1821–1902) who first coined the term. Virchow noted that as the cells in our bodies die, bone density, the resilience of skin, and internal organs all became weaker. The human body became susceptible to external injury, infections, and disease, and to internal collapse due to the ageing process, along with less and slower blood-supply to the tissues and main organs.

Thus, while the body continued to function well, the ageing process posed ever-higher risks to the anatomy. The pathology was a given. So, even a form of muscular Christianity such as Sydney Anglicanism, or for that matter other forms of (seemingly) endlessly renewable and ever-youthful faith, will be subject to necrosis. The Irish Protestant identity goes some way to explaining Sydney Anglicanism's rise and eventual fall. It accounts for the blending of anti-Catholicism and yet the same social conservatism that is resistant to same-sex unions. It explains the tribalism, and also the "spiritual snobscape,"[90] which was elitist and classist.

In their time, Irish Protestants were the wealthy minority, and at home in the upper echelons of the British class system. Thus, charming, mannered, fiscally secure, public-school (boarding) educated, and with extremely strong ingrained attitudes to gender—the right kind of masculinity (muscular, cerebral, anti-emotional) is prized.[91] So too is the right place for women (submissive, pliable, and rooted to roles in the home). This is all accompanied by an abhorrent fear and loathing of male same-sex relations.[92] The ascendancy of such religious outlooks is not hard to comprehend, in the same way that their eventual disintegration is also entirely predictable.[93]

We have noted the Orange Order credentials of T. C. Hammond, and the quasi-Masonic elements of Grand Orange Lodge merit some mention. They are male-only affairs, as are the Masons. Many Freemasonry traditions survive in the Orange Order, such as the organization into lodges. The Order has a similar system of degrees through which new members advance. These degrees are scripturally sourced in the Order (something Freemasonry does not permit). There is ritualism of higher degrees, such as the Royal Arch Purple and the Royal Black Institutions, which have specific dress codes—sashes, aprons, gloves, and distinctive tailoring, and other regalia.

In terms of belief, the Order differs from Freemasonry on explicit expressions of religion in rituals, and also overt political campaigns, the Orange Order being permissive of both, and also active. Again, if one wants to understand how it was quite so easy and obvious for the Sydney Anglican hierarchy to contribute a million Australian dollars to the "no to same-sex legislation" campaign in that country, the Orange Order roots provide the template for a public demonstration and intervention in the interconnections of politics and religion, in a way that Freemasons would not ever countenance.

The Irish Orange Order have always considered the Fourth Commandment to be sacrosanct, which forbids Christians to work, or engage in non-religious activity generally, on Sundays. Even to the extent that when the 12th of July falls on a Sunday, Orange Day Parades are held over to the next day instead. Even in the twenty-first century, the Orange Order has opposed agricultural shows held on Sundays, and of course regards shopping, sports, and entertainment on the Lord's Day as unwholesome. Such Sabbatarian approaches survive amongst some Chapters of the Gideons (also male-only).

Apparent relaxation of the rubrics for belonging to the tribe need careful discernment. The tribal elders are savvy. For example, previous rules specifically forbade Roman Catholics and their close relatives from joining the Order. More recent drafting of the rules adopts wording to exclude those of any "non-reformed faith" instead. Converts to Protestantism can join but must appeal to Grand Lodge. Some branches of the Order will make public assurances that Roman Catholics can join. However, given that swearing an oath not to enter a Roman Catholic Church is still a condition of admission to the Order, potential Catholic applicants will find themselves in a quandary.

Character and Culture in Congregations

The fairest characterization of Sydney Anglicans engaging with other provinces in Australia and the wider Anglican Communion is deliberate disassociation from the Anglican tradition, coupled to intensive missionary endeavor. Here, it closely follows the pattern of the Brethren "meetings" of the mid-Victorian era onwards. Indeed, Sydney Anglicans will use the term "meeting" interchangeably with "service." Many churches in the diocese do not use a prayer book or a liturgical form of service. Few churches sing canticles and responses.

But the striking feature of all church services is the reverence for the Bible, which teeters on the brink of falling into a kind of idolatry. Their Bible has a "totemic status." It is God-like: it cannot err, is perfect, pure, and is to be reverenced as though it were. Correspondingly, no formal liturgy is used, since it may detract from the worship and adoration of Scripture. Some elements of Anglican liturgy may still be used for congregational participation, such as a corporate confession of sin, the saying of creeds, and some corporate prayers. Lay participation in Sydney churches also occurs through Bible readings, leading intercessory prayer, leading the meetings, testimonies and interviews, singing and playing music. In many parishes alcoholic communion wine has been replaced with grape juice. Usually, the reason given for this is to be sensitive to people for whom alcohol may cause a problem.

Brethren rubrics also surface in the wearing of vestments. Or rather, not wearing them. The Irish-influenced anti-Catholic and anti-ritualistic Evangelical Brethren DNA of Sydney Anglicanism expressly forbids the wearing of the chasuble. This is a legal prohibition that originated with Archbishop Wright, an English Evangelical strongly influenced by Irish Protestantism. Wright deemed the vestments were "Romish" and illegal, for which he relied upon decisions of the English ecclesiastical courts as finally upheld in the Privy Council in Read vs. Edward King, the bishop of Lincoln (1892). The main objection to chasubles in the mind of Sydney Anglicans is the association with the High Church idea of a (Romish) "sacrificing" priesthood. Archbishop Wright's practice is codified in synodical ordinance, which makes Sydney the only diocese in the entire Anglican Communion that bans the wearing of chasubles (with the exception of Ireland).

Paradoxically, perhaps, the cope was never banned, and is often worn at the (small) number of Sydney Anglo-Catholic churches where the celebrant at the Eucharist would otherwise wear the chasuble. Most clergy in the diocese, however, dispense with robes or any clerical attire, conducting church services in street clothes ranging from a suit and tie to smart-casual attire. As previously noted, Sydney Anglicanism has more morphological resonance with the Plymouth Brethren (and its Irish sectarian expressions) than any other denomination. If you can close your eyes and imagine an upper-class Australian version of the Revd.

Ian Paisley (pre-Good Friday Agreement), you will have captured an essential essence of the leadership of the Diocese of Sydney. Their motto, or perhaps mantra, is: "Wherefore come out from among them, and be ye separate, saith the Lord, and touch not the unclean thing; and I will receive you" (2 Cor 6:17).

As any student of congregational studies, anthropology, or ethnography will confirm, generalizations can only be made after extensive and intensive grounded fieldwork. Immersion is key. There are some high-quality anthropological studies of Sydney Anglicanism now beginning to emerge, and here I will simply mention a few of the key observations from those conversations, as well as my own interactions with clergy and laity in the Diocese, and corroborating my own "thick" conversations.

First, the local Sydney Anglican congregations are diverse in character and composition. Members of congregations I spoke with personally talked quite freely about pushing the clergy to preach for eight to twelve minutes, and would regularly or frequently tell their clergy that twenty-minute sermons tended to be flabby and repetitive. Clergy I spoke with thought that anything less than twenty minutes was (merely) a homily, and so not "proper teaching."

Second, most of the laity I spoke with thought that subjects such as women and sexuality were not issues that concerned them, but rather something that consumed the minds of the clergy. Many laity reported that they disliked being told (every week, I was assured by several of them) that they were "sinners." They spoke longingly for hearing a message that was hope-filled, inspirational, relevant to their actual lives, and wise. Despite this, laity spoke appreciatively of their clergy, and expressed affection for them—though clearly not in agreement with them.

Third, one anthropological study was intrigued by the mode of pedagogy that was used to teach laity. Sermons—often lasting thirty to forty minutes—would frequently be reinforced with PowerPoint illustration, with questions (and the "correct" answers) flagged in relation to the subject being addressed. Attendees are often given handout sheets for the sermon, comprising headlines, questions to follow-up, with blank spaces provided to fill in the answers.

Fourth, the anthropological reflection on the "sermon slot" notes how the approach to teaching adults has more in common with Sunday School or kindergarten, with take-home sheets to fill-in, and mutually reinforcing patterns of authority, ensuring (literally) that everyone is on the same page. The communal reinforcement of the sermon's message is explicit—"turn and share with your neighbor what you have just heard and learned" (in other words, reinforce the lesson by repetition).

Fifth, an attitude to Scripture that is a form of pseudo-science. Or, is perhaps better understood as a specific mode of congregational engineering. The Bible is read as a "manual," and applied to the breakdowns, repairs, and maintenance in the life of a Christian. Thus, if facing the prospect of a divorce (family or friend), you may hear "turn to chapter X and verse Y of Book Z" as the answer and the means of resolution. The attitude taken to the Bible is that it is a factual manual, and therefore to be learned and applied, as one might take a manual to a car, domestic appliance, or heating system.

Sixth, Sydney Anglicans—clergy and laity I spoke with—were decidedly lukewarm to the new "province of the Southern Cross," with some openly expressing cynicism and disinterest. Likewise, Global Anglican Futures Conference (GAFCON) was a subject that meant very little to the people I spoke with, some of whom suggested that this might be an ego-trip for the leadership, but had nothing to do with the clergy and congregations of the Sydney Diocese.

Seventh, both clergy and laity I spoke with expressed profound dis-ease at the declining numbers of young people engaged in church life. They were divided, however, on the causes. For example, the largest university church in the city (St. Barnabas Broadway) saw the students threaten revolt and secession over the stance of the diocese on same-sex unions. They compelled the rector to make their views known to the hierarchy, and he (reluctantly?) obliged.

Eighth, numbers from recent census data indicate that Millennials and Gen Z are unpersuaded by the Gospel According to Sydney Anglicanism. This mirrors the current situation of churches in Ireland. The authority of the clergy and church hierarchy has been eroded and rejected due to revelations of abuse and malpractice. Yet the church still presuming to instruct the population on what to vote for and against. The people vote with their feet.

According to the sociologist David Martin, the condition of much British Christianity can be characterized as a form of "sweaty semi-Pelagianism." Pelagius (354–418) was an Irish-British monk whose teachings stressed the role of human choices in salvation. Concerned about the moral laxity of Roman Christianity, Pelagius (contra Augustine) stressed personal rational choice and strict moral rigidity as vital ingredients for attaining salvation.

Sydney Anglicanism is essentially Pelagian in character. In *theory*, it is committed to salvation by grace alone. In *practice*, like many forms of sectarian Protestantism, it is also intensively driven by works as one of the main "signs" that signals an individual is saved. The more intensive and extensive the works are, and visible too, the more signage a believer possesses that their salvation is authentic and true. A "lazy believer" is virtually an oxymoron. If you are not working hard for the Lord, you are probably back-sliding, distracted by the world, or worse, losing your salvation. "By grace alone" may be said and sung with great gusto. But the reality for theological worldview of many that hail from the Exclusive Brethren and Sydney Anglicanism is that works matter far more than such believers may wish to concede.

For those who closely adhere to the theological construction of reality within Sydney Anglicanism, salvation is definitely not by grace alone. Terms and conditions apply. Your salvation may be withdrawn for any number of reasons at any time, including apostasy, sexuality, divorce, or the nefariously slippery term "back-sliding." Disagreeing with the clergy might also indicate you are on some road to apostasy and damnation. Moreover, if you don't work very, very hard for this salvation, you may well find that God is very, very angry with you, as God tends to be with the rest of the world.

The rendering of John 3:16 for quasi-Pelagians goes something like this: *"For God so hated the world that he killed his own Son, what whomsoever does not fear this divine wrath being visited upon themselves at any point will certainly perish, and be subject to eternal damnation."* In other words, disobey at your peril, and make sure you earn enough loyalty points to get your bonus, which is eternal salvation. Sydney Anglicans will be regularly reminded that many churchgoers don't have rewards cards, because they're not proper members of God's club, which has an eternal-rewards-scheme. But the good news is that Sydney Anglicans are members of this exclusive club. They can earn credits for being good and loyal, no matter what the cost. And please note again, for the avoidance of doubt, that you can lose all your hard-earned rewards points if you break the terms and conditions of the loyalty scheme. If you have any doubts about anything, see your leaders, and they will explain what is wrong with your doubts, and how to eliminate them. The price for forfeiting your membership of this club with its benefits does not bear thinking about.

The socio-cultural roots of Sydney Anglicanism helps us to understand the theological priorities. God, as Father, is a reserved, unemotional, rational authority figure, given only to anger and the necessary corporal punishing of sin as and when required. Jesus, the Son, is subordinate, and eternally so. The function of the Holy Spirit is to help the believer stay in line as obedient and compliant. Emotions and relationships must therefore be constantly policed, and sexuality and gender are particularly fertile fields for emotions and relationships to lead the unsuspecting into sin.

Some opine that Sydney Anglicanism is fundamentalistic. I find this to be a valid label in the overall diagnostics. True, in fundamentalist communities it is never the Bible that rules. It is always the interpreter. And for sure, Sydney Anglicans in the pews will struggle to articulate reasonable theological dissent and remain within the tribal fold. Conflation is the curse that many who are raised in fundamentalist communities only discover too late, when the price of believing, belonging—and leaving—are all far too high.

In fundamentalist churches, the preacher will usually tell you what the Bible says, and also oblige you with what he insists the text means. Or rather, what God meant by what God wrote. So, don't argue with this, please—it is what God says. To disagree with the preacher is therefore to disagree with God's word. And that means if you disagree with the preacher, you are disagreeing with God. At that point, your options are limited: repent, back down, . . . or leave quietly. Conflation between ideology and power is a problem in any authoritarian regime. In fundamentalism, it is the divine–human conflation (i.e., how can you tell the difference between interpretation and revelation?).[94]

Endgame: Sectarian Secession

We know how this ends. There will not be a leaving card, with a small reception to wish you well on the next stages of your faith journey. More likely is that your name will not be mentioned again, and any question as to where you have been of late will be met with "Ah yes, s/he's left our fellowship, because they turned away from God, and from his word . . . so sad. But we continue to pray s/he will return to the Lord, and come back to us." This is, of course, a highly sectarian theology. One tribe has the Truth; the rest are the damned. Sectarianism is often labelled as "religious" or "political," but the reality of a sectarian situation is usually much more complex.

In its most basic form, sectarianism is the existence within a locality of two or more divided and actively competing communal identities, resulting in a strong sense of dualism that unremittingly transcends commonality, and is both culturally and physically manifest. Sectarianism arises in religious, political, or cultural conflicts between groups. Factors such as prejudice, discrimination, or hatred will quickly come to dominate in such conflicts. Most members of sectarian groups are preschooled into believing that they are *necessarily* engaged in the conflicts that beset them, and their struggle is therefore characterized by fright, flight, and fight. Fear is the key; fleeing impurity essential; and fighting error and apostasy a noble crusade.

Sydney Anglicanism is sectarian, for sure. But the roots of this stem from antagonisms locked into early Irish Brethren secession, and a complex spaghetti of class-related issues. On the one hand, Sydney Anglicanism behaves like a lower-class or lower-middle-class dissenting brand of Nonconformity. It has a strong Protestant work ethic, and all the hallmarks of that Weberian classification. Its behavior also mirrors its nemesis, the Roman Catholic tribe, in areas such as family life and marriage, attitudes to entertainment and recreation, work and leisure, social and cultural trends, and religious hierarchy. And while they can collaborate on campaigns rooted in social and political conservatism, and both are theologically ultra-conservative, neither regards the other as an expression of "the true faith."

Sydney Anglicanism continues to be shaped by the residual attitudes still found in working-class and middle-class Irish Protestantism, including its Ulster branches with Orange Orders (more formally known as Loyal Orange Institution, and meeting in Orange Halls or Orange Lodges). Yet Sydney Anglicanism is also wealthy, elite, and well-connected to the upper echelons of Australian society. This is partly through schooling, with fee-paying single-sex denominational boarding schools still accounting for some of the very best education money can buy. Add the colleges and the welfare organization (Anglicare) into the mix, and the history of the Church of England in that continent, and you can easily see why Sydney Anglicanism has a permanent seat at the high tables of Australian society. Thus, on the one hand, the polity functions and behaves like a disenfranchised sectarian minority, but, on the other, it continues to wield the kind of clout that upper-class Anglicanism can still muster in England.

In terms of character, the muscular, masculine Victorian-Edwardian Christianity comes through at every level. This is an excarnational faith, not incarnational; any notion of the "social gospel" will be treated as some abhorrent apostasy. Sydney Anglicans are anti-ritualistic and anti-aesthetic. They are suspicious of the realm of feelings and emotional embodiment; psychotherapy will be treated with wariness. The suspicion of feelings is highly gendered (and vehemently anti-feminist), and the apotheosis of the father figure—a distant dictator who is capable of enormous anger—the obvious anthropological root of the favored Sydney Anglican theological construction of reality.

If this community were a patient, it would be diagnosed as one with a material-prosthetic faith, with props to sustain its beliefs as an alternative and complete system of rationality, equal or superior to the sciences or any other discipline or discourse. In some respects, the Christian Scriptures are treated in a manner (arguably) akin to the Qur'an. That is to say, this word of God is held to be in some sense created out of nothing. This is akin to Arianism, which recognized the Godhead as immutable, but held that the Son, who is mutable, must, therefore, be deemed a creature who had a beginning, but who has been called into existence out of nothing. Sydney Anglicans regard the Bible, as the word of God, in a similar way.

However, Sydney Anglicanism is modern, functionalist, and pragmatic. Hence, the Bible is treated like a car repair manual. The Scriptures are there to maintain the vehicle, fixing the problems, breakdowns, and the broken. True believers—who are schooled into the Bible-as-manual-mentality—know that if you maintain your faith, life, and soul as the manual stipulates, you will be safe and secure, and your faith will endure. The preacher is a kind of senior mechanic, and church is a weekly service (in the vehicular sense). Trying out other vehicles is definitely not allowed, and is seen as apostate. There is intense brand-loyalty.[95]

Treating Scripture as a homogeneous text in which every single chapter and verse is equally authoritative is a bizarre approach to the Bible, and not one that Scripture ever asks of its readers. The Bible has no self-conscious identity—the title of this sacred book being applied long, long after its (disputed) component parts were assembled and broadly agreed. (Though please note, "broadly," not definitively.) Treating each verse of Scripture as comparatively, equally, and absolutely authoritative is a strange approach to take to texts that are variegated in origin, genre, and intention, and have not asked for or demanded this approach.[96]

Poetic language about the weather is not equally authoritative to a weather forecast that relies on satellite data. They are not easily compared—any more than statistics should be given equal weight to moral absolutes, or metaphors to history, or comparing science to poetry. As I (infamously) noted in Dan Brown's *The Da Vinci Code* (chapter 55), fundamentalists regard the Bible as if written in heaven, and faxed by God to trance-like robotic scribes who merely transcribed what was given. This theory of divine authorship is not biblical, but is a modern form of pseudo-science.

The Bible cannot be literally translated, but it is still literary. Your version cannot be faultless (no translation of *any* text is ever "perfect"—because language does not work like that). But that does not mean that the message of God's word cannot come through to you clearly.

The Geneva Bible manages to summon over forty references to "tyrant" or "tyranny" in translation; the King James Bible (Authorized Version), by contrast, redacts the term altogether. Those ruling over churches as fundamentalist leaders will not want their congregations mulling over Scriptures that mention "tyranny," lest the laity should wonder that the leader-interpreter himself is the despot. The Authorized Version is therefore the usual preferred choice of traditional fundamentalists. This translation avoids awkward terminology that invites suspicion of hierarchy and monarchical exercises of power. The translation sounds ancient, and happily, already carries the label "authorized" with its associations with authority. The Authorized Version is Old World. The text of the Geneva Bible is the translation critical of that old order.

Sydney Anglicanism is sectarian, secessionist, and authoritarian, but also has monarchical postcolonial empire DNA baked into its polity. An absolutist approach to Scripture needs an elite cadre of interpreters who cannot err. However, a faith where it is hard to *critically interact* with the Scriptures (as that means disagreeing with the preacher-interpreter, and thus with God) may have limited traction in the future. Such authoritarian custodianship is unappealing. Millennials and Gen Z have other values; because their world is different. It is diverse, inclusive, and open-minded. Sydney Anglicans have similar problems to those experienced by Ulster Orange Orders unable to recruit young people who no longer subscribe to the tribalism of their forbears. The mitigating factor for Sydney Anglicanism is their relative social and fiscal stability, and the relative lack of proximate alternatives.

Yet the writing is still on the wall. Like Northern-Hemisphere Christianity, secularism and secularization have less agency than many within conservative faiths claim for themselves. But this is temporal. Sydney Anglicanism faces the same problems as the Church of England. An indifferent citizenry who are clearly moral, spiritual, and good, but who have better things to do than listen to a preacher fighting yesterday's wars with a Dawkins or a Darwin. Conservative Anglicans who point to the light of their own stars—preachers, teachers, and church leaders, and their latest initiatives—would do well to remember that starlight only comes from dead planets. All such light fades over time.

The archbishop of Canterbury's eventual abdication of the primacy ("primate of primates"—first amongst equals) within the Communion will merely represent a timely recognition that the Church of England, in a postcolonial era, cannot stake a claim to be the head of a national church and an international denomination. Popes do not have to be Italian in order to be the bishop of Rome. Recent history has served up German, Polish, Argentinian, and American Pontiffs. None of them are required to head the Italian Roman Catholic Church at the same time. That business belongs to the Italians.

It is therefore quite odd for any archbishop of Canterbury to opine that the leadership of the national Church of England can be led by someone who does not share in national identity or interests. Were the role of archbishop of Canterbury to be split between heading the national church and global Communion, it is plainly easier to retain identity in respect of the Church of England than it is to assert extensive international authority.

The Outlook

Since 1784 signaled an end before there was even a beginning—that one can be an Anglican bishop without referring to or drawing upon the Church of England, or acting in deference to the archbishop of Canterbury—postcolonial Anglicanism has been unstoppable. It may not be what was intended, but the Protestant Episcopal Church of the thirteen colonies led the way, a century before the Anglican Communion was established on the back of the expansiveness of the British Empire. Even before that empire, there was a postcolonial province doing things differently. As the British Empire has gradually dissolved, so has the Anglican Communion. The Commonwealth (founded 1926) was a stop-gap in the dissolution of an empire, and a mere prelude to its eventual termination.

In the meantime, the legacy of the British Empire ripples on. As I write this, the Church of St. Mary Redcliffe (Bristol) has unveiled some new stained-glass windows commemorating the Bristol Bus Boycott of 1963. Sixty years ago, citizens initiated a four-month boycott of the Bristol Omnibus Company, since it refused to employ Black or Asian bus crews in the city. Thousands of ordinary Bristolians boycotted the buses and rallied, until racial discrimination was ended. Fifty years earlier, one Rosa Parks was born to impoverished parents in Montgomery, Alabama. Parks become an activist the National Association for the Advancement of Colored People (NAACP) in 1943, aged thirty. And just twelve years later was the "just cause" for the bus boycotts in Montgomery, Alabama—and in many respects, the spark for the modern Civil Rights movement.

In Britain, and through public outrages such as the Windrush scandal (a political debacle in 2018 concerning at least eighty-three people who were wrongly detained, denied legal rights, and threatened with deportation), the Empire has been striking back at Britain. The *Empire Windrush* ship carried just over a thousand migrants to the UK in 1948. It became a symbol of a wider mass-migration movement. Many of the "Windrush Generation," as the migrants became known, experienced a remarkably cool reception from Church of England congregations. That many of the migrants had nascent or active membership of the Anglican Church through the earlier centuries of enslavement and colonization appeared to count for little in Britain. But perhaps this should not surprise us.

As we noted earlier, part of the English blindness towards its role in the slave trade was that nobody could, legally, be a slave in England. Plantation owners who might bring a slave home with them while on furlough consistently discovered that English law did not protect their ownership and power in respect of human "property," if on English soil. (The colonies were a different matter, however.) The English, as a nation, have generally lacked self-awareness in respect of their slave-trading legacy. Indeed, some of the incomprehension could be said to be rooted in the fact that the experience of first-generation African and Afro-Caribbeans in Great Britain was primarily through immigration. In contrast, the first-generation Africans in America were primarily slaves.

There is a world of difference between economic or political motives for immigration, and enforced enslavement.

All that remains is postcolonial independence and self-determination. As the Nigerian author Chinua Achebe prophesied in his 1958 novel *Things Fall Apart* (with the book title borrowed from W. B. Yeats's gloomy poem-prophecy[97] "The Second Coming"), context is all. Yeats wrote his words in 1919, just after the collapse of empires in the wake of the First World War—the Russian and German revolutions—and the British beginning to lose Ireland. Yeats saw that the center could no longer hold. Passionate intensity would drown out and overwhelm any hesitancy in conviction.

Yeats's words apply to the Church of England, and the Anglican Communion. Canterbury and Lambeth Palace once constituted some kind of center. It has not held. It matters no more to Anglicans in Uganda or Guyana than the location and function of the Commonwealth Secretariat, or what the headquarters does, and who the secretary general is. At the time of writing it is, incidentally, the estimable Baroness Patricia Scotland, who is the sixth secretary general. Baroness Scotland was born in Dominica, and the Commonwealth Secretariat is stationed in Pall Mall, London. The motto for the organization is "56 countries working together for prosperity, democracy and peace." Sydney has only followed an older path that was first trodden by eighteenth-century American Episcopalians, with Scotland providing the means. With the recent emergence of GAFCON, the Diocese of the Southern Cross (another Sydney initiative), and the Anglican Church of North America (ACNA) network, the consequences of the Empire have struck back at the progenitor of the Anglican empire. It is to the consequences of this that we now turn, as we also explore the alternatives.

Rampant Sacred Irrationality

> [Jesus] spake also a parable unto them; No man putteth a piece of a new garment upon an old; if otherwise, then both the new maketh a rent, and the piece that was taken out of the new agreeth not with the old. And no man putteth new wine into old bottles; else the new wine will burst the bottles, and be spilled, and the bottles shall perish. But new wine must be put into new bottles. (Luke 5:36–38a)

Decanting the new wine of democracy and open, transparent government into the old wineskin of monarchical governance is a recipe for bursting the wineskin. Revolutions are the consequence—splits and much spilling—until the new wine can be accommodated into some new vessel. Governments and constitutions can be patched up over decades, even centuries. But eventually, the wear and tear require something entirely new. The monarchical–democratic tension is an old–new wineskin conundrum. But underpinning such tension is something more surprising: the sacred.

By "sacred" here, we do not mean God. Rather, we mean that value, idea, foundational myth, or revelation that cannot be questioned. It is held to be fundamental, and the rights to it inalienable. The claim of the right of an individual to free choice in matters surrounding birth, sexuality, and gender will invariably conflict with those who say these are not matters of unlimited choice, but, rather, are constrained by God-given boundaries.

The psychologist Jonathan Haidt notes that when a group of people make something sacred, the members of the group with its system of belief (which includes political belief) quickly lose the ability to think clearly about it. He notes that just as morality binds, it also blinds.[98] Rampant sacred-irrationality is everywhere, or so it seems. It describes the current state of abortion debates. Both sides are vehemently pro-life. Gun control in the USA is similar. Both sides believe gun purchase and ownership should be controlled, but have very different ideas about who should have a gun, when, where, and why. Pro- and anti-Trump voters have comparable difficulties with dialogue. If we follow the sacredness to its source in a belief system, we discover what is ultimately sacrosanct. That is what people gather around, and because it cannot be questioned, there is licensed rampant irrationality. RSI (rampant sacred-irrationality) is also the acronym for repetitive strain injury. The two have some similarities, the most obvious of which is that they are painful, wearing, and exhausting.

In the United Kingdom, Brexit delivered in spades on rampant sacred-irrationality. Did Britain's best interests as a nation lie in one version of freedom and identity (that was anti-EU) or the other version (that was pro-EU)? People who have family—or who had been friends for decades—have split irrevocably on the pivot of rampant sacred-irrationality. Like some ancient or modern civil war, we find kith, kin, neighbors, and friends creating dividing lines that separate those who adhere to their sacred-irrationality (which cannot be questioned or debated) and those that challenge it (who must be repelled at all costs).

Debates on gender, sexuality, ethnicity, and religion also pivot on rampant sacred-irrationality. If my experience and chosen identity is my right to own, and cannot be questioned, then it becomes sacred. To challenge it, or seek compromise, will be interpreted as a violation. Suddenly, and somehow in contemporary culture, we have reached a point where everyone has a sacred right to be entirely believed.

But how are churches—and the Church of England, especially—to resolve persistent divisions within a culture soaked through with rampant sacred-irrationality? There are lessons to be learned from the past. The American Civil War (1861–1865) pitched the Southern Confederate states against the Northern Union states. The practice of slavery in the United States was one of the key political issues of the nineteenth century, and it was a primary cause of the Civil War. For Anglicans—Episcopalians in the USA—the division was painful. The economy of the Southern states depended to a large extent on slavery. The Northern economy did not. Episcopalians split down the middle on this, albeit only for the duration of the war. But the legacy continues to this day. Incidentally, all denominations split like this during the Civil War, and many in the Church of England supported the separatist Confederates.

At the outbreak of the American Civil War, the Confederates only possessed a single factory for making armaments. The supply of guns and cannon was largely from the British, who effectively supplied and armed the Confederates. We cannot ignore that British support for the Confederacy came decades *after* the votes to abolish slave trading and slave ownership had been passed in Parliament. Yet Britain armed the proslavery Confederacy, and effectively extended the war by several years.

The Church of England has been unable to come to terms with the current issues posed by internal rampant sacred-irrationality. The Church enshrines the rights of those who oppose equality on gender and sexuality. The separatists are protected—including their own bishops—because it is held that their beliefs and right to self-determine their identity cannot be questioned. Rather like the Confederates ordaining their own bishop to care for the pastoral needs of slave owners, it becomes impossible to question the relationship between personal legitimacy and corporate agreement. At the end of the American Civil War, the Episcopal Church was reunited, and meekly accepted, fully, that Confederate bishop as an equal.

The seeds for ecclesial division—one faith, two worlds—lie well beyond the boundaries of Anglican parochialism, and are deeply rooted in diverse cultures and histories, which are then primarily responsible for producing the distinctive ecclesiology that characterizes TEC or the Church of England or other parts of the Anglican Communion. The end of the eighteenth century, and the birth of an independent American Episcopal Church, witnessed two quite different approaches to change emerging. The one favored by many British was conservative, gradualist, and reformist, with change coming about incrementally and evolving. Movements for emancipation and representation were gradualist and temperamentally moderate in tone, if not outright cautious.

Revolution, in contrast, will usually result in anything from civil war to mass migration, depopulation, the settling of accounts between rival groups, segregation, violence, and long-term social trauma. Revolutions create new worlds, and they invariably displace or destroy the contexts and cultures from which the revolt emerged. Some revolutions are organized. Others are popular, and while not disorganized, can justly claim to be unorganized. The sexual revolution of the 1960s and the Industrial Revolution of the late eighteenth century fit into this category. Mao's mid-1960s Cultural Revolution in China is a combination of organized and unorganized, and tapped into populism.

The American Revolution that emerged in the 1770s–1780s began long before 1775, and as we have seen, the French Revolution was also the result of a steady accrual of profound dis-ease with the hierarchy. The English Revolution of the 1640s was also rooted in longer-term problems. Broadly, each of these revolutions could be said to be caused by the persistent failures of reform, whether initiated by the hierarchy, or demanded by the people, only to be resisted or reneged upon by the hierarchy. The success of a revolution usually depends on some longer-term history of failures, and there being some widespread consensus that the hierarchy are no longer fit to govern, will only rule in their own interests, or are unprepared to listen to calls for reasonable and proportionate actions to bring about a more just, equitable, and open society.[99]

Thomas Hobbes' *Leviathan*—or to give its longer title: *On The Matter, Forme and Power of a Commonwealth Ecclesiasticall and Civil*—was written during the English Civil War and published in 1651. Hobbes (1588–1679) made the focus of his work the structure of society and legitimate government. Although Hobbes was a monarchist, his reflections on the state and nature of the commonwealth would be manna for the early American

Patriots in the late eighteenth century. Hobbes argued that everyone must give up total freedom to gain limited guaranteed freedom. He then expounded three types of commonwealth that deliver this freedom.

First, a representative man or individual, one who is for all and who embodies the law, justice, mercy, faith, good order, and virtue—namely, a monarch. Second, there could be an assembly that is for all—a parliament or council that is democratically appointed, and also guarantees democracy. Third, there could be a partial assembly—a group or cadre that delivered social order, but was neither monarchical or democratic, such as an aristocracy, plutocracy, or dictatorship. Many would argue that the governance that emerged in eighteenth-century Britain was a movement from the first to the second model, while maintaining a degree of ongoing hybridity.

While that may be so (although personally, I think it contestable), it is more than reasonable to suppose that were Hobbes writing of Church of England governance today, he might have serious concerns. Bishops retain baronial powers, are unaccountable, and not subject to censure or regulation. They are, de facto, above ecclesiastical law, and seldom subject to public or secular law. General and Diocesan Synod are faux-democratic bodies, with meetings bearing more resemblance to a party political conference than a proper parliament that can hold ministers to account.

The General Synod we see now is a theatre in which bishops and ecclesiastical officers perform, inform, and groom the delegates. There is no meaningful democracy when the executive sets the agenda, makes and interprets the rules that govern debates, and even pick who speaks. The executive cadre of officials who prescribe policies and proscribe polity are likely to correspond to Hobbes's third type of commonwealth. Freedom is limited by all the options, but only the second model of commonwealth gives an authentic voice to the people.

Enlightened Church Governance

It took John Locke (1632–1704) in his *Two Treatises of Government* (1689) to argue against the idea of absolute monarchy. Sometimes regarded as the "father of liberalism," Locke proposed a theory of social contract that recognized the basic freedoms and rule of law required for a representative government. Locke influenced many of the Scottish Enlightenment thinkers as well as Voltaire, Rousseau, and others—and those drafting the Declaration of Independence in the breakaway colonies of America. The seedlings for republican democracy were set out in Locke's work, and it is worth recalling that just as the citizens of France and America were arguing for democracy, independence, freedom, and revolution, the ferment of debate was lively in Britain. Many British writers and political philosophers supported American independence.

A decade before 1776, Benjamin Franklin (1706–1790), one of the leading political philosophers of his day, and a founding father of the United States, was setting out the arguments for American independence in a letter to Henry Home (Lord Kames). Home was a leading figure in the Scottish Enlightenment, and a patron of David Hume, Adam Smith, James Boswell, and William Cullen. In Franklin's letter to Henry Home of February 25, 1767, he writes,

> I am fully persuaded with you, that a consolidating Union, by a fair and equal Representation of all the Parts of this Empire in Parliament, is the only firm Basis on which its political Grandeur and Stability can be founded. Ireland once wish'd it, but now rejects it. The Time has been when the Colonies might have been pleas'd with it; they are now indifferent about it; and, if 'tis much longer delay'd, they too will refuse it. But the *Pride* of *this People* cannot bear the Thoughts of it.
>
> Every Man in England seems to consider himself as a Piece of a Sovereign over America; seems to jostle himself into the Throne with the King, and talks of OUR *Subjects in the Colonies.* The Parliament cannot well and wisely make Laws suited to the Colonies, without being properly and truly informed of their Circumstances, Abilities, Temper, &c.
>
> This it cannot be without Representatives from thence. And yet it is fond of this Power, and averse to the only Means of duly acquiring the necessary Knowledge for exercising it, which is desiring to be *omnipotent* without being *omniscient.*[100]

For Franklin, the sovereignty of the king was easily understood. But, argued Franklin, nothing was more common in the thirteen colonies than to talk of the *sovereignty of Parliament*, and the *sovereignty of this nation* (i.e., Britain) over the colonies. Franklin was not against sovereignty, but rather wanted to assert the primacy of a sovereignty that protected the "common Good of the Empire," and regulated laws and commerce. Change was in the air. The reforms Americans sought were reasonable, rational, well-argued, and measured. They could not achieve such ends, however, without revolt.

Thomas Paine (1737–1809) was English-born, but became an American, and a prominent political activist, revolutionary, and philosopher. His *Common Sense* (1776)—a forty-seven-page pamphlet—was probably one of the most influential arguments for American independence, and certainly inspired revolutionaries. For Paine, monarchical power was well past its sell-by date:

> The most plausible plea which hath ever been offered in favour of hereditary succession is, that it preserves a nation from civil wars; and were this true, it would be weighty; whereas it is the most bare-faced falsity ever imposed upon mankind. The whole history of England disowns the fact.
>
> Thirty kings and two minors have reigned in that distracted kingdom since the conquest, in which time there has been (including the revolution) no less than eight civil wars and nineteen Rebellions. Wherefore instead of making for peace, it makes against it, and destroys the very foundation it seems to stand upon.[101]

Such sentiments could easily be applied to the eighteenth-, nineteenth-, and twentieth-century bishops in the Church of England, in trying to operate an ecclesial Commonwealth or Communion (or to keep the Methodists down, and eventually, out). Sovereign power was either being slowly reformed, or overturned by revolution. The days when bishops were regarded as all-powerful and all-knowing were waning, and the demands for subsidiarity and independence growing.

The postcolonial era in the life of English Anglicanism has been a narrative of steady-but-gradual depletion, punctuated by occasional revolt, and an increasing recognition that revolution leading to democracy is preferable to the kind of deity and domination enshrined in the office and role of lord, prince, and baron bishops.

As indicated earlier, the early American lobbyists for reform were Whigs, Patriots, and conservatives. We should therefore see the revolutions of France and America as representing failures in gradualist approaches to reform. They took the law into their own hands. The Scottish consecration was a further iteration of the American Revolution, breaching the power of English ecclesial patrimony.

If one is looking for the causal villain of the fracture in Anglican/Episcopalian identity and unity in the twentieth and twenty-first centuries, one has to engage with the chasms that slowly emerged between democracy and monarchical hierarchies in the late eighteenth century.

Philosophers, climate events, economics, politics, wars, cultural evolution, the Industrial Revolution, and more besides represent the unseen mass of the iceberg.

The ecclesial splits are just the tip of the iceberg, and no more. Monarchical governance slowly unraveled, but was less apparent due to the age of competition in European empires, and the social and economic advances of the Industrial Revolution. It is really only in the postcolonial era, which is relatively recent, that the past begins to catch up with the nations that exploited their former colonies.

But the seeds for dissipation were present long before the postcolonial era. Consider, for example, the New University Library at St. Andrews, Fife. On the wall is a quotation from James Wilson, dating from Philadelphia in 1768. Wilson grew up in Fife. In the New World he became the leading legal authority and helped frame the independence declared from 1776. His words are staggering in their Enlightenment simplicity:

> All men are by nature equal and free. No-one has a right to any authority over another without his consent. All lawful government is founded on the consent of those who are subject to it.[102]

Biblical Governance?

But perhaps what is most surprising to modern readers of Paine's *Common Sense* is the amount of space he devotes to Scriptural reasoning. Paine points out that the monarchy, for the Jews, was an idolatrous delusion contrary to Mosaic law. It is described by Paine as one of the "sins of the Jews," and the request for a king over the Israelites represented a moral and spiritual weakness. The preferred form of governance for the Israelites was that of the Judges—Joshua, Gideon, Deborah, and others—who placed themselves under the law, and were clear that it was "the LORD God who rules over you."

Gideon declined to be anointed king (cf. Judg 8) and also told the Israelites that kingship was not theirs to bestow upon him. Gideon regarded kingship as "heathen," and was also against dynastic, inherited kingship. For the early Americans like Thomas Paine, it is perhaps not surprising to find that a considerable percentage of a tract like *Common Sense* is therefore anti-monarchical yet pro-democratic, rooted in a lengthy exegesis of Old Testament texts.

It is hard for twenty-first-century readers to comprehend how much weight the proponents of new governance in late eighteenth century America would ascribe to the Old Testament. But as America was, for many, a promised land, with religious liberty enshrined under law, and the "heathen" driven out, conquered, or converted, we can perhaps imagine how ordinary citizens configured their identity and destiny through the sweeping narratives of the Old Testament. The resistance of the colonizers to rule by kingship was, therefore, rooted in a kind of sacralized rationality.

For many of the colonists of early America, the Old Testament was rich with illustrations and barely coded examples of righteous individuals speaking truth to power. Nathan the prophet calls out King David for his infidelity, duplicity, and complicity in the death of Bathsheba's husband. The Books of Proverbs and Ecclesiastes represent, in some sense, the democratization of wisdom, with the Psalms doing the same with praise and lament. Knowledge is power. And what the early American believed and practised was that this was levelling. Priests were not above their people. Religious faith itself was now in the hands of all faithful believers, and provided they followed the laws, statutes, and commandments of God, they were assured of salvation.

This was hardly some new epiphany, since many of the early reformers in Europe, fleeing religious and political persecution, held to such truths. There was an in-built equitability in the congregations and sects that emerged in sixteenth-century Europe, and it is that spirit that found a home—in multiple places, and in a wide variety of guises—across the settlements of seventeenth- and eighteenth-century America. In many respects, the scriptural warrant for this would be plainly apparent to the settlers. They were broadly drawing on Jewish tradition—the writers of the Old Testament, who promoted a notion of freedom that was not founded on reforming their mistreatment, or even necessarily liberation from tyranny, or striving for some new political autonomy or equality. Rather, it was on arriving in some new promised land, settling and cultivating what had been given to them—indeed, predestined for them—and abiding by the will of God.

The biblical authors of the Old Testament, rather like the founding mothers and fathers of America, promoted a form of "positive liberty" that was based on a just social order.[103] Leviticus, for example, demands that those who lose their livelihoods are supported by their neighbors. The lives, lands, and livestock of the vulnerable are protected. The Old Testament holiness code is one that promotes interdependence. The Deuteronomic law also limits the power of the monarch. The king must be one of your kin (Deut 17:14–20), and not above the citizens. Crucially, the only role the monarch has is to study, practice, dispense, and obey the law.

The laws themselves are understood to be directly mediated revelations from God. They represent the covenant between God and humanity, and turn the legal code into an apotheosis of sorts. The monarch must be subject to that law too. The covenant is also a dynamic reminder of Israel's fate when it was denied rights and legal protection: "Remember when you were a slave in Egypt . . . God redeemed you from there. I, God, therefore command you to observe and protect the rights of the orphan, widow, alien, and vulnerable" (Deut 24:18–22).[104]

What was crucial to Jewish identity (and arguably remains the case to this day) is not whether an individual believes in God, but rather, do they observe the law? The obligations to obey the law are fundamental. In the birth of America, this was transmuted into a fundamental respect for the law, judges, legislature, and the jurisdiction of the state. For Americans, politics is semi-detached from this orbit. It is the law that is the ultimate authority, with politicians, including the president, constrained by the Constitution. Within our one-faith-two-worlds paradigm, Americans sacralize the state to the extent that religion has no part of it. The sacrosanct nature of the American state requires no one religion to be privileged above another, or to exercise a position of power or influence, lest it lead to tyranny. Church and state are separate; but church and politics can mix freely. In Britain, without a written constitution, church and state are baked in together, but there is a deep aversion to any mixing of politics and religion.

There is a sense, then, that Americans are "people of the book" in a way that the British are not. But what book, exactly? Yes, every newly elected president of the USA is sworn in by making an oath, with their right hand on the Bible. British prime ministers have no such public ritual. But "people of the book" should be taken more generically here. In the 2015 film *Bridge of Spies*,[105] the plot details the American–Russian prisoner exchange at the height of the Cold War. The title of the film draws from the Glienicke Bridge in Berlin, where such swaps were made, and the exchange is life-for-like: Rudolf Abel (a KGB spy convicted and imprisoned in the USA) for Gary Powers (the pilot of a U2 spy plane shot down over Russia).

The focus of the film is, however, on James Donovan, the American attorney appointed to represent Abel. Donovan acts as a good lawyer must—with integrity, and the presumption of a fair trial and an innocent-until-proven-guilty client. Later in the film, a CIA agent, Hoffman, attempts to coax Donovan into conceding Abel's case. The coaxing soon turns into some mild menacing of Donovan as defense attorney. Why is Donovan doing such a good job? Does the CIA "need to worry about you [i.e., Donovan]?"

Donovan's response to Hoffman is terse: the law is superior to political expediency. Hoffman states that the accused deserves the best defense under the law, and that is what makes America a free country committed to equality and fairness. America is a law-abiding democracy, not a whimsical tyranny. Not even governments get to decide who lives and dies. There are courts of law for that. Although Abel is found guilty, Donovan succeeds in petitioning the judge to spare his client the death penalty. He is sentenced to imprisonment for thirty years, which is subsequently commuted in a prisoner exchange. But the justice and the law were upheld throughout.

The English Civil War was meant to end the tyranny of unaccountable monarchy, and replace it with the sovereignty of Parliament. Yet after the execution of Charles I, the Army Council running the new Commonwealth moved swiftly to control the press, and shut down dissent, with the only publications allowed being those that praised Cromwell's regime, and barely mentioned the massacres of Catholics taking place in Ireland at the hands of the New Model Army. Meanwhile, an atrocity against an Irish Protestant was given full and lurid coverage in the media. Long before Vladimir Putin or publications such as *Pravda*, there was Cromwell.

Those backing the parliamentary cause against the Royalists quickly discovered that they were under a military dictatorship, complete with a theocratic and primogeniture succession that bears more resemblance to North Korea than any modern democratic nation state. It is ironic that some of the same people who ushered in the British republic, were, within less than a decade, working hard to restore Charles II to the throne—provided, of course, that Charles II would recognize that Parliament was now sovereign.

But Britons would have to wait more than a couple of centuries for democratic process that enabled everyone to vote for an elected representative in Parliament. In 1918, the only Britons who could vote were property-owning males, which excluded two-thirds of adult males and all female voters. Perhaps with an eye on the revolution in Russia (1917) and Germany in 1918, Parliament, monarchy, and establishment headed off revolution and reformed with the Representation Act, permitting all adult males over twenty-one and all women over thirty to vote. But long, long before that, America was independent; the seventeenth and eighteenth centuries' revolutionary political shifts had begun to lead to a new world of democracy, just as the old world of monarchy slowly slipped away.[106]

Today, many Americans would argue that the tyranny of violence is just as manifest in a state that conflates monarchical power with legal authority, since it mashes divine and human power in ways that are open to abuse. To be sure, democracy is hardly a perfected polity. We know that as a system, it is not as simple as one-person-one-vote. As recent American presidential elections have shown, democracy rests no less on checking who counts the votes, and who says whose votes count. For that, there needs to be good law and unimpeachable judges. For all its faults, democracy is less aloof, capricious, and precarious than any rival monarchical power. And insofar as English Anglicans and American Episcopalians are concerned, democracy and monarchical governance are divided at this point. Anglicanism is one faith, but two worlds. America represents the world of new wine. England is of the old wineskins.[107]

Beginnings and Endings

It is hard to imagine the Church of England hanging on to its powers and privileges in the next fifty years, or even in the shorter term. Especially since the majority of citizens expect equality and accountability from their institutions as any prerequisite for trust. Moreover, as the numbers of "paid-up" members of the Church of England has already effectively fallen off the cliff-edge—and there is no sign that this decline is temporary or seasonal—serious questions have to be asked. These relate to the fitness and role of an established church in one nation, yet within a devolved union of three nations, and Northern Ireland.

To some extent, the underlying problem is rooted with England itself. The United Kingdom is not a union of equals. Around 85 percent of the UK live in England. Economically and politically it dominates the other nations. The parliaments of Wales, Scotland, and Northern Ireland were, until quite recently, subsumed into the single entity at Westminster. Subsidiarity and devolution in the non-Westminster assemblies is only partial, and subject to Westminster veto. Scotland voted by a majority of over 62 percent to remain in Europe, and Northern Ireland likewise by 55 percent. But with Brexit marginally carried in England, all four home nations were made to leave. The English domination of politics over the past three centuries has seldom factored in the Whig-Conservative, Anglican-Protestant hegemony that rides on the tail of this nationalism. The Acts of Union in 1707 (Wales, Scotland, and England to make Great Britain) and 1801 (to add in Ireland to form the United Kingdom) were intended to prevent French invasion and suppress any potential for Roman Catholic insurrection.

The present state of the Church of England—the national church only for England, and not the other home nations—cannot quite see itself as others do. As a national church, it would pose an enormous challenge for the very best estate agent to elicit serious interest. True, the Church of England is not for sale. But it is constantly on the lookout for long-term and loyal tenants who will take care of the storefront as though they were the owners. Upkeep, appearance, productivity, regional-brand-compliance, and purpose are devolved to the local occupiers, who mostly do an extremely good job on very tight budgets.

For all their labor, laity and clergy will receive little thanks from their somewhat distant landlords, who are only interested in the productivity and turnover. And compliance too, unless diversification delivers growth. We now have a situation in which the Church of England's senior leadership are re-mortgaging the church on a regular basis. In this, they are banking on the past and borrowing from the future to try and resolve the present crises. As many will know with their own homes, it is risky—and only makes sense if the value of your property goes up. But as the social, moral, spiritual, and intellectual capital of the Church of England remains in a kind of stubborn negative equity, there may be a default at any point.

There is very little that the Anglican Communion or the Church of England can do about the cultural weather that perpetually rains on its parades. Prayer won't alter the winds, storms, rain, floods, and heat that lie ahead. The currents flow, and the tides are coming in, no matter what Canute's courtiers may have hoped for. The weather cannot be altered, nor wished away. Yet there is arguably no such thing as bad weather—only the wrong selection of clothing, and a lack of preparation. What churches must do now is avoid making heavy weather of the challenges that lie ahead.

We have contrasted the model of "Old World" Church of England (post-revolution and a slow-reformed monarchical establishment), with that of the "New World" democratic entity that quickly evolved in early America, thereby giving us two complementary but quite different forms of polity. These two worlds had entirely incongruent outlooks. The Old World believed in the pre-eminence of a God-willed monarchical authoritarianism. The New World believed in an inalienable right to democratic equality. The Old World offered monarchy—and even if one that was benign, kind, and good, its citizens were still "*subjects* of a realm." There were those who were just born to rule over others.

The New World is not perfect, for sure. But it is democratic, and governance and government can be changed with the will and consent of the people. All are equal. There are no subjects, only citizens. As the Old World passes away, with its classism, elitism, and entitlement—it is dying even in Britain—the New World is also subject to insidious contemporary threats.

Conclusion

Reading Church and Culture

To some extent, what emerges from a study of the life and times of Samuel Seabury is a kind of cultural theory of Anglicanism. What proved to be a remarkable privilege in researching the material for this book was to be able to see Seabury's own first-hand accounts of his pastoral engagements over the course of his episcopal ministry, which ended with his death in 1796. Up to that point, Seabury's diaries, handwritten prayers, and annotations provide us with invaluable clues as to how pastorally engaged his ministry was as a bishop.

For example, his prayers for the consecration of grounds to build a new church or chapel, or to bless the building itself, are finely attuned to the language of the 1662 *Book of Common Prayer*. His prayers for a mother who has lost a son at sea, or for others living in fear, grief, with illness, and struggling with hardship, give us a rich insight into the life and work of an early American bishop. His prayers for his clergy and his frequent meetings with them to encourage their ministry mark him out as a true apostle of the Episcopal Church. Perhaps this should not surprise us, as the role of an early American Episcopal bishop did not have any scope for laying aside local pastoral responsibilities and the running of a church and congregation. When Seabury had returned to America in 1785 as a bishop, he still had to function as a parish priest. His episcopal ministry was inherently grounded in the day-to-day "cure of souls."

Samuel Seabury's consecration in 1784 by a group of Scottish non-juror bishops had caused alarm in London, who feared a Jacobite church emerging in America. It was this act that caused the Church of England to consecrate the next tranche of bishops. So, by the time Seabury took on the additional responsibility of being bishop of Rhode Island from 1790, he did so with the blessing and support of three other American bishops who had been consecrated within the Church of England. Seabury's first ordinations had already been conducted at Middletown in August 1785, and it is clear that in reading the early accounts of his ministry, Seabury was essentially creating an entirely new Anglican culture that had to work outside the authority of the Church of England.

We can see this, to some extent, in the re-assemblage of liturgical provisions. For Seabury, the apostolic succession was vital for maintaining the unity of the church—one faith, but now practised somewhat contrarily in two different continents. For example, Seabury had tried to order an episcopal miter in London, before returning to America. This being the Hanoverian era for the Church of England, Seabury was coldly informed that none had been manufactured or tailored since the Reformation. No Hanoverian bishop wore them.

But Seabury's sense of catholic orders prevailed, and after finding various drawings in archives, one was made. Seabury, however, was mistaken in thinking that a miter was everyday attire for a bishop, and widely lampooned for wearing his when walking the streets of New York. He was the first bishop in modern Anglicanism to have a miter. It was made out of black beaver skin. On the back crown of the miter, in gold filigree, is sewn a crown of thorns—consistent with Seabury's high eucharistic theology.

Liturgically Seabury believed that all eucharistic celebrations were derivative of the bishop's "celebration" of the Eucharist, and he further believed that the bishop celebrating the Eucharist completed the sacrificial act of Jesus on the cross. Seabury believed, in effect, that his cathedral was wherever he was. Today one might regard this as a kind of theological narcissism. But we should not be surprised at this egocentric approach to episcopacy. He might have picked some of this up from Scottish Laudian theology and the entitlement of the English episcopal establishment. But at the same time, Seabury's monarchical leanings also came from him being a dedicated monarchist and High Tory. He had been chaplain in the king's army and was imprisoned during the revolution.

Ecclesiologically, Seabury did not believe in representative or democratic governance. He was opposed to lay people having a role in the governance of the church. Clergy could gather in convention, though, to hear the direction of the bishop ex cathedra. It is interesting to note that it was not until the 1970s that the Diocese of Connecticut admitted lay people to its Standing Committee. Seabury was uncompromising in his regal airs, and in 1789 he only agreed to work with fellow-bishop William

White and to attend a general convention in Philadelphia provided the bishops could sit together in a separate house from the laity.

Perhaps Seabury was reacting to his deeply internalized oppression living as a minority Episcopalian in Puritan, establishment Connecticut. Seabury's High Church, monarchical, episcopal sentiments were a response to his perceived oppression. Seabury's father, who had been a Congregationalist minister, was part of the Yale apostasy, becoming an Episcopalian—and as a separatist he suffered for it. This was a reactionary theology and ecclesiology with respect to the Puritans. Seabury's grandson, Samuel Seabury, was a defender of slavery while a professor at General Seminary, writing *American Slavery Distinguished from the Slavery of English Theorists, and Justified by the Law of Nature.*[108] Plainly, entitlement had been passed down the family line in the Seabury lineage.

In terms of liturgy, however, Seabury's legacy has been remarkable even to this day. *The Book of Common Prayer* (1662) is a mixture of Calvinist, Catholic, and Orthodox elements and doctrines. Seabury, in adopting the *Scottish Book of Common Prayer*, took on the more Catholic theology of the Eucharist that had been favored by the Stuart monarchy, especially under Archbishop Laud. At a stroke, therefore, the revisions of Thomas Cranmer (1549 and 1552) were reversed by Seabury's *American Prayer Book.* Seabury went further, and exhorted congregations to participate in regular, weekly Eucharists. At that time in the Church of England, the Eucharist would have been received at Christmas and Easter, and perhaps also on the first Sunday of every month. Otherwise, the liturgical fare was non-eucharistic.

Structurally and organizationally, however, the Episcopalian churches of early America were self-funding, self-organizing, and enjoyed high degrees of local autonomy. In many respects, their polity is more akin to a Presbyterian model of the church, save only for the addition of bishops. Local decision-making remains, to this day, as important as any diocesan dictations. Though as we have seen, Seabury was no champion of democracy himself.

Seabury's Later Ministry

In June of 1785 Bishop Samuel Seabury arrived in Newport, Rhode Island, on his way to New London, Connecticut. There he took up residence as rector of St. James's Church, his father's old parish, and remained in this office for the rest of his life. Cathedrals, bishops' residences, special provisions for bishops, salaries were all things that lay far in the future for the American Church. The first American bishops were supported as rectors of parishes, and often held other employment too, as did Seabury (he was a medical doctor).

Early in August the clergy of Connecticut assembled in Middletown to receive formally their bishop. In a matter of days he had ordained four men as deacons, delivered his first charge to his clergy, and officially convened them as an organized body. Seabury worked hard to build up the Church in Connecticut. There were also many demands on his attention. Despite also being bishop of Rhode Island from 1790, the Episcopal congregations in New England had to look to Seabury. He normally undertook a long trip at least every spring and fall. His itineraries were usually arranged so as to include attendance at the Connecticut diocesan convention in the spring, or an additional convocation of the clergy in the fall, visitations to numerous parishes, ordinations, and other activities. His diaries record his travels, ordaining a person in one town, settling a dispute in another, consecrating a new church in the next place to visit. Seabury was often accompanied by his daughter Maria, or son Charles—the latter sadly predeceasing his father.

An itinerant bishop was a distinctive innovation, and not a model copied from Europe, where bishops mostly kept to their palaces and cathedrals. Seabury had neither, and with the communities of Connecticut being so scattered, the only way to connect with congregations was to seek them out. This made Seabury's ministry intensely pastoral.

His other major innovation was to recontextualize the American Church, and to read the culture differently. Up until 1776, Anglicanism in America was the Church of England abroad. Seabury, however, regarded the post-revolution American Church as directly descended from earlier catholic models, and not dependent for its parental lineage as some offshoot of the Church of England. His adoption of the Scottish liturgy consolidated that sense of the Episcopal Church being Anglican, but *not* the Church of England. Furthermore, his encouragement of weekly eucharistic observance also consolidated this new sense of identity. Throughout this period, Seabury continued to be a parish priest and medical doctor. He gave free medical aid to the poorest of the parish, thereby setting another example of Christian charity.

This period as bishop was, however, challenged and marred by his relationship to Episcopalians in other states. Churchmen in the Southern and Middle Atlantic states had pursued a rather different course from their brethren in Connecticut. After the Revolutionary War, some sought episcopal ordination from the Church of England. There was, after all, Bishop Charles Inglis (1734–1816) in Canada to consider. Inglis was an Irish High Tory, and had been rector of Trinity Church in New York. In response to Seabury's consecration, George III directed that Inglis would be consecrated as the first "official" bishop of North America. Inglis was consecrated in 1787.

Did the American Episcopalians *really* need to be that separate from the Church of England? Charles Inglis's ecclesial patrimony suggested not. Consecrated as the first bishop of North America, he was based at Halifax in Nova Scotia. Inevitably, some Americans questioned why a handful of newly independent states needed ecclesiastical autonomy. Others resented the apparently undemocratic organization and unilateral actions of the New England Church. So, for several years, Anglicans in America were often on the verge of dividing. General Conventions of the Southern and Middle states were held in Philadelphia in 1785 and 1786. Thereafter it was agreed to meet every third year, as is still the custom.

In 1787 the Middle states were strengthened when two bishops were finally consecrated in London. Of these, William White of Pennsylvania was always conciliatory toward New England. Samuel Provoost of New York, on the other hand, refused point blank to recognize Scottish ordinations or to have any dealings with Seabury. The prospects for the proposed Convention of 1789 were hardly hopeful. But as it was, sickness prevented Provoost from travelling, and in his absence at the Convention, Seabury was unanimously recognized and affirmed. In the autumn of 1789, the Convention met again in Philadelphia, and the union of the Church agreed. A House of Bishops was constituted, and Seabury, as senior, had the honor of being first presiding bishop.

The new union bore immediate fruit with a welcomed revision of the Prayer Book. On Holy Communion, the Convention took proactive and creative action. A new service was compiled, based on the ancient liturgical principles represented in the Scottish liturgy. By the time the next General Convention met in 1792, James Madison had been consecrated in England as bishop of Virginia. The House of Bishops consisted of Seabury, White, Provoost, and Madison. White tactfully arranged a courteous meeting between Seabury and Provoost, and Seabury generously ceded the presidency to the bishop of New York. The four prelates then joined together to consecrate Thomas John Clagett as bishop of Maryland. The union of the American bishops was there formally established.

As it turned out, neither Seabury nor any other New Englander attended the 1795 Convention, as an epidemic prevented travel to Philadelphia. The united Church was, however, quite secure, and through Bishops White, Provoost, and Clagett, the sacred succession of the episcopate was eventually passed on to several new bishops and so to later generations down to the present.

Bishop Samuel Seabury passed away on an ordinary day of parish visiting on Thursday February 25, 1796. There was no prior warning, and no obvious underlying health condition. Seabury had spent the morning visiting parishioners in New London, Connecticut. In the late afternoon, he had walked with his daughter, Maria, to the home of one his churchwardens. Taking tea, he suddenly experienced a sharp pain in his chest, and despite a nearby doctor being called, nothing could be done, and Seabury died. He was buried in a family plot, very close to his place of birth some sixty-seven years earlier.

Cultural Theory

From the vantage point of social and cultural history, we can now see that the American Episcopal Church emerged quite pragmatically. This is not a criticism. Sometimes the best kind of divine agency is consecrated pragmatism, and what we see in Seabury's ministry is faithfulness to the tradition, the past, and to the Scottish and English Anglican antecedents. We also see a degree of sentient spiritual opportunism in which the moment is seized. We see democracy at work too, right from the very first General Convention. We should remember it would take another couple of centuries for the Church of England to half-heartedly experiment with democracy in the form of its own General Synod, which is not to the liking of its bishops.

Social and cultural theory also shows us that the Anglican Communion was effectively broken long before it was made. Once it left the factory, it looked like it might work in the age of the Empire and imperialism. But in a postcolonial era, where subsidiarity is normative, any and all attempts to impose otherwise will be experienced as oppressive. We note that the divisive issues in the Anglican Communion—around sexuality, gender, liturgy, reform, power, and authority—are merely the visible tip of an enormous iceberg. The mass below the surface is much more significant, and that coalesces around democratic polity, equality, individual freedom, cultural crises, political change, and revolution. Such factors underpin most debates on Anglican polity in almost every decade, and the lack of cultural comprehension leads to countless, but equally entirely predictable theological misunderstandings.

Are they avoidable? Probably not. But they are negotiable. That is why this book has aimed to be broadly educational, showing how climate change and crises, social and political revolution, and religious and theological upheavals have all interacted. In so doing, we have made several assumptions about this kind of interaction, to form a critical cultural theory of Anglican identity and its travails.

First, that culture and the socio-political can drive, change, and transform ecclesial and theological understandings and practices.

Second, that big changes to weather patterns invariably lead to transformations in politics and religion, and to social upheavals.

Third—and this has been somewhat implicit—the theological roots of modern social thinking, whether monarchical or democratic in outlook, are still influential.

Fourth, and likewise implied, is that the very categories of "religion" and "science" are themselves very modern (i.e., late nineteenth century), and have much fuzzier edges than most might imagine, and are also closely related, whether in complementarity or competition.

Fifth, the theological roots of liberalism and conservatism find expression in contemporary politics. For many, the religious right and the political right are known to overlap, but the same is also true of the left, lest we forget. Unconscious theological assumptions still, to this day, shape sociopolitical outlooks.

Sixth, the position of the theological and environmental right and left have more in common than they imagine, since both espouse a form of "progressive dominion theology" (often abbreviated as PDT).[109] One could arguably characterize both Christian sides of the slavery debate as holding to progressive dominion theology. The same is true for climate change today, and remains so for debates on governance and national polity (i.e., social democracy or reformed monarchy?). Deep religious convictions with nascent theological outlooks are to be found in both of worlds. They are not exclusive to the left or the right.

Seventh, a sizeable amount of Anglican theological reasoning on sexuality, gender, and other social "problems" could be recategorized as a form of progressive dominion theology. When a denomination seeks to impose a putatively global solution to a set of specific regional and cultural issues, some attempt at dominion will be close to hand, and in the name of being progressive. The first Lambeth Conference was an exercise in progressive dominion theology, yet despite that, the rubrics for establishing normative Anglican theological positions on polygamy still proved to be elusive. In the time-honored English and mannered way, such topics are no longer discussed at the episcopal dinner-party table. To raise the issue is impolite—just like talking about money or politics.

Eighth, science and religion are not engaged in some kind of warfare as many might wish to characterize their relationship. Their interrelationship remains integral to how the natural world is understood and interpreted, and although their cohabitation in the modern world is sometimes fractious, there has never been a divorce. The two parties—the two worlds—are on speaking terms, and share custody of a wide range of subjects, issues, concerns, and hopes.

Ninth, we are delving beneath the surface of debates on topics such as climate crisis, revolution and polity, and social upheaval, in order to illustrate how the changes we experience on the surface are in fact stirred from depths that we cannot see. So in some respects, I agree with Paul Tyson when he notes that theology is like an iceberg: "It is not the obvious bit that you can see that will sink your ship."[110] The iceberg motif is more pertinent than one might imagine. The iceberg cools the sea, and has significant benefits to all manner of life—marine, mammalian, and plant.

At the same time, the fact is that the iceberg floats free at all points to some natural phenomenon. Or, to a growing crisis of frequency in icecaps melting, caused by global warming. This is hardly an exclusive claim regarding theology as being iceberg-like, since the same dynamic applies to social, political, and religious change. It is what we cannot see, below the surface, that should concern us. For it is that which has the power and magnitude to sink an ocean liner such as the *Titanic* (1912), simply by floating in the sea.

As with icebergs, sometimes only the tiny tip of an enormous mass is visible. For example, the developed-world view of human identity assumes a sovereignty over the natural world. It presumes a freedom and determinism that licenses humanity to act upon the world as though external agents, rather than as a consequence and aspect of nature. Such views founded in superiority are rooted in both religious narratives and scientific outlooks. Likewise, assumptions centered on individual freedom and self-determination are ancient theological constructions of reality as much as they are the bedrock of Enlightenment philosophies and politics. Yet such enlightened outlooks don't necessarily translate into a commitment to equality.

Consider fiscal issues for a moment. With the Seven Years' War all but over by 1763 (Treaty of Paris), Americans might have hoped for some respite. However, war is expensive, and debts needed to be repaid to the creditors. The British Crown and government resolved to tax their peoples in order to balance the books. Levies were placed on goods. The colonies were the target for raising new tax revenue. The Sugar Act of 1764 taxed goods that were not British yet still imported into the colonies. Some favorite food and drink staples quickly became unaffordable luxuries. The Stamp Act of 1765 taxed newspapers, pamphlets, legal documents, and playing cards. The Quartering Act of 1766 required the colonist to feed, house, and pay for British soldiers ostensibly there to serve and protect them. The Declaratory Act of 1766 gave the British government carte blanche to make binding laws within America and subject its citizens to any taxation London saw fit to impose. The Townshend Acts of 1767 taxed lead, glass, paint, paper, and tea.

Likewise, consider the Great Slave Auction of early March 1859, which saw one of the largest sales of slaves to take place at a single event in the USA. The auction took place on a racecourse near Savannah, Georgia, over the course of two days. The mass "fire-sale" of around four-hundred-and-sixty slaves was prompted by the wealthy plantation owner, Pierce Butler, needing to pay off his substantial gambling debts and satisfy his creditors. The Butler family were staunch Episcopalians, and originally from a wealthy Irish Protestant Anglican family, but who fought with the revolutionaries in the War of Independence. For the auction, the slaves were housed in the horse stables, and the two hundred or so buyers were permitted to inspect and price up bids for individuals and family units before the sale began.

The Butler family were among the largest slave-owning families in the USA, and had been politically active in securing property rights and federal compensation to be paid to owners for any escaped slaves. The advertisement for the Great Slave Auction that appeared in the *Savannah Republican* announced, "For Sale—Long Cotton and Rice Negroes." The advertisement goes on to explain that those purchasing slaves must "pay one-third cash" up front, and they will be "charged interest on the balance owing from the date of purchase in equal installments." Mortgages, loans for purchase, and personal security are also required to complete the transaction.

This almost casual contractual rhetoric, which is entirely familiar to most people today for any other normal purchase, can only remind us of Hannah Arendt's notion of the "banality of evil."[111] As we noted earlier, British support for slave trading continued long after the Acts of Abolition in 1807 and 1833. Britain supported and armed the proslavery Confederacy during the American Civil War (1861–1865). Such support was motivated by economics as much as by politics, and British military intervention in the war cannot be set apart from the core cause of the war: slavery.

It is perhaps difficult for modern readers to engage with the incongruity of slave ownership. In Confederate states long before the Civil War, Black and White would worship together in the same services across the mainline denominations. Under the dominating Christian paternalism of the time, and certainly prevalent during the eighteenth century, the slave owner would be seen as a kind of "father" to the whole household of the slave and the free. The prevailing assumption of the time was that "the Negro race is inferior to the White race," and that left to their own devices, the Black population would fail to provide for itself and descend into anarchistic self-extermination.[112]

It is beyond the scope of this book to relay the causes of the American Civil War. What we should note, however, are the legal disputes that ramped up the tensions between North and South in the decade leading up to the outbreak of hostilities. The 1850 Fugitive Slave Act gave federal assistance to Southern slave owners who had lost slaves to the sanctuary of Northern states. Free persons who assisted slaves escaping their owners were liable to a thousand-dollar fine. The Baptist, Methodist, Presbyterian, and Episcopalian denominations were divided North–South on the issue of slave ownership. Such divisions were not healed for decades. Ironically, with the end of the Civil War, and the arrival of emancipation, Sunday worship became the most segregated day of the week, as Black and White rarely worshipped together.[113]

So elements in the compound of what lies beneath the surface of ecclesial change are wide-ranging and include: slavery and its legacies, revolutions, racism, classism, climate crises, social dis-ease centered on governance, postcolonialism, the ending of empires, the emergence of independent nations, and global currents in secularization.

Waiting for Change

One obvious area where there is a glaring lack of accountability and transparency in the polity of the Church of England lies in safeguarding. Monarchical rule thrives in contexts of opacity, and in safeguarding the Church of England's hierarchy has developed a range of processes that can be leveraged against clergy, almost like some punitive charge of treason might have operated in a medieval court. What we can say about safeguarding is that it is feared, not trusted, capricious, and easily weaponized to become malicious and vindictive. Yet, rarely, the hierarchy is ever subject to the machinations of safeguarding. As such, it operates as a perfect vehicle for discipline and punishment. As things currently stand, the Church of England has most clergy subjected to multiple and properly organized and professional risk assessments. Yet some clergy appear not to be subject to regulatory control, and can then be "rewarded" with large sums of money to leave ministry if misdemeanors are uncovered. The case of Canon Andrew Hindley was instructive.[114] Accused over several decades of acts of sexual abuse, with minors, and with multiple risk assessments conducted by reputable, authorized professional agencies, he nonetheless continued in ministry until 2022. He was paid a reputed £250,000 to withdraw from his post at Blackburn Cathedral. Hindley was able to leave with his pension intact, and without having been through a full Church of England disciplinary proceeding (CDM).[115]

One Church of England judge—Sir Mark Hedley, a colleague of the archbishop of Canterbury who was honored in 2022 by Lambeth Palace for his legal contribution to the Church—declined to prosecute Hindley for engaging in "non-consensual sex" (i.e., statutory rape?) with a young man. This disconcerting decision was reached on the grounds that Hedley could not be sure if Hindley's alleged victim was under age at the time. According to one report from the BBC,

> In April 2020 Sir Mark Hedley, Deputy President of Tribunals, made what appears to be a startling ruling. He documented that while he thought that it could be proved the case involved non-consensual sex, he could not be sure if the alleged victim was 17 or 18 at the time, so the case could not go forward to a tribunal.[116]

At the same time, other clergy have been subjected to multiple false accusations and falsified risk assessments, and forced into early retirement, with some even taking their own lives, yet there is no compensation from the Church and no consequences for their accusers and the forgers. Sir Mark Hedley again, in one case, declined to consider clear evidence of falsified risk assessments when conducting an inquiry, and declined to disclose his potential conflicts of interest or record a relevant register of interests that might impact the work of the inquiry. The inquiry did not go ahead. In the same proposed inquiry, Sir Roger Singleton (a former director of the National Safeguarding Team, and under whose watch the false risk assessments were manufactured) was also to play a leading part, as though this constituted no conflict of interest.

It should not be necessary to ask a British judge to abide by the laws and codes of practice that govern secular law. But this being the Church of England, it operates as a law unto itself. Hedley is a member of a private dining club—Nobody's Friends—that often meets at Lambeth Palace. So is Sir Roger Singleton. Founded in 1800, Nobody's Friends is one of the oldest dining clubs in London, with roots in the High Church tradition, Conservative Party, and Freemasonry, drawing its membership from senior clergy, senior ecclesiastical civil servants, Church lawyers, and other members of the "establishment." Membership is 50–50 clergy–laity.[117] The motto of the dining club is *Pro Ecclesia et Rege*—"For the Church and King."

This private dining club is flush with ecclesiastical lawyers and leading figures from the establishment, and it might well be above board. Then again, the absence of a transparent, accountable, and open "conflicts of interest" policy or proper "register of interests" for the Archbishops' Council, senior ecclesiocracy, and many bishops does invite speculation on why such a void exists in the twenty-first century. Indeed, in the absence of any explanation, joining the faint dots in this chasmic governance vacuum merely seems precautionary. Despite concerns over this potentially unlawful vacuity in the governance of a major charitable foundation, questions raised at General Synod about these issues are deflected and deferred by individuals answering for the Archbishops' Council who are also members of the private club. The church lawyers also bat the questions away from the podium at General Synod. The main law firm (Winckworth Sherwood, founded 1777) serving the archbishop of Canterbury's work at Lambeth Palace and several other southern provincial dioceses had, until recently, offices located in Oxford adjacent to where the University of Oxford Freemason's Lodge met.[118]

Of course, there is no way of knowing if Canon Hindley was ever a member of Nobody's Friends, or had personal support from any of its members, though the latter seems highly likely on the basis of associations. Hindley, as a High Churchman, senior canon, and being well-connected would certainly fit the profile. Certainly, the existence of the dining club and its previous record on protecting alleged and proven perpetrators of sexual abuse was noted by Alexis Jay at IICSA in 2018.[119] More recently, the conservative Evangelical clergyman Jonathan Fletcher (colleague of John Smyth QC, and both involved in allegations of abuse against young boys attending Iwerne Camps over many decades) emerged as another member of Nobody's Friends, as was his father, Lord Fletcher.

Predictably, bishops in the Church of England have doubled down on the problems posed by the failure of the disciplinary proceedings against the likes of Canon Hindley, and called for risk assessments registering concerns to be sufficient grounds for removing clergy. The bishop of Blackburn, Philip North, made such a call in the *Church Times*,[120] although his plea is somewhat problematic on several grounds.

First, North was bishop of Burnley in the Diocese of Blackburn for several years while Hindley's alleged abuse was known of, yet little was done, seemingly.

Second, if it is to be made easier to remove clergy for safeguarding abuses and failures in policy and practice, then bishops should be subject to those same rules—though North says nothing on this.

Third, North himself is strongly supported by the same senior lawyers at Lambeth Palace who are members of Nobody's Friends. This group represents a clandestine alliance of High Churchmen opposed to the ordination of women, and enjoys significant financial leverage through their organizations, including one simply known as The Society, of which Bishop North is a key member.

Fourth, the opacity of episcopal decision-making does not inspire trust and confidence.[121] Bishops in the Church of England, without exception, have consistently presided over catastrophic safeguarding procedures. Yet Bishop North argues for even more powers for the bishops, and is seemingly unaware of their lack of competence, insight, expertise, and accountability. (Far less episcopal power—or better still, none—would be preferable.)

Fifth, just as fundamentalist communities are ruled not by the Bible, but by the interpreter with the authority to prescribe the true meaning, so bishops would be left in charge with interpreting risk assessments and CDM judgments. There are already examples of bishops making mercurial decisions as to what a CDM determination means. The judge may say, "No case to answer," and the bishop may say, "But I don't see it like that" and proceed to act contrary to the legal process. Clergy and victims would be at the mercy of fickle episcopal judgments (as they already are).

Sixth, and to emphasize these points, there is plain evidence of clergy being subject to false accusations, subject to vexatious and manipulative processes and forged allegations,[122] as well as falsified risk assessments, which invariably bishops and senior legal figures in the church will try to conceal or even endorse.[123]

Seventh, and finally, bishops continue to use Non-Disclosure Agreements (NDAs) to eliminate dissent and conceal egregious safeguarding errors. These are charitable funds, used to silence victims or the falsely accused.[124]

Here the autocracy shifts to being a "vetocracy"—some things can never be changed, and will be subject to perpetual veto by the leadership. In all of this, any of the vested interests between private dining clubs, secret societies, types of churchmanship, financial and legal powers are not subject to open scrutiny or any form of accountability. As though this were not bad enough, the presiding culture at Lambeth Palace will also resort to deploying public-relations organizations and arrange for media briefings against individuals. There is evidence of PR agencies such as Luther Pendragon (who also number Winckworth Sherwood as a client) being retained to spread false stories about individuals that the leadership of the Church of England wants to see removed or punished. False allegations of "safeguarding risk" and "alcoholic" are known to have been weaponized by church media officers and public relations agents against individual clergy.

As I have argued before, the Church of England just looks askance at the civil law that binds all other citizens on equality, sexuality, gender, data protection, personnel, employment, safeguarding, and the like.[125] As the blogger Stephen Parsons noted many years ago, calm elitist arrogance sits with suspected quiet tolerance of toxic evil and the failure to protect and defend victims of that cruelty. As a law unto itself, it can do so, since it sits outside English law by virtue of its position as "established by law," and so enjoys many exemptions under normal law. In such a bubble, quasi-regal pretensions and the monarchical culture of patronage that accompanies it are easier to develop.

Yet a weak autocracy is arguably the worst of all worlds. The key courtiers that surround the monarchical figure—the archbishops in this case—have access to unrivalled financial powers, legal and public relations resources, and significant leverage. The culture of patronage presides over the culture of preferment, and while that is made to appear as though it is democratic, transparent, accountable, and open, the reality is otherwise. Those favored by the patronage are fine. Those who find themselves at odds with it can easily find they are subject to secret campaigns or vendettas. As there is no operational "conflicts of interest" policy or "register of interests" amongst the highest echelons of the leadership of the Church of England, concealment of malice is relatively straightforward.

Some in the field of ecclesiology may wonder why the polity of governance in the Church of England has developed like this. I think the answer partly lies in its protected elite status, its quasi-regal operatives, multiple forms of episcopal-monarchical simulacra, aloofness from normal civic law and professional codes of conduct, high-handed lofty entitlement, and also its faith-based hubris, which is simultaneously anti-modern and yet also lays claim to be progressive and cutting edge. This paradoxical, some might say oxymoronic, position will usually present itself as close as possible to being omniscient and omnicompetent, and will offset its rare displays of omnipotence with fetishized pastoral beneficence.

But for victims of abuse, and those abused by the (so-called) "systems" of the Church, this will all be reified as systemic and harrowing re-abuse. In turn, protests about that will be met with protestations of well-meaning innocence. Diagnosing this ecclesial polity—it is a kind of social-mental condition of the soul of the church—is complex. But the diagnoses would lie somewhere in the terrain of dissociative identity disorder (DID), with bishops and senior ecclesiocrats alternating between possession and non-possession. While that is tormenting for the patient, it is terrifying for those made to live under such leaders, as the episcopal-corporate mentality is at least schizoid, if not in fact (analogically) suffering from a kind of multiple personality disorder. If one is subject to a safeguarding complaint, is your bishop your pastor, supporter, prosecutor, investigator, judge, jury, or jailer? Frankly, it is a lottery.[126] Add in the hubris—some might say with a large slug of corporate narcissism concerned only with *appearances*—and the recipe for the leadership in perpetrating further abuse is fully set. A final heavy seasoning of certainty-orientated Evangelicalism or "father-knows-best" High Churchmanship completes the fare on offer.

Strange though this may seem, there are instructive ecclesial parallels. The Christian Science Church was certain of its superiority to modern medicine. It refused modernity's interventions, and in its own way, also enshrined being "a law unto itself." Exactly parallel to the Church of England's safeguarding history, however, Christian Science quickly appropriated the terms of modern medicine. There were Christian Science physicians, nurses, carers, diagnoses, prognoses, and even nursing homes. Just as the Church of England's safeguarding has its Core Groups, Lessons Learned Reviews, national panels, officers, advisors, investigations, audits, assessments, and determinations.[127]

The similarity is striking here, because in both cases, none of the practitioners have any independence from the institution they represent. Nor are they subject to any external professional independent regulatory body, work under proper codes of practice, or have any need to demonstrate accountability, transparency, justice, or competence. Safeguarding in the Church of England, exactly like the "medicine" of Christian Science, is not related to any external teaching, training, or research-based body that confers recognizable qualifications or assesses expertise. The person who is subject to the Church of England's safeguarding is ultimately in the same position as any ill "patient" under the care of Christian Science. Being seriously unwell and in great pain within a Christian Science context has been likened to "Jonestown in slow motion." Being subject to the Church of England's safeguarding processes is the equivalent of Guantanamo Bay in slow motion—continual captivity, with no prospect of freedom, truth, justice, or eventual release.

Perhaps the only difference between these two polities to note at this juncture is that those who opt in to Christian Science teachings and beliefs probably do so consciously, and having some knowledge of the risks they undertake in doing so, and what security they forego. But the same can seldom be said for those who are served by the Church of England's safeguarding. The unwitting will assume that their experiences of the Church of England, as the established church of the land, will have some secular-normative foundation, and correspond to normal professional standards drawn from public life. Yet the unwitting will be cheated by the Church at this point. There is no correlation between what secular safeguarding policies and practices deliver and what the Church offers. Even those inside the Church of England's governance just cannot see how detached their systems are from normal functional reality.

Meanwhile, the Church of England continues to adopt hollowed-out secular terminology in the name of keeping up *appearances*. This is an endemic trend in the leadership of the Church of England, with its appropriation of terminology including "mission statements," "vision statements," "strategy," "healthy organization," "KPIs," and the like.[128] Lessons Learned Reviews in the Church of England are, on average, delivered more than 750 days late (and rising), cost hundreds of thousands of pounds, are heavily redacted by the secretariat and legal staff at Lambeth Palace (even when they have set the terms of reference for the work), and result in absolutely no change in culture or practice, or any identifiable lessons being learned or implemented. *The Makin Review*, which was meant to focus on the abuse perpetrated at Iwerne Camps, was eventually published over fifteen hundred days late. It subsequently led to the resignation of the archbishop of Canterbury, Justin Welby.[129] This was largely due to sustained public and media pressure, and it does suggest that there is now little appetite in contemporary English culture for an aloof monarchical polity that is unaccountable, elite, seemingly above the law, and non-transparent. Indeed, the same sense of public outrage that brought down Archbishop Welby in November 2024 was also apparent in the case of Prince Andrew, the Duke of York, in October 2025. The public has had enough of an entitled monarchical polity that seems to operate outside the rules and sees itself as above the law.

Denial and Resistance: Churches and Change

What cannot be seen, of course, can often be denied. The climate crisis, the impact of slavery, the effect of monarchical rule on social and political conduct, the angry ferment for revolution rather than another reforming tweak—these can all be subject to denial by the powers-that-be. The denials themselves are, however, not quite what they seem. A Religious Right that denies climate change or plays down the legacy of slavery will still be committed to a doctrine of creation and humanity. The visceral rejection of these overt agendas is rooted in the fear of what (really or truly) might lie beneath their causes—secular environmentalism, reactionary discrimination, wokeism, or covert political, moral, and theological attempts to overthrow the past, perhaps? Then again, it may also be the fear of diversity, accountability, transparency, and fairness, and what that could expose in those who currently hold power.

Political activism is common to both the Old World and the New. We move closer to revolution when the status quo is manifestly failing, yet still perpetuated through power, and further denials and self-justifications are deployed to suffocate the voices for change. Such dynamics can lead to the bringing down of governments to the left and the right of the political spectrum. In the distant and recent past, the same elitist tone-deafness to those clamoring for change has emptied churches and spawned entirely new breakaway denominations. It creates schism too, and can inadvertently promote secularization. When religious leaders no longer listen, nor speak truthfully with integrity and authenticity, it is unlikely that the disenchanted will seek an alternative spiritual harbor.

Both the Old and the New World stem from the same, one faith. God is manifestly present in the Declaration of Independence, and likewise in the Crown that the signatories to the Declaration rejected. There is one faith, but two worlds. Theology was central to both. It is central for the oppressed just as much. For as the enslaved Black African population in the Confederate states began to turn to Christian faith, the repertoire of spirituals included songs with coded melancholic sentiment. "Swing Low, Sweet Chariot" is a song about being swept up to heaven, "coming to take me home." Likewise, "Steal Away" glorifies those who "steal away home to Jesus!" and who "hain't got long to stay here." Slaves knew perfectly well that the penalty for running away could be death, or torture, punishment, and beatings that could lead to death. So to "steal away" meant either an escape to freedom or a one-way ticket to heaven.

Tempting as it may be to compare the current perils facing global Anglican polity to the ill-fated *Titanic*, and even to suggest that all attempts to save it are as hopeless as the proverbial rearranging of the deckchairs, I am not convinced that the colossal ocean liner of 1912 is the place to locate our concern. Of far greater significance, it seems to me, is the iceberg, the seas, and the reality and parable of global warming for ecclesial life. A focus on the cultural environment, in other words, is going to be far more profitable than meditating on the fitness of the ship. The ship can be made safer, and refitted as needed. It is the *oceans* that need to cause global Anglican polity concern. For none of the bishops can change the weather.

Even the briefest survey of Anglican moral reasoning at Lambeth Conferences concludes that Anglicans do eventually work out that they do better if they adapt and evolve. While that is good news, the bad news is that this is normally too late to avert the further depletion of confidence by the public in their moral, social, and spiritual expectations of the Church. While Anglicans debate—again and again—sexuality (an issue they cannot resolve), they erode their public intellectual capital.

There is more bad news for the wider Communion too, and the Church of England. Anglican bishops proceed as though they are somehow protecting the vulnerable, and that without their intervention, society will unravel. The late nineteenth- and early twentieth-century statements on women reflect concerns the (male) bishops have *for* women. Debates on birth control are concerns *for* the family and society. Later debates on sexuality were, likewise, narrated as concerns *for* natural order, stable family life, and Christian "tradition."

However, suffice to say, the moral reasoning of the Church of England ignores basic principles of jurisprudence, legal accountability, oversight, and governance. The small cadre of lawyers working in the discreet field of ecclesiastical law maintain the separatism of the Church from wider accountability and regulation. The bishops still presume to lecture the wider world on what is good for it, and what it should avoid. But any talk of regulating unaccountable bishops, introducing equality into personnel problems within the Church, and otherwise acting fairly, as a public body should—well, the silence from the bishops will be deathly. What ultimately comes to pass is quite sobering. Bishops resisting normative progressive cultural currents are destined to become footnotes in history.

So what exactly are the emerging crisis points for the worldwide Anglican Communion? As we have argued over the course of this book, the apparently divisive issues of liturgical reform, sexuality, and gender are second-order matters, and symptoms of the deeper social and cultural malaises affecting all of the mainstream denominations across the world. Money, sex, and power are always with us as divisive issues. Psychologists sometimes point to the phenomena of "distraction-devaluation" as a default coping mechanism for individuals and groups, when inimical and complex forces threaten to overwhelm and undermine.

This has been true for the Anglicanism for over 250 years. The oath of fidelity to the reigning British monarch was no longer needed. The binding of obligation and loyalty were attenuated in politics, and simply copied into the church. The forces of secularization, globalization, urbanization, consumerism, individualism, liberalism, and increased strength of progressive democratic polity has undermined elitist monarchical command-and-control ruling. Autocracy may be tolerated, but it is very rarely chosen. Bishops, and their churches, by remaining aloof and unaccountable, and hoping that their mystique will camouflage their lack of transparency, are no longer protecting the church. They are, in fact, unwittingly accelerating its decline and depleting its identity.[130]

Just as there is a geopolitics of slow catastrophe emerging in the analysis climate change, so it is in ecclesial life. The presenting divisive issues of gender, sexuality, and crises in authority have emerged from much deeper causal currents. A slow ecclesial apocalypse is now evolving, which will see a rapid decline in respect for, inclination towards, and membership of the church. It is hard to imagine any kind of novel initiative in evangelism or mission stemming this tide. The only remaining option would be for the churches to recover their sense of integrity, and be honest about the remorse, repentance, and reparation that are owed to its victims and those it has abused. There is no sign of this happening anytime soon.

The seismic shifts of power ushered in by the Industrial Revolution have resulted in incalculable discrepancies over the last three centuries between land and labor, rural and urban, vocation and profession. The Church of England has 75 percent of its churches in rural areas, while the nation has 75 percent of the population living in suburbs and cities. The days of Parson James Woodforde—an English clergyman ministering in Somerset and Norfolk parishes and author of *The Diary of a Country Parson*—are behind us. Woodforde knew all his parishioners by name, whether or not they came to church. But there were only 360 of them. Today, there are fifty-six million people living in England, and eight thousand paid clergy. That yields a ratio of 1:7000.

There are other tipping points too. Just as the statue of John Colston was tipped into Bristol Harbor, so now—and this is very recent—are congregations beginning to ask prescient questions about the endowments, ornate memorials, and artefacts that have enriched churches. In 2020, Britain's National Trust reported that at least one-third of its historic houses had direct links to slavery. Some of these houses—Castle Howard and Harewood, to name but two—were able to commission work from the likes of Robert Adam, Capability Brown, and Thomas Chippendale. Or to hire Joshua Reynolds, the preeminent portrait artist of the day, leaving some of these new country houses with art collections worth millions.

The wealth for these houses came from estates whose wealth came from income streams in Barbados and plantations in the West Indies. The newly monied slave merchants were elevated to peerages by successive monarchs in the eighteenth century, and were often upgraded from baronets to become earls. Slave trading paid handsomely. The Church of England also benefitted with dividends offered by those keen to ingratiate themselves further into the establishment. Such wealth survives to this day. Recently, a divorce settlement was required for the owners of Castle Howard, necessitating that some of most important works of art be sold. A Michelangelo sketch went for $8 million, while Joshua Reynolds's *Portrait of Omai* (a captured Polynesian, the art dating from 1776) sold for $14.6 million.

A History of the Future

Historical crises tend to arrive unseen and uninvited. Like climate events, they are beyond our control, yet demand a response.[131] The 2019 United Nations Intergovernmental Panel on Climate Change (IPCC) Special Report on the Ocean and Cryosphere in a Changing Climate defined a tipping point as "a level of change in system properties beyond which a system reorganizes, often in a non-linear manner, and does not return to the initial state even if the drivers of the change are abated." A 2021 IPCC Report defined a tipping point as a "critical threshold beyond which a system reorganizes, often abruptly and/or irreversibly." The change can be brought about by a small disturbance causing a disproportionately large alteration to the system. In ecosystems, as with social and political systems, a crisis can trigger a regime shift, a major systems reorganization into a new stable state. Or, it can spawn a revolution.

All that said, it is not difficult to be humorous about the modest and temperate proclivities of English Anglicanism. Rather like the climate of the nation that gave birth to its national church, it is often overcast with light drizzle; but it is also sunny and raining, with warm spells. As a nation, the English heavily over-narrate their weather. In reality, however, England's climate is temperate. As Bill Bryson wryly observed,[132] the rest of the world sniggers when English newspapers carry headlines such as "Phew, What a Scorcher!," or perhaps more risibly "Britain Sizzles in the 70s." In many parts of the world, this is not even warm, let alone hot.

Kate Fox's *Watching the English*[133] discusses English "values" (fair play, courtesy, and modesty), which she claims are designed to combat and address social dis-ease. Fox speculates on the cause of this complex potage that comprises the English character, and suggests that climate, island-identity, and history may be factors. To conclude her book, she spends a fortnight queue-jumping in the ticket office at Waterloo Station. The English are a nation proud of their queuing skills, and the associated forbearance and patience required. She notes that the queue consistently acts with mild reticence and negligible challenge to her conduct. What is worse, the queue-jumping, plainly, is causing a scene. She suggests the English would rather let the queue-jumper get away with it, merely commenting that they plainly "don't know the rules" (which, like the British Constitution, are unwritten).

In terms of ecclesiology, the climatology of a denomination or church, together with its optimum emotional temperature, is an important interpretive key in comprehending ecclesial life. So in terms of mood, refracted through a climatological motif, we can instantly see, for example, how mild or cold "fronts," when encountering "hot winds," create storms. Indeed, in intra-ecclesial disputes—the Global South Anglican provinces versus those of the North on the issue of human sexuality comes to mind—we might be witnessing a clash of moods and temperaments as much as we are also seeing explicit theological differences emerge.

Indeed, the emerging ecclesiastical climatology in the Anglican Communion witnessed at the beginning of the twenty-first century, like the rest of the planet, now finds itself exposed to extremities. Normal and temperate weather configurations seem to have given way to immoderate and excessive patterns of behavior that are driving a new agenda. The sense of "furious religion" has returned. Cool, calm religion—that beloved export of Europe for so many centuries—is giving way to hot and sultry expressions of faith that despise moderation and temperateness. And Anglicans of all hues are caught up in the new extremes of spiritual weather. Ecclesiastical global warming has arrived.[134]

Some churches, of course, thrive on intensity and heat; it is a sign of vibrant life and feisty faith. But others who are of a more temperate hue find this disturbing: heated exchanges, anger, and passions seem to dismay more than they console. Anglicanism, then, as a *via media* expression of faith, finds the soul of its polity profoundly troubled by excess.

By so doing, we are able to see how theology and church development (or evolution) are usually some consequential response or reaction to changes in the environment, and very seldom causal of the cultural change. We have also sought to utilize the reality of changes in weather, as well as using climatology in the service of the analogical imagination, to show how a world that is warming, or ablaze, will invariably struggle to remain composed and complete.

To some extent, weather maps are of some help here. The first published weather chart appeared in *The Times* on March 31, 1875. It was prepared by Sir Francis Galton (1822–1911). Galton was a polymath extraordinaire, and amongst other feats, he devised the first system for classifying fingerprints, experimented on the efficacy of prayer (he concluded it only helped the petitioner, as prayer contributed nothing to the longevity of others), worked on meteorology, the science behind a perfect cup of tea (seriously), and coined the phrase "nature versus nurture." Francis Galton was also a pioneer of "scientific" racism and proponent of eugenics.

Galton's 1875 weather map was of Northwest Europe, and we note with interest the terminology applied to the illustration of weather fronts. These include "dull" (NW Scotland and London), "smooth" (Irish Sea, North Sea, and English Channel), "fine" (NE Scotland), "thick" (Denmark), "clear," "overcast," and "slight swell" (Bay of Biscay). While the weather might have been all of these things in late March 1875, the terms used by Galton are suggestive of a particularly temperate English outlook, and calibrations that represent a characterization of mood and sentiment as much as anything else. Overall, Galton's chart provides *reassurance* to readers of *The Times*. The weather map reveals the English climate to be "calm" and "mild." The chart offers some ideal indicators and conditions in the collective national sentiment, irrespective of any actual inclemency.

So what of the future of the Church of England here, in the wake of Seabury's consecration? As the historian Mark Harrison noted of the Soviet Union, when leviathans evolve towards becoming ever-more secretive, and any rules, checks, and balances are removed from public scrutiny, everything that matters happens behind the scenes. Indecision becomes incentivized, and vested interests are never called out. The citizenry withdraw their trust, and a tiny elite just focus on making sure the entire system does not collapse. But collapse it will. Largely, like the bureaucratic imperialism of the Soviet Union, under the weight of its inefficiency, corruption, and cover-ups.[135]

Imperialism as a mode of governance can be found in capitalism and communism, monarchies, and republics. And in churches seeking to rule and reign without accountability, transparency, or integrity. Yet in retaining all powers to itself and their cadre of bureaucrats, imperialism still thrives amongst many congregations and denominations. But what history teaches us for the future is that for Protestant denominations such as the worldwide Anglican Communion, and for American Episcopalians too, democracy really matters. Bishop Samuel Seabury modelled a kind of regional pastoral-teaching ministry for his episcopacy that did not overburden or interfere with the local churches in his care. Seabury did not carry—in his spiritual DNA—the kind of quasi-regal sense of entitlement that many English Hanoverian bishops possessed. Liturgically and theologically Seabury was more Catholic than his English counterparts. Organizationally he was more of a democrat that his English counterparts, who were still invested in monarchy.

In a postcolonial era, there is no space or place for the archbishop of one nation to preside over all other provinces in other nations, even if only in some symbolic way. The archbishop of Canterbury could still function as the head of a English Church, but there is no need whatsoever for any such church to be established. The nation needs a church that upholds the law of the land, and is therefore subject to it. The present situation is democratically unconscionable, where the Church of England exempts itself from laws on equality, accountability, data compliance, transparency, sexuality, and gender that it doesn't like. It cannot continue.

Especially when, at the same time, the Church of England enjoys enormous privileges (including tax, finance, etc.) in the country it is meant to serve and represent. One can no longer justify a church that exempts itself from the rule of law, yet presumes to be the national guardian for moral well-being. With so few of the nation offering the Church of England any mandate for its privileges, the time has come to disestablish. The Irish, Welsh, and Scottish Anglicans have managed this. England can too.

The archbishop of Canterbury's eventual abdication of the primacy within the Communion will merely represent a timely recognition that the Church of England, in a postcolonial era, cannot stake a claim to be the head of both a national church and an international denomination. It is therefore quite odd for the previous archbishop of Canterbury to opine that the leadership of the national Church of England can be led by someone who does not share in national identity or interests. Were the role of archbishop of Canterbury to be split between heading the national church and global Communion, it is plainly easier to retain identity in respect of the Church of England than it is to assert extensive international authority. In the meantime, the Church of England limps on, hampered by the inability of its leaders to make moral decisions. In compromising, the bishops seek to keep control through mercurial and ill-conceived mediation. Every time the General Synod of the Church of England makes a decision—often after years of debate and anguish—the bishops will take the decision away for further reflection, or find a means of undermining it, or making substantial space for exceptionalism.

Consider this parallel example in public life relating to smoking. A small minority of people still like to smoke cigarettes (approximately 11 percent in the UK). Smoking remains lawful. But restrictions on smoking in enclosed public spaces is legislature that came into force some decades ago (2007). Society reached a mind—by majority—on how the personal choices of a few might infringe the liberty of all. Smoking in public spaces was no longer a private issue—a matter for the conscience or manners of the smoker to make a judgment on how nearby non-smokers might react. Smoking in public is deemed to be "anti-social," and the legislation recognizes that one person's liberty to smoke infringes on the well-being of others.

Discriminatory views on grounds of race, gender, and disability are similar. You may think what you like in private, but you can't implement such views and practices on the public. So, smokers remain free to light-up in private. But they are no longer free to share (or inflict) their habit on the wider public. Smokers effectively lost their familiar freedoms—so that wider society could gain equality of experience with fresh air in enclosed shared spaces. There was no feasible compromise here.

It was not illiberal to regard "designated smoking zones" inside restaurants as offensive and antisocial. Nor would it be "illiberal liberalism" to resist new requests for alternative shared spaces being opened up for smokers, in order to compensate for their loss of old customary public places. We don't seek to balance the losses of privilege for smokers by yielding them some new public space. We don't say, "Well, we banned smoking in all pubs, but as reparation, you can now smoke in certain restaurants." Or, for that matter, set about re-designating all trains as smoking zones once again, and reintroduce specified non-smoking carriages. Nor do we suggest that smokers can light up in *your* private space, which was hitherto smoke-free.

As for passive smoking and public spaces, the claim that smokers only impact their own health has been widely refuted. In the same vein, a male bishop opposed to women priests will invariably have a widespread impact on the "air" of the whole diocese—clergy and laity alike—quite independent of any personal or public compensatory gestures they attempt to make. That's because theological positions are inherently influential and powerful. They are liminal and subliminal; explicit and implicit. Theology affects mood and morale. Even privately held theological convictions will send unconscious coded signals that shape culture, churches, and congregations: communicating acceptance or rejection, faith or doubt. So we need to know that our bishops fully affirm the ministry of *all* their clergy—irrespective of their gender.

Likewise, imagine for a moment King Solomon (see 1 Kgs 3:16–28) saying to two mothers upon the death of one infant, and the ensuing custody battle raging over the remaining child, "Look, I can see you are both grief-stricken and hurt, and you might both have legitimate claims. So, how about coming to some kind of co-parenting or child-sharing arrangement, where the infant lives with one mother for half the week, and then goes to the other mother for the remaining half? That way, nobody loses. The child can then decide whom it wants to be with when it has come of age." There is a certain "balance" and neutrality here. We may praise Solomon for his impartiality. Yet in our re-imagined scenario, asked to referee this dispute, he prevaricates; then declares a score draw, and does not make the *decision* required.

We should recoil at this quirky rendering of the story, although it has a familiarity—exactly the kind of compromise and fudge that a group of English Anglican bishops would manufacture. But it does not exhibit wisdom. Impartiality is not what the Old Testament extols. Wisdom is "other," and it requires thought, calm, and decisive care, and sound judgment. Wisdom requires comprehending moral agency, acting with courage, compassion, and resolve. Wisdom must sometimes be brave. Some decisions and judgments that must be made cannot please all those we care for. But most Church of England bishops prefer compromise. It keeps them aloof and in power, in some fantasy of ostensibly keeping the peace. (Thank God they were not at Nicaea or Chalcedon; just imagine the fudging!)

Ecclesiology Reconsidered

Part of the labor in this book has been to draw our attention to how ecclesiology can and should be done in the present. Rather like tracing family lineage or drawing family trees, ecclesial history is a matter of ancestry. True, there is no such thing as "ecclesial DNA." But knowing what ancestry our denominations have—the theological unions and traits we have inherited to the present—are of enormous assistance in stripping away the kernel-myths from the core-grain-reality. Ecclesiology done well is, also, an opportunity to engage in some light *sliding doors* speculation. If

Seabury had been consecrated by English Anglican bishops rather than the Laudian-Jacobite Scots, what character might have imbued early American Episcopal identity? If Seabury had received his episcopal orders from the Danish Lutherans, would Anglicanism have survived in continental America? (Yes, but it would probably have become a very different ecclesial species.)

Ecclesiology done from the inside—by its own confessional champions—instinctively roots for narratives and assumptions based on some purist pedigree foundation. Done by outsiders, rivals or opponents, ecclesiology can offer a highly prejudiced treatise of ecclesial ancestry. Our approach takes a middle path, rooted not only in historical realism but also taking account of culture and context. Imperialism, racism, classism, sexism, nationalism, and other forms of discrimination play a significant role in how churches and denominations come to evolve. It is unwise to think about the origins and identity of ecclesial bodies without taking into account such factors. The ways in which theologies, aesthetics, and ideologies merge and spawn also play a significant role in the formation of ecclesial identity.

While the personal study of ancestry might assume—and even enjoy—taking account of such factors, ideological ecclesiology often presumes that the identity of a church is some kind of exclusively theological affair. Yet it rarely is, and much like family ancestry, we find that accidents, chance meetings, missed and seized opportunities, external factors, choice and lack of choice all play a large part in how a church or denomination eventually emerges.

For example, I tend to date the Church of England from 1534—with Henry VIII divorcing from Rome and assuming the headship of the national church. But the average English person did not, thereafter, introduce themselves as being "C of E." That perhaps began a century later, and even then, only very haphazardly. When did Anglicans start using that nomenclature for themselves? Not until the seventeenth century at the earliest. In the sixteenth century, English Christians realized (relatively fast) that they were no longer Roman Catholic and were now Protestant. But any notion of being Anglican took decades to crystallize, and several more decades to enter into their common vocabulary. Methodists can follow a similar story in tracing their ancestry.

Since New Testament times, churches have been analogous with "the body of Christ" (cf. 1 Cor 12), and this allows for a playful interpretative approach to ecclesiology. The congregations I have studied—fieldwork, site visits, and ethnographic studies—can be both big-hearted but weak-minded, or vice versa. Some congregations and denominations positively radiate their emotions, but at the expense of the cerebral. A believer can be left feeling famished, with the ache of intellectual hunger unmet. Others are averse to emotional displays of any kind and like to approach worship and preaching as a largely cerebral engagement. Structurally, denominations can carry inherited conditions that are passed down the body-politic line. Frail inner structures (when the skeleton of the denomination is weak), slow reflexes, tendencies towards obesity or anorexia are all observable in the body politic.

With rare exceptions, the body in question—church, congregation, or denomination—sees itself as normal, and those at variance with it as abnormal. For Protestants—who inherently carry the DNA of individualism and separatism in their polity—the puzzle is how to be catholic without being Roman Catholic. For more than half a millennia churches have struggled with their familial identity as bodies of belief, trying to figure out their commonality with others, and yet at the same time how they are different, and why that matters. Grounded ecclesiology can help illuminate the characteristics and traits of ecclesial communities as they wrestle with their distinctive identities, and their fitness for adaptation with contemporary culture.

But there are other reasons why honest historical realism is important for the enterprise of grounded ecclesiology. Naturally, it provides some kind of inoculation against becoming captive to myths and fantasies regarding origins. But perhaps more importantly, like the ancestry of a family, we find that sin and grace are encountered in equal measures, as are accidents and intentionality. Such an approach also forces us to face up to histories we'd rather forget. The history of slavery is a stream of oppression, cruelty, racism, and exploitation. As the writer David Leigh recently noted of the beauty and grandeur of Balintore Castle, which nestles in the Glens of Angus in the foothills of the Grampians in Scotland, we can marvel at the exquisite architecture forever and an age. But we must also reckon with the monetary fortune that built this Scottish castle, with the wealth coming entirely through the Lyon family, who were slave owners with large plantations and estates in Jamaica.

Jamaica is a particularly pivotal island for the history of slavery. The "Baptist War" in Jamaica of 1831 convulsed the churches and the role Christians played in eventual abolition. Earlier slave rebellions in Jamaica, and their brutal, cruel suppression, destroyed the case for gradualist reform. Many in the churches had supported gradualism. It avoided paying substantial compensation for slave owners and also evaded potential risks to trade, plantations, and produce. Gradualism, it was held, improved the lives of slaves, but avoided potential political risks imagined in wholesale emancipation. Yet it was only extreme violence and atrocities that destroyed the preferred gradualist approach.

Like the ancestry of a family, or binaries that might pitch the colonized against colonizer, or winners versus losers in empires, it is hard for any denomination to separate out the good and the bad in the construction of their ecclesial identity. It is only the passage of time that enables us to look back and make a measured assessment on the ethical identity of an institution. For the Church of England in the eighteenth century, right through to the present day, there has been a marked reluctance to engage in a forensic account of its debt to slavery and slavery's by-products. Despite the Church of England being an overt, frequent, and multiple beneficiary of slave trading, there is no indication that the denomination can see itself as an agent in the construction of "Anglican imperialism."

Indeed, as Rowan Strong points out,[136] bishops were apt at condemning the transatlantic slave trade as "a commerce disgraceful to the human species," but stopping short of condemning slave ownership, as there was no clear mandate in Scripture for doing so. In contrast, American Episcopalians went from being overt apologists for slave ownership to much more profound and more reflective self-criticism. As Jennifer C. Snow notes in her outstanding work,[137] the development of America went in tandem with the history and culture of the Episcopal denomination.

Slavery was also a different prospect on either side of the Atlantic. English slave owners rarely saw or met slaves, and many who invested in the trade and ownership only did so through London-based brokers, insurers, and financial agents. Slaves were commodities that produced an annual yield with a guaranteed return. Mortgages and loans were available for such investments, as one might purchase properties to rent out.

Americans, by contrast, were hardly remote from their purchases. Slaves worked their land and also functioned as servants in their houses. Financially, slaves fell under different legal and commercial categories, those reserved for chattels and stocks. Like agricultural produce or clothing, slaves could be bought and sold as goods. Indeed, in eighteenth-century small ads in American newspapers, slaves were not advertised under land or real estate, but under chattels.

So, while one could take out a loan to acquire such human resources and also insure against their loss, slaves were essentially chattels. When they went missing, they were classed as lost or stolen goods. In England, slaves had a different value and were a potential financial investment offering a good return. In America, slaves were an expendable resource, and a means to an end. Loans and insurance were available, but the value and legal identity of slaves were different. These kinds of detail might account for why the American Episcopal journey on race, exploitation and slavery has been more marked and thorough than its English counterpart.

Bluntly, Americans were forced to face up to the value (or rather the lack of it) that was placed on slaves and those oppressed because of the color of their skin. The English journey is more ambiguous and, frankly, less honest. It lacks that self-critical retrospect that seems to drive post-imperial American history and ecclesiology. The English cannot see themselves as oppressors but rather only as investors and opportunists who brought benefits, albeit occasionally going too far or getting it slightly wrong.

Americans, in contrast, have had to face up more squarely to their racism and oppression. This has led to the kind of healthy self-criticism we encounter in Jennifer C. Snow's work, which has yet to emerge from within the Church of England's ecclesiology. Perhaps this can only change when the English are freed of the myths and legends that seem to be baked into their identity and their perceived national history. Until then, English Anglicanism will struggle to be free of its prevalence in claiming preeminent pedigree for its ecclesial identity and is unable ever to imagine its role and agency as an oppressor at home, let alone abroad.

As we have indicated in this brief discussion, there are forces at play that have a profound impact on the shaping of ecclesial life and identity. This is especially observable at times of social, political, and environmental trauma. In our section of illustrations, we give a graphic example of this with the hand-redaction and candle wax used to change the prayers for the monarchy in the *Book of Common Prayer* into prayers for the president and people of the new Republic of America.

Lest English people assume some steady-state ethos, Britain itself had a decade where it experimented with a republican form of governance. As Alice Hunt notes in her *Republic: Britain's Revolutionary Decade, 1649–1660*,[138] the "dangerous monarchy" was abolished, and swept away too was the House of Lords. This was an era of unprecedented change and instability, and it left its mark on the Church of England too, which lurched from Laudian theology and polity to something much closer to Presbyterianism. Fundamental assumptions about sovereignty, liberty, and polity were debated and implemented, and entirely new forms of radical politics became commonplace conversations in the coffee houses and meeting places for ordinary citizens.

In many respects, this radical decade formed the foundation for what was to emerge later as the Enlightenment. Once the old forms of autocracy had been dismissed, the stage was set for a new compact between leader and led. Indeed, there is an argument to be made that the American Declaration of Independence and the establishment of post-revolutionary independence owes more to the settlement of Britain from 1649–1660 than any other exemplar. For sure, even after Oliver Cromwell's death in 1658, there was little appetite to return to the old monarchical autocracy that many felt had been thrown off by the English Civil War. Yet despite widespread support, the collapse of the British Republic came in 1660, and with it some return to the patterns of polity in church and state that had remained familiar and within collective public memory.[139]

What we are left to reflect on in closing this section is the kind of ecclesial polity the emerges from a republican rather than a monarchical context. It seems reasonable to characterize it as follows. In a republican context, the ecclesial culture will draw on democratic assumptions that are open to radical and even revolutionary outlooks. In a monarchical context, the ecclesial culture will permit a moderate level of democratic governance, provided that it remains subordinate to an unelected head of state, or the head of the Church. Any notion of radicalism or revolution will be resisted and narrated as contra-ecclesia, or even against God. In a nutshell, this helps us to understand the deep tremors—earthquake, frankly—that Seabury's consecration represented in the late eighteenth century. Consecrated by non-jurors, with Jacobite sympathies that inferred sympathy with Catholicism, and the emerging tremors of revolutions and republicanism (American, but in no short time French too), the Church of England took the measures it deemed necessary to remain in power, and reluctantly recognized Seabury's episcopacy. Thus, the Anglican Communion was born. Not out of vision, but out of division and disquiet. In the restless history of Anglicanism, such forces have simply continued to the present. The past is never behind us. History is with us now, and it will be our tomorrow.

Grafting: The Parable of the Phylloxera

Pale-yellow, sap-sucking insects that attack vineyards might seem a curious place to bring our reflections to some kind of conclusion. However, the story of the Great French Wine Blight of the 1850s offers us an analogy of some aspects of the pathology of ecclesiology we have been exploring in this book.

The early French colonizers of Florida in the seventeenth century had hoped to grow vineyards and enjoy some of the comforts that their wines, vines, and vignerons gave them in France. However, they were repeatedly thwarted in trying to cultivate vines. The aphids went largely unnoticed to French-American farmers seeking to plant vines. All they saw were the results. The roots rotted quickly, and the leaves of the vines dried out. Wine production failed. No one at the time knew the cause. It was assumed wine could not be made, despite the soil and the climate all appearing to be conducive to wine-making. The puzzle persisted well into the eighteenth century.

With changes in sea-faring in the nineteenth century—the shift from sail to steamships—journey times across the Atlantic were reduced dramatically, and to a large extent this resulted in increased trade, faster travel, and greater profits. But as epidemiologists would later testify, the faster the transatlantic crossings, the more likely it was that hidden diseases could move from one continent to another, unseen and unchecked.

Phylloxera is a native East Coast insect that breeds on vine leaves and eventually attaches itself to the root system. American vines eventually evolved a resistance to the larvae of the insect, so native American wine production was possible in the eighteenth century. But European vines, with no exposure to the disease, were at the mercy of the insect eggs. Some vineyards—in sandy, slate, or volcanic soils—seemed to be immune from the blight. But the vast majority of vineyards failed, as the disease proved to be fatal to the European vines. Few were exempt from the blight, though curious examples (e.g., Bollinger) did emerge.

The potato famines that had swept Europe decades earlier (caused by another insect blight, *Phytophthora infestans*, and probably originating from Mexico and Southern American states) had produced mass starvation, spawned revolutions, and triggered mass migration. The French Wine Blight was not in this league, but the consequences for the industry were devastating. Around half of the businesses were lost, wages halved, and migration to North Africa and the Americas increased. Farmers switched to the production of raisins, or to entirely new crops.

By the 1870s, some sort of solution was emerging for French vineyards. It was discovered that by grafting disease-free French vines onto blight-resistant American rootstock, the vineyards could begin to recover. While some American rootstock struggled with the chalky soils of French vineyards, the recovery was well underway, and *Phylloxera* eventually eliminated.

One obvious reading of the *Phylloxera* analogy is to note how the inculcation of monarchical governance in America failed. And arguably, what has allowed monarchical governance to survive in Europe—only just, mind—is the grafting of American democracy into European polity. The same might be said of ecclesiology too. Namely that were it not for the grafting of spiritual and religious consumerism to create a kind of "market-model" ecclesial ecology across Europe, the religious landscape on that continent might be more defiantly secular, atheistic, and anti-religious.

These are speculations, of course. But the *Phylloxera* parable invites us to contemplate the myriad of ways in which regional or national polities and cultures are unable to resist foreign "blight." It is only with the introduction of another alien ingredient that eventual resistance can be cultivated. But that requires grafting, and with that process, the identity of the original vine is forever changed. It cannot go back to what it was.

Because the shape of ecclesial life is to some extent determined by the contextual ground in which it is located, and as the socio-sacred synergies grow and develop over time, so we discover new patterns of polity emerging that could not have been easily foreseen. Moreover, these new and emerging patterns require careful explication and explanation. What seems apparent on the surface often requires some kind of deeper reading in order to understand something of the shape and dimensions of ecclesial life.

What emerges from the parable of the *Phylloxera* is something quite remarkable. Namely, that the source of blight was also to become the source of salvation, and eventual recovery. Without American rootstock that had evolved to be resistant to *Phylloxera*, the European wine-making industry would have been extinguished. The lesson for global Anglicanism might be similar.

Could it be that the very forces of the late eighteenth century that separated church and state—severing the connections between Crown and colony in America, and going on to develop a non-monarchical, democratic, and profoundly republican ecclesial polity—might be the rootstock that needs to be fully grafted into the rest of the proverbial Anglican vineyard? That unless that is done, English Anglican polity will be for sure undone. Could it be that American Episcopalianism might therefore be the instrument that saves global Anglicanism from its own blight?

That would indeed be a remarkable journey for the evolution of Anglicanism. To become a different kind of global denomination that did not hinge on monarchy, imperialism, and empire. And instead became an expression of Christianity that was both episcopal and democratic, without compromise to either. Perhaps then, and only then, the curse of the blight that English Anglicanism currently struggles with might finally be beaten. But to do so requires the grafting of authentic American Episcopalian rootstock (Isa 60:21; John 15:4–8; Rom 9–11).

Endings and Beginnings

As I write, it would seem that democracy is under threat as never before. Autocracy can reign in democratic states, as several modern states can bear witness. The potential for tyranny never entirely vanishes, and when democracy finds itself under the heel of autocracy, the only defense of freedom that is left lies with the law. Autocrats know that too, and will turn on the judiciary, prorogue the parliament, change the laws, suspend the constitution, and seize hold of "emergency powers."

Crises of any kind can be the occasion for mounting a coup against the citizenry. The church is no different. Many in the Church of England have given up counting the number of livings and frontline parish jobs suspended, or established committees sidelined or made redundant, in order that the new agenda for numerical growth—"essential for survival" is the language—can be implemented. Such decisions have displaced or overturned the basic character of the church. Here, the New World being ushered in starts to look like a more sinister version of the Old World. This time it will not be Charles I reigning by some "divine right." It will be an executive committee with more power and authority than any Stuart king could have dreamed of.

In the present age, the Church of England is hopelessly caught between models of governance and oversight that blend plutocracy, autocracy, and despotism with monarchical and democratic ideals. It has grafted an ontologized quasi-managerialism into a new ecclesiocracy, and then christened it as leadership. The result leaves the episcopacy stranded as resented rulers who no longer represent the will of the people in pews. Furthermore, the continued extension of democratization through the information revolution means that clergy, laity, people, and nation are not required to take the word of their respective religious leaders as gospel. They may tolerate monologues, but it does not follow that they accept or trust the word of a bishop. Many recent social surveys indicate that the people certainly don't—no more than they trust the word of a professional politician.

The Jesuit scholar Walter Ong has identified a further problem in relation to information, knowledge, and power.[140] The first information revolution was *writing*, namely the Axial Age (the eighth to the third century BCE), referring to the transition from oral cultures and languages to written, thereby creating an independent bank of social and communal memory. The second revolution was *mass printing*, which in the sixteenth century enabled the Reformation. Religion thrived, diversified, and expanded across these two eras. The third revolution is the present. Namely, one of *instant, ubiquitous, universal information overload*, such that even "alternative facts" can flourish in a post-truth aeon.

Faith communities, their leaders, and their religious identities are struggling with this third age. The constant flow and overload of information increases choice and empowers democracy, but it also increases the possibilities for individualism. The third revolution, like the first two, questions the need for intermediaries to hold or interpret knowledge. People can decide for themselves. Anxiety and even anger tend to increase, and authority only becomes more flustered as it loses the trust and confidence of its former adherents.

Church leaders, typically, tend to double-down at this point, and seek to reassert old patterns of power and authority on a new order. Rather like trying to travel back through time, and govern the church as though there was no printing, the challenges of the third information revolution have yet to be computed by those leading (or revolting within) the Anglican Communion. This third age cannot be countered by charismatic, executive, or bureaucratic expressions of quasi-regal power lodged into the episcopacy. Nor will it prevent schism. The culture of patronage is limited in what it can bestow, and as the stock value of the archbishops and bishops in the Church of England continues to decline, fewer will want a share in what the institution represents.[141]

In the meantime, the power and leverage of the alternative-right is in decline. Sydney Archdiocese is merging parishes, cutting costs, and struggling to draw in new, younger clergy. Having staked out its ground on the issues of sexuality and gender, we can now see that the real anxiety—one shared across the world of developed-nation Protestant denominations—is not sex, but rather money and power. Whoever has the power and the money has the leverage to make the rules on sexuality and gender. Sex and gender would be much easier to handle if money and power were levelled up. Bishops and ecclesiocrats won't do this, so sexuality and gender emerge as the proxy-conflict for what is actually at stake in the internecine ecclesial wars. Like most wars and zones of conflict, the people fighting it most bitterly won't know that. Each side hopes for victory.

Yet the real war hasn't begun. Sexuality and gender are classic signs of displacement. In the Church of England the deeper fear is the lack of money, the collapse of power and prestige, and the inability to cope with standard-issue democratic demands—accountability, scrutiny, regulation, transparency, and fairness. This is the elephant in the room. But while the Sexuality Wars continue to be stoked (or "managed and maintained" into some perpetual non-resolution to keep the bishops in a central presiding role even by those in charge of Protestant denominations such as the Church of England), all this does is to delay any action on what is essentially the real front line, and the more serious conflict yet to come. While this is not explicitly surfaced, the drain of older people, younger people, and the growing distances between congregations and their denominations will continue. The signs of fragmentation are everywhere, and they appear to be irreversible.[142]

I suspect in trying to resolve any of this, matters will be taken out of the hands of the Church of England in the near future. Indeed, the sheer boldness of the GAFCON declaration issued in October 2025 suggests that this moment has arrived, since GAFCON proclaims that the Anglican Communion will now be reordered, with only one foundation, namely the Holy Bible, "translated, read, preached, taught and obeyed in its plain and canonical sense, respectful of the church's historic and consensual reading."[143] The consequential renouncing of primatial power or authority over the provinces of the Communion is more descriptive of the present than prescriptive for the future. That said, abrogation of an international primatial role would bring an end to the catholic fiction that Anglican/Episcopalian identity and polity is more akin to Roman

Catholicism (especially in the ontology of ordination) than it is to Protestantism. The Church of England has tried, for centuries, to play a pivotal international role by claiming to be a *via media* between Catholic and Protestant ecclesiology. Up to a point, that constituted a worthy goal. But the goal has proved to be unattainable, and the game is plainly now over.

The social, political, and cultural consequences of Seabury's consecration are still being worked through. It is fair to say that in the present, neither the wider Communion nor the Church of England have comprehended the complex cultural drivers that shaped the Old World and the New World, yet allowed adherence to one faith—which across the continents they most certainly practice differently. The consequences for the Anglican Communion cannot yet be known. But a final story might help.

During President Richard Nixon's visit to China in February 1972, he was received by the Chinese premier, Zhou Enlai. At a diplomatic lunch hosted by Zhou, he was asked what he thought about the French Revolution. He paused, and then famously remarked, "It's too early to tell." The quip is striking, for we do not know what the impact of that event—more of a process—has really been. Likewise, the American Revolution. It is possible that Zhou thought the question referred to the student-led protest movements in Paris during May 1968, rather than the bloody revolution of 1789. But to my mind, "too early to tell" helps us to see the contingencies and consequences of events in context.

History is not in the past. It shapes the present and the future. The more we understand about how our culture has been and is being shaped, the more likely it is that the beliefs, commitments, and ideologies that we adhere to can be read in a way that does not pre-determine our next steps. To my mind, the Anglican Communion is still dealing with the effects of the American Revolution, Samuel Seabury's consecration, the Scottish non-jurors, the decline of English pre-eminence, and the end of the British Empire. It is also dealing with the decline in deference to inherited power (whether by bloodline or ontological lineage), and the assent of democracy. It really is too early to tell where this will all lead. But it is never too early to start the critical work of engaging with such complexity, and working out how to live together as a real Communion, despite the cultural differences.

That said, I want to close by reflecting on the stark genesis of what, in part, prompted this project. Namely, researching archives and seeing small ads that offered ten-dollar rewards for the return of "lost property," which are then listed as "Negroes." Slave owners advertised like this every week across the USA. In 1854, with the help of Democratic president, Franklin Pierce, elite enslavers managed to push through the Kansas–Nebraska Act. The new law overturned the Missouri Compromise that had previously kept Black enslavement out of the American West since 1820. The US Constitution guarantees the protection of property by almost any means, including violence—and so that meant the enslaved, treated as property, would now be extended across the USA. Enslavers were quite clear that this was their goal. Their denominations and clergy were mostly more than ready to endorse and legitimize such positions.

To the slave owners—and that meant Samuel Seabury and his descendants too—it was absurd to suggest that "all men are born equal." Once the Kansas–Nebraska Act was passed, almost three dozen members of Congress gathered to strategize on how to overturn this Act. They included Edward Dickinson of Massachusetts, whose daughter Emily was already writing poems that would place her at the forefront of American literature. The group dispersed to their homes across America, determined to make their stand for democracy and the power of those who opposed slavery. But it was to take a lawyer and political rising star in 1858—one Abraham Lincoln—to lead the resistance. Lincoln prevailed, however, and was then elected president in 1860, much to the chagrin of Southern slave-owning powers. The Civil War was already close. By the time of the 1863 Emancipation Proclamation, which ended the American system of human enslavement, the Civil War was already well underway.

From the 1860s to the 1930s, many Americans worked tirelessly for democracy, equality, and freedom. They were opposed by those who saw it as their God-given right to enslave others, and regard others as lesser. They continued to be active throughout the Civil Rights movement, and beyond, to this day. In the twenty-first century, America and the wider world once again finds itself facing an existential crisis. Politically and culturally, the stakes could not be higher—namely to affirm the fundamental principle that all are born equal and free. Our churches, denominations, and other faith communities once again find themselves faced with a choice. As do Episcopalians, who were divided on the issues of race, equality, and freedom in the nineteenth century. The question now is, "How shall we live?" Or, perhaps even more sharply, "What Would Jesus Do?"

Illustrations

Artefacts from Episcopalian Life

Courtesy of the Virginia Theological Seminary Archives, Bishop Payne Library.

Bishop Payne Divinity School (Whittle Hall, above) was a racially segregated Episcopal school for African American ministerial students. The seminary is named after Bishop John Payne, the first Episcopal bishop of Liberia. The seminary was the only Divinity School in the Episcopal Church devoted exclusively to the training of "young Negro men" for the ministry. The seminary began in 1878, with the first graduate being James Solomon Russell, who though called to ordained ministry, was prohibited from training at the then all-White Virginia Theological Seminary.

MORNING PRAYER.

may be ~~to do always that is~~ righteous in thy sight, through Jesus Christ our Lord. *Amen.*

¶ *In Quires and Places where they sing, here followeth the Anthem.*

¶ *Then these five Prayers following are to be read here, except when the Litany is read; and then only the two last are to be read, as they are there placed.*

President U.S.

¶ *A Prayer for the ~~King's Majesty~~.*

O Lord, our heavenly Father, the high and mighty Ruler of the universe, who dost from thy throne behold all the dwellers upon earth; most heartily we beseech thee, with thy favour to behold and bless thy servant, the President of the United States, and all others in authority; and so replenish with the grace of thy holy Spirit; that they may always incline to thy will, & walk in thy way: Endue them plenteously with heavenly gifts; grant them in health & prosperity long to live; & finally, after this life, to attain everlasting felicity, thro' J. C. our Lord.

Almighty God, the fountain of all goodness, we humbly beseech thee to bless our gracious Queen *Charlotte*, their Royal Highnesses *George* Prince of *Wales*, the Princess Dowager of *Wales*, and all the Royal Family: Endue them with thy Holy Spirit; enrich them with thy heavenly grace; prosper them with all happiness; and bring them to thine everlasting kingdom, through Jesus Christ our Lord. *Amen.*

P. for the clergy & people

Almighty & everlasting God, from whom cometh every good & perfect gift, send down upon our bishops & other clergy, and upon the congregations committed to their charge, the healthful Spirit of thy grace; and that they may truly please thee, pour upon them the continual dew of thy blessing: Grant this, O Lord, for the honour of our Advocate and Mediator Jesus Christ. *Amen.*

¶ *A Prayer of St.* Chrysostom.

Almighty God, who hast given us grace at this time with one accord to make our common supplications unto thee; and dost promise, that when two or three are gathered together in thy Name, thou wilt grant their requests; Fulfil now, O Lord, the desires and petitions of thy servants, as may be most expedient for them; granting us in this world knowledge of thy truth, and in the world to come life everlasting. *Amen.*

2 Cor. XIII. 14.

THE Grace of our Lord Jesus Christ, and the love of God, and the fellowship of the Holy Ghost, be with us all evermore. *Amen.*

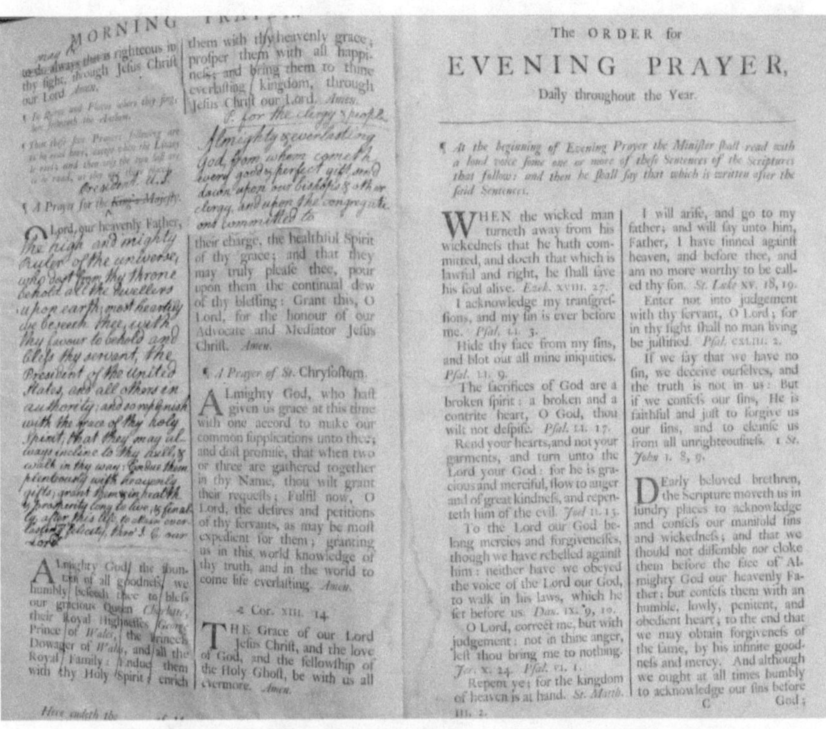

MORNING PRAYER.

righteous in thy fight, through Jesus Christ our Lord. *Amen.*

¶ *A Prayer for the* ~~*King's Majesty.*~~ President U.S.

O Lord, our heavenly Father, the high and mighty Ruler of the universe, who dost from thy throne behold all the dwellers upon earth; most heartily we beseech thee, with thy favour to behold and bless thy servant, the President of the United States, and all others in authority; and so replenish with the grace of thy holy Spirit, that they may alway incline to thy will, & walk in thy way: Endue them plenteously with heavenly gifts; grant them in health & prosperity long to live, & finally after this life to attain everlasting felicity, thro' J. C. our Lord.

~~Almighty God, the fountain of all goodness, we humbly beseech thee to bless our gracious Queen *Charlotte*, their Royal Highnesses *George* Prince of *Wales*, the Princess Dowager of *Wales*, and all the Royal Family: Endue them with thy Holy Spirit; enrich them with thy heavenly grace; prosper them with all happiness; and bring them to thine everlasting kingdom, through Jesus Christ our Lord. *Amen.*~~

P. for the clergy & people

Almighty & everlasting God, from whom cometh every good & perfect gift, send down upon our bishops & other clergy, and upon the congregations committed to their charge, the healthful Spirit of thy grace; and that they may truly please thee, pour upon them the continual dew of thy blessing: Grant this, O Lord, for the honour of our Advocate and Mediator Jesus Christ. *Amen.*

¶ *A Prayer of St.* Chrysostom.

ALmighty God, who hast given us grace at this time with one accord to make our common supplications unto thee; and dost promise, that when two or three are gathered together in thy Name, thou wilt grant their requests; Fulfil now, O Lord, the desires and petitions of thy servants, as may be most expedient for them; granting us in this world knowledge of thy truth, and in the world to come life everlasting. *Amen.*

2 Cor. XIII. 14.

THE Grace of our Lord Jesus Christ, and the love of God, and the fellowship of the Holy Ghost, be with us all evermore. *Amen.*

The ORDER for

EVENING PRAYER,

Daily throughout the Year.

¶ *At the beginning of Evening Prayer the Minister shall read with a loud voice some one or more of these Sentences of the Scriptures that follow: and then he shall say that which is written after the said Sentences.*

WHEN the wicked man turneth away from his wickedness that he hath committed, and doeth that which is lawful and right, he shall save his soul alive. *Ezek.* XVIII. 27.

I acknowledge my transgressions, and my sin is ever before me. *Psal.* LI. 3.

Hide thy face from my sins, and blot out all mine iniquities. *Psal.* LI. 9.

The sacrifices of God are a broken spirit: a broken and a contrite heart, O God, thou wilt not despise. *Psal.* LI. 17.

Rend your hearts, and not your garments, and turn unto the Lord your God: for he is gracious and merciful, slow to anger and of great kindness, and repenteth him of the evil. *Joel* II. 13.

To the Lord our God belong mercies and forgivenesses, though we have rebelled against him: neither have we obeyed the voice of the Lord our God, to walk in his laws, which he set before us. *Dan.* IX. 9, 10.

O Lord, correct me, but with judgement: not in thine anger, lest thou bring me to nothing. *Jer.* X. 24. *Psal.* VI. 1.

Repent ye; for the kingdom of heaven is at hand. *St. Matth.* III. 2.

I will arise, and go to my father; and will say unto him, Father, I have sinned against heaven, and before thee, and am no more worthy to be called thy son. *St. Luke* XV. 18, 19.

Enter not into judgement with thy servant, O Lord; for in thy sight shall no man living be justified. *Psal.* CXLIII. 2.

If we say that we have no sin, we deceive ourselves, and the truth is not in us: But if we confess our sins, He is faithful and just to forgive us our sins, and to cleanse us from all unrighteousness. 1 *St. John* I. 8, 9.

DEarly beloved brethren, the Scripture moveth us in sundry places to acknowledge and confess our manifold sins and wickedness; and that we should not dissemble nor cloke them before the face of Almighty God our heavenly Father; but confess them with an humble, lowly, penitent, and obedient heart; to the end that we may obtain forgiveness of the same, by his infinite goodness and mercy. And although we ought at all times humbly to acknowledge our sins before

C God;

Even before the American War of Independence was concluded, copies of the Church of England's *Book of Common Prayer* in use by Americans struck out the prayers for the king's majesty and, using wax and ink pen, replaced the redactions with prayers for the president and people.

The original Virginia Theological Seminary building, 1827.

Bishop John Payne, 1815–1874: the first Episcopal Bishop of Liberia.

Bishop William Meade (1789–1862) was the third bishop of Virginia and the founder and first president of Virginia Theological Seminary, where he is buried.

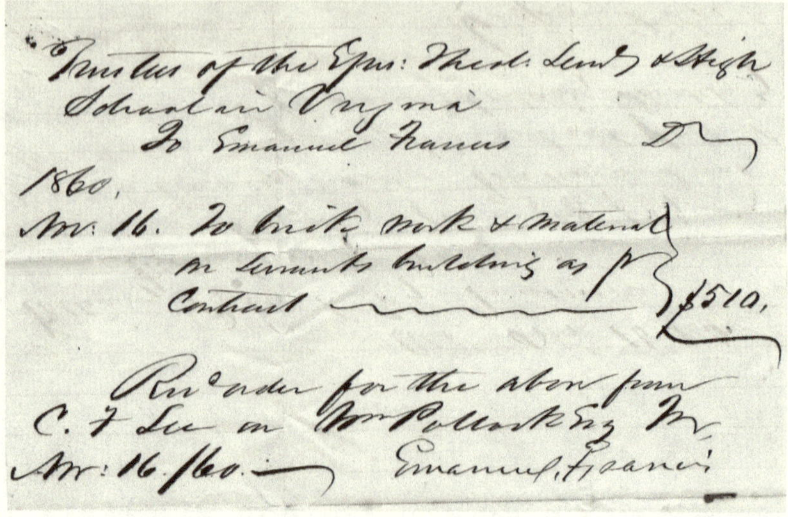

Trustees of the Epis: Theol: Semy & High
School in Virginia
To Emanuel Francis Dr
1860.
Nov: 16. To brick work & material
on Servants building as pr
Contract —— $510.

Recd order for the above from
C. F. Lee on Wm Pollock Esq Tr
Nov: 16 /60 — Emanuel Francis

The bill for constructing the slave quarters, Virginia Theological Seminary.

The slave quarters at Virginia Theological Seminary (no longer extant). A single building around the size of a car garage, segregated on the inside by a wall to separate men and women. The building contained no fireplace, stove, privy, or other amenities.

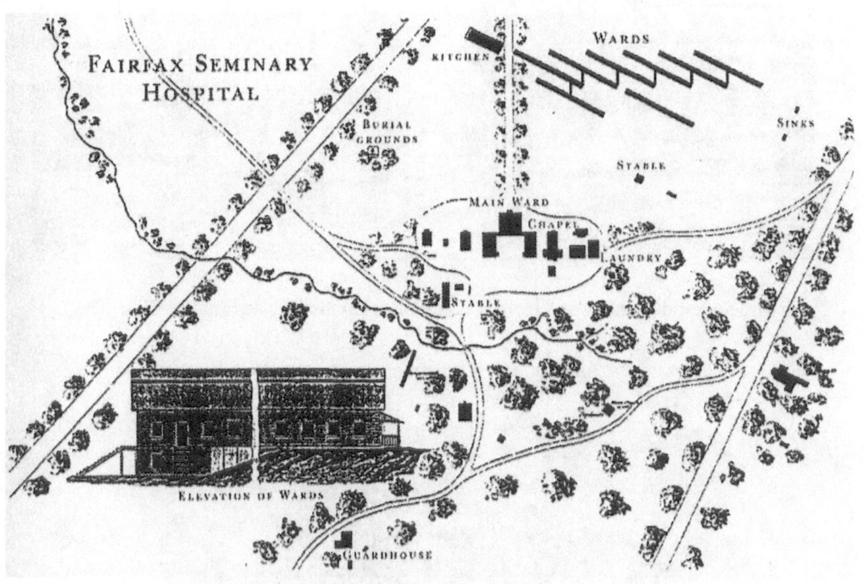

Virginia Theological Seminary during the American Civil War became a hospital for wounded combatants.

The hospital wards at Virginia Theological Seminary in an early photograph.

The hospital laundry at Virginia Theological Seminary during the Civil War.

Bishop Payne Divinity School Faculty, c. 1890. Despite the segregated context of the time, four of the five faculty are White. From 1905 to 1922 the president was Corbin Braxton Bryan, a White supremacist who believed Whites had a responsibility to offer Black people the benefits of Christianity. The last graduation class of the school was in 1949. Virginia Theological Seminary started admitting African American students in 1951.

John Walker, the first Black Virginia Theological Seminary seminarian to graduate, with fellow graduates, 1954.

Bishop Samuel Seabury, very much as a bishop from the British Georgian era would be portrayed. Note the lack of miter, pectoral cross, ring, or other episcopal ephemera. The bishop has a preaching scarf and bands—"dog-collars" did not appear until the nineteenth century.

Virginia Theological seminarians (entrants) 1954, after segregation had finally been lifted.

CODA

Form and Function

Past, Present, Future

Pope Francis passed away on April 21, 2025, after a short illness. It was Easter Monday. He had occupied the See of Rome for a dozen years, with courage, humor, a light touch, and deep public concern for the poor, for refugees, for the stigmatized, and for the broken. His pontificate was marked by compassion and care for those outside the Church. Inside the Church, Pope Francis somehow managed to keep *Pax Romana Ecclesia* intact, despite the divisions on dogmatism and culture wars that have rent asunder most Protestant denominations.

Global Anglicanism is proof of that. It is mired in disputes about membership and identity, which is part of the proxy war on sexuality and women's ministry that continues to cripple the reputation and ministry of the wider Anglican Communion. Meanwhile, as a denomination, English Anglicanism is badly out of step with the ordinary public moral standards enshrined in English law. It's not just on gender issues either—employment rights, safeguarding, and other spheres across the Church of England are also increasingly perceived as alienating and unjust.

Archbishop Welby left office on January 6, 2025 in the wake of the public outcry and scandal over the inaction relating to John Smyth QC, one of the Church of England's most prolific serial abusers. The earlier *Makin Review* addressed aspects of the Smyth abuses and led Welby to resign in November 2024. This was a Canterbury Saga worthy of Chaucer—"The Rueful Tale,"[144] perhaps?—though that pilgrim journey seems to have no obvious end destination. However, it left a legacy of several unresolved issues.

First, this was the only time the officeholder had left due to public pressure and been made to resign. Over fifteen thousand people signed a petition calling for his departure, and his resignation is symptomatic of a public mood that has turned decisively against an unaccountable episcopacy and its ecclesiocracy. If the Church resists scrutiny and external regulation, it will repeatedly fail as a credible public body and never be trusted.

Second, the resignation pointed to a much deeper malaise for the Church of England. This is not so much a church in crisis as a body nearing the end of its natural life. Like all organic bodies, institutions have a lifespan too; death is a normal part of the existential cycle. If there is to be a resurrection—not just endless attempts at resuscitation and rejuvenation—death must be embraced. The Church of England preaches this. In the future, it must live it too.

Third, the Church of England continues to live and flourish locally. All life is there, and that is truly hopeful. However, as a national hierarchical institution and international denomination, it is in an advanced state of decay. It is also deeply mistrusted, often stoking emotions of rivalrous fear and resentment. Death avoidance only means that the Church of England spends more time in a self-imposed purgatory of painful palliative stasis.

Current Challenges—Comparing and Contrasting

For some in the media, the recent movie *Conclave*[145] and the slightly older *Two Popes*[146] are what the wider public will draw upon for their frames of reference when it comes to choosing a pope. It is safe to say that a movie on how future archbishops of Canterbury are chosen would lack the basic drama for box-office success, but probably score high on farce and irony. But more concerningly, it could be a tale that not even Chaucer could have conceived of. Though it is tempting, I am bound to say, to start drafting a version of "The Committee Member's Tale" as a kind of *Satirecclesia*. As the playwright David Hare conceded in one revealing press interview prior to the opening of his play *Racing Demon*[147] (a comedy-drama focused on rivalrous clergy in London), he had initially proposed writing a play about the General Synod of the Church of England and had even observed several sessions for background research. However, he quickly concluded that General Synod's machinations were so farcical and convoluted that no audience would ever believe them.

This structural problem for the Church of England is wholly Protestant in the making, and the absolute antithesis of Roman Catholic ecclesiology. The next pope will live in the Vatican in Rome, Italy, but he need not be Italian. Furthermore, even if the next occupant of the See of Rome were an Italian, he would not lead the Italian Catholic Church. That role falls to Cardinal Matteo Zuppi, appointed in 2022. Certainly, Canterbury is not the Vatican, although Lambeth Palace shows worrying Curia-like inclinations and is increasingly shaped by ultramontanism in outlook.

The new archbishop of Canterbury, Dame Sarah Mullally, has all this on the agenda before she turns her attention to global Anglican affairs, and with the North–South splits on sexuality and gender remaining unresolved, this is likely to lead to a scenario that will see the role of the head of the Anglican Communion significantly recalibrated. Some have already suggested that the archbishop of York takes on a more executive function as "primate of all England" (one of his/her titles), and that the holder of this role leads the Church of England. That would leave the See of Canterbury open to international primatial competition after Mullally retires, in order to lead the wider Anglican Communion. At first glance, this looks promising. But it leaves a set of unresolvable constitutional questions.

For example, at some stage in the future, could a non-British prelate sit in the House of Lords and also act as a very senior member of the Privy Council? What if that bishop or archbishop came from a country that was a republic, and the candidate were not supportive of monarchical polity in modern democracies? How could such a person take the loyal oath or vote in Parliament on domestic affairs or foreign policy, when this was not their country? What would happen in the event of international conflicts of interest arising? Could a pro-Beijing candidate be considered, or one from a country more aligned with Russia, Israel, the USA, Palestine, Rwanda, Argentina, or Europe following Brexit? What would a foreign spiritual leader of the Church of England say or do in such eventualities, and on behalf of whom? The list of questions is lengthy, and the answers unresolved.

The rigor, drama, and seriousness of a conclave (upon the death of a pontiff, around 135 cardinals meet until a candidate is identified and has accepted the nomination) could hardly pose a sharper contrast to the work of the Church of England's Crown Nominations Committee (CNC). The former is soaked in prayerful discernment. The latter is secular–Protestant to its core, albeit a process committed to prayer.

The same DNA is wired into choosing Church of England bishops, and despite the recent (though entirely predictable) stasis that has developed over several unresolved or delayed selections for appointing current candidates to diocesan bishoprics, the system is unlikely to change.

In contrast, Roman Catholicism has developed a serious history of spiritual discernment in its conclaves, and its substantive historical annals testify to that. The modern *Canterbury Tale*, however, takes us to a very small committee that meets a few times in London. This is a very *English* way of choosing a candidate to run some aspect or arm of the UK government. Except in the case of the archbishop of Canterbury, this committee is also choosing a kind of world leader, albeit one that bears little comparison to the See of Rome.

Glancing at the *Roman Catholic Cycle of Prayer* and comparing it to the *Anglican Cycle of Prayer* is instructive. Roman Catholics have 3,200 dioceses and 650 archdioceses, 225,000 parishes, over 400,000 priests, 50,000 permanent deacons, 650,000 monks and nuns, and nearly 3,000,000 catechists for their 1.3 billion followers. But it manages to get by with only 5,340 bishops. Believers who use the *Roman Catholic Cycle of Prayer* will pray for nine dioceses daily. Pope Francis opposed increasing the number of bishops yet continually encouraged his episcopal colleagues to spend all their time with their parishes, priests, and people, and "as shepherds should smell of the sheep."

Anglicans have around 55 million followers (80 million is often claimed, but that includes 25 million in the Church of England, where attendance is down to just over 0.5 million, and two-thirds of the laity are now retirees). Global Anglicanism has 855 dioceses, meaning believers pray for around two each day if using the *Anglican Cycle of Prayer*.

Globally, Roman Catholics outnumber Anglicans by over 25:1. In percentages, Anglicans constitute about 3.5 percent of what Roman Catholicism represents. Anglicanism is 96.5 percent smaller. Yet the Anglican Communion had amassed almost 900 bishops by 2025, despite its relatively small size. There is one bishop for every 0.25 million Roman Catholics, in contrast to one Anglican bishop for every one of its 60,000 followers. Not for nothing is the denomination referred to as "Episcopalian" outside England. It seems that when it comes to bishops, Anglicans cannot get enough of them.

The Anatomy of a Crisis

The last serious attempt to break the deadlock around the office and role of the archbishop of Canterbury was the review led by Lord Hurd, and published in 2001. *To Lead and to Serve* (the Hurd Report)[148] was far-reaching, though its assumptions and presumptions would not be shared now. It is something of an English conceit to assume that one of their number is the natural option to represent the rest of the world—that (of course) someone from the English nation is innately suited to lead foreigners. *To Lead and to Serve* assumed precisely that, and focused its attention on making the global-CEO-type *primus inter pares* role of the archbishop more manageable in England. Naturally, it is another conceit of upper-class entitlement not to ask the English what they might want.

Hurd's review[149] recommended that the archbishop's ordinary diocesan duties be devolved permanently onto a bishop in Canterbury. The report recommended "a strategic distancing from the current degree of his [*sic*] day-to-day involvement in the detailed administrative affairs or management of the Church of England in England." It further recommended developing the role of the archbishop of York in the overall governance of the Church of England in England, such that "leadership of the Anglican Communion will remain one of the principal modern roles of the Archbishop of Canterbury." To do that, it would be necessary to establish a post at episcopal level at Lambeth, funded by the Anglican Communion to act as the archbishop of Canterbury's right hand in Anglican Communion affairs, with a view to its holder deputizing wherever practicable for the archbishop in the Anglican Communion.[150]

It is another conceit of upper-class English elitism that such reports are welcomed and promised "to be considered," but then quietly filed away and forgotten. In fairness, this is a general trait found in institutions and traceable in other denominations. As Garrison Keillor notes, when Lutherans respond to a request from their local pastor or vestry with "'Well let me think about that, and if I decide to [go ahead] I'll give you a call' . . . in Lake Wobegon [that] means 'No.'"[151] English Anglicanism is no different:[152] "Let me think about that and then form a working group" is coded episcopal-speak for "No."

If one were re-running Lord Hurd's review today, attention would need to focus on the fires burning at home. English Anglicanism is in a parlous state. Leaving aside the intractable debates and divisions on sexuality, gender, equal marriage, and the like, the structures and finances of the Church of England are broken. Trust and confidence in episcopacy—from within the church and abroad in the wider public—is at a crisis-level low, and there are no signs of that changing.

Some have clung (out of desperation?) to the news that there are some small and encouraging signs of younger people returning to church, though it is far from clear that this will be of lasting benefit to the Church of England.[153] But one swallow does not make a summer, and talk of growth and resurgence feels more like a single sunny-day interlude in the midst of an interminable, bitter winter that shows no sign of ending. Though the population of England grows in the twenty-first century, vocations for ministry have continued to decline. Clergy have few rights, too much responsibility, little support, and pitiful stipends and pensions to look forward to.

Volunteers for roles in parishes are also declining. The elite English ecclesiocracy and episcocrats have created a church where the "bosses" are essentially secure, unaccountable, unregulated, and generally well-paid. But the clergy and volunteers are heavily over-regulated, held accountable for virtually anything and everything, and have reportedly never felt more undervalued and vulnerable. Evidence shows many are leaving.

This is a denomination where morale has collapsed to the point of dissipation and despair. Yet, the Church of England leadership is essentially in denial and shows no sign of engaging with the mood on the ground, let alone of resolving the problems. The suspicion is that the leadership does not know what to do, so it avoids conversation on the key issues that concern parishes and clergy. This accelerates the decline, which increasingly feels more like a dire ecclesial vortex.

There is also a heavy element of cognitive dissonance at work in English Anglicanism. Its leaders believe the Church is in recovery and can reverse decline. The same leaders refuse to learn from other declining denominations, because they believe the Church of England is a special case. The ecclesial polity finds itself inhabiting two parallel, conflicting universes. One knows it is declining. The other has to believe it isn't, and the recession is only some blip. Even more risibly, the leadership of the Church of England believes and promotes the idea that it is on some kind of par with Roman Catholicism, despite the chasmic differences in scale: 1.3 billion versus 55 million. Likewise, the Vatican is an independent state with a diplomatic corps (the pope appoints an apostolic nuncio to each nation). Canterbury does not have diplomats, and the British apostolic nuncio relates to the UK government, not Lambeth Palace. Reality is dawning and, as cognitive dissonance leads to bifurcation or implosion, morale, trust, and confidence will continue to collapse.[154]

Thus, and as I have argued before,[155] were the Church of England to accept its core Protestant identity (since the denomination began in 1534 after the legal split with Rome), then it would be freer to see that its pan-Anglican international organization, operation, and identity are considerably closer to that of arrangements for other larger Protestant denominations such as the Lutheran, Presbyterian, and Methodist. Stated bluntly, global Anglicanism does not need its "head honcho" to reside in England. There is no theological or deep ecclesiological rationale for the head of the Anglican Communion to lead from Canterbury or Lambeth Palace in the way the pope must be at Rome. Some "titular" headship could still preside (i.e., holding or constituting a purely formal position or title without any real authority, in much the way that the reigning British monarch is titular head of the Church of England). But as for leadership, there is no reason why the head of the worldwide Anglican Communion (NB: not the Church of England, which remains "by law established") cannot be determined with some election by the primates, and the office holder running for a limited term. Anglicanism could be led from Hong Kong or Cape Town, for example.

Here we note one of the core principles of design, that "form follows function," which states that the appearance and structure of a building, machine, structure, or object (i.e., its architectural and built form) should primarily relate to its intended function or purpose. Global Anglicanism, and the fudgy process that recently took place in 2025 to choose a new Canterbury archbishop, was the opposite of this: far too many functions are looking for some form. It could not work and was effectively doomed to disappoint.

History is clear enough. There was no Anglican Communion in 1534. There was barely one in 1784 when Samuel Seabury was consecrated, and only the nascent outline of an ecclesial imperial network in 1834 when Newman was writing *Tracts for the Times*. The functions of the archbishop of Canterbury hardly changed from 1534 to 1834. Today, there are far too many functions operating ineffectively without any form; they are homeless. Arguably, it was the architect Louis Sullivan who first coined the modern maxim "form follows function," in the way we now understand the phrase and its meaning. Sullivan drew on the theory of his friend and mentor John H. Edelmann to assert that a rationally designed structure may not necessarily be beautiful, but that no building can be beautiful that does not have a rationally designed structure.[156]

What cannot be addressed by any incumbent of Lambeth Palace is the unresolved nature of the Church of England's identity. Since 1834, many Anglicans have bought into the myth that it has two pedigrees. On the one hand, it is Protestant Reformed. On the other hand, it is Catholic. Some Anglicans go further, and entertain fantasies of reunion with Rome, forgetting that the core theology of the Church of England is Reformed Protestant, and that the supreme governor of the Church is the reigning English monarch, not the occupant of the Vatican.

This confusion of identity cuts no ice at the proverbial Church–Crufts Show. Anglicanism is a hybrid; a mongrel denomination that is sartorially and liturgically Catholic, but theologically and organizationally Protestant. Anglican bishops dressed in purple are left stranded in the middle, trying to hold together two slowly bifurcating tectonic plates. Today, most English Anglican bishops enjoy unchecked executive power but have almost no theological pedigree. Their real authority lies in pastoral praxis, but few have the energy to inhabit that aspect of their role. Today's bishops are often found to be desk-bound bureaucrats, firing off emails and issuing shiny policy documents with fanciful vision statements, warding off the panic attacks.

Any incumbent of Lambeth Palace could do worse and take an honest, serious look at the identity issues that have remained unaddressed since the Church of England severed its ties with Rome in 1534. Anglicanism is essentially a branch of Protestantism. True, and unlike other Reformed churches, Anglicans kept their bishops, and some of their clergy and churches still continue to adapt their liturgies and clerical dress codes from Rome. Others opt for a more "happy-clappy" style of worship. Some Anglican churches avoid using the prayer of confession in liturgy. Others have liturgies of baptism that feel more like exorcism services. There is no liturgical uniformity. Nor is there any central power or authority in Anglican polity to counter the exercise of such freedoms. Theologically and organizationally, Anglicanism is essentially a Protestant expression of Christianity and is unable to police its diversity.

What the Church of England now needs is serious, authentic clarity. It is time to stop pretending that global Anglicanism is like Roman Catholicism and is in the same global orbit. It isn't. The process of choosing any new archbishop of Canterbury in the future will never attract affection, trust, or faith. The Crown Nominations Committee is a crystallization of the confused mindset that reflects the state that the Church of England is in.

Thus, no archbishop of Canterbury is likely to emerge from a conclave during the next fifty years. Nor, alas, from the kinds of democratic, open, and transparent election processes that some other parts of global Anglicanism already adopt for bishoprics. An elitist English Anglican establishment will always shy away from egalitarian ecclesiology. But if the Church of England owned its Protestant identity more explicitly, it might find that a genuinely democratic synod would attract more public support than some secretive committee ever could.

Past: Emerging from the Crossroads

The Church of England and wider Anglican Communion stand at a crossroads. Can it be a comprehensive and catholic global church, or is it destined to become a Protestant federation and umbrella organization, mired in divisions over past abuses, sexuality and gender, and other issues? Now facing seemingly unprecedented challenges, we need to consider some of the scenarios going forward.

Undoubtedly, the nation (by which I mean England) is at a turning point in history and culture. In 2034, the Church of England—a national Protestant church that decisively broke from Rome—will be five hundred years old. Lambeth Palace has no plans at present to mark this event, as Anglicans are divided on whether this is their quincentenary. Some Anglicans think that the Church of England is a continuing Catholic church.

That is not how the Vatican views this national Protestant denomination founded on Swiss-German Reformed theology. Unable to explain itself, the Church of England hierarchy stays quiet on such issues, doubtless hoping that keeping up appearances (literally, by dressing up like Roman Catholic clergy in everyday attire and liturgical wear) will obfuscate the reality. (NB: The stained-glass window featured on the cover of this book shows how eighteenth-century Episcopalian bishops usually dressed—in black gowns and preaching bands. Readers will have noted the lack of any modern liturgical accoutrements for the bishops depicted in the window—no pectoral cross, miter, episcopal ring, purple cassock, or dog collars—all of which were vestments originating from Victorian ritualism and Roman Catholicism, and not adopted by Episcopalians until well into the late nineteenth and twentieth centuries, in the wake of the influence of the Oxford Movement and its variegated liturgical cultures.)

Another bicentennial that comes to mind is also a few years away. In 1832, the British Parliament introduced the Reform Bill, designed to level up the status and rights of other denominations. The Bill sought to overturn the Test Act of 1673, which had effectively barred Roman Catholics from holding public office and even attending university. The government had been chipping away at religious discrimination since 1828, with Nonconformist denominations being extended some equality measures.

But in 1832, the Church of England stood its ground on privilege, and despite broad religious support for change, bishops in the House of Lords voted against change to help defeat the Reform Bill on its first reading. Cue protests and mayhem. The archbishop of Canterbury was heckled in public, the carriage of the bishop of Bath and Wells was stoned, and a crowd of almost ten thousand turned up to watch an effigy of the bishop of Carlisle being burned. On the third reading of the Reform Bill, no bishop was found to be in opposition.

The Victorian era marked a sea change in how the public viewed the Church of England. The first census of 1851 found that of the eighteen million population of England and Wales, around a quarter were Anglican, only fractionally more than those who identified as Nonconformists. Pressure to reform led to the disestablishment of the Church of Ireland (overwhelmingly Roman Catholic) and, eventually, of the Church in Wales in the Edwardian period. The changes were slow but inexorable.

Perhaps the most significant shifts were directed towards the entitled, lofty elitism often displayed in the Church of England's hierarchy. The USA had acquired its native bishops in 1784 following the defeat of the British in the American War of Independence. Yet, well into the nineteenth century, Church of England bishops declined to recognize and affirm visiting American clergy, insisting they should be regarded as laypeople since they could not affirm allegiance to the Crown. This "religion of class," as John Henry Newman dubbed it, still believed in *Rule Anglicana*, and presumed to treat other denominations as inferior species, and even other parts of the Anglican Church outside Britain as second-class citizens.

There is continued pressure on successive British governments to reform the House of Lords and, with that, address the anomaly of Church of England bishops sitting in the legislative chamber as of right. The establishment has its stock of old canards to meet such demands. These include all the arguments about Church of England schools, and even occasionally, a conservative commentator might venture that bishops in the House of Lords go back to feudal times.

In truth, the history is more complex. Wales only gained parliamentary representation in 1536, Scotland in 1707, and Ireland in 1801. The anomaly of English bishops sitting in a UK Parliament looked even stranger when the Irish and Welsh Anglican bishops were removed in 1869 and 1920, respectively. Scottish Anglican bishops have never been represented in the House of Lords.

Reforms to bishops sitting in the House of Lords are nothing new. The Clergy Act, also known as the Bishops' Exclusion Act (effective from 1642), prevented clergy from exercising any temporal jurisdiction or authority. It was repealed in 1661 with the restoration of the monarchy under Charles II. In the twenty-first century, under Charles III, there is no case for privileging English peers in the House of Lords, let alone a tiny group known as "Lords Spiritual" who cannot conceivably represent the interests of Wales, Scotland, and Northern Ireland.

One can contemplate the lengthy wish list compiled for any future occupant of Lambeth Palace in the decades to come. Many will call for ecclesial calibration and balance based on high–low, left–right, liberal–conservative calculations. One assumes prayerfulness, wisdom, compassion, pastoral care, depth-inspiring spirituality, and theological nous would always be taken for granted. Let us hope so. But I think the one important feature that will be needed in the future selection processes during the remainder of this century will be new: *realism*. Faith in and for the future rests on that. The Church of England will not need another rallying call for revival. The people's hopes in the pews now rest on authentic and honest candidates who do not deny reality.

The church will need archbishops of Canterbury in the future who recognize that less will be more. Cutting back on the hierarchy and top-down management of churches—"heavy pruning," to borrow a phrase from Jesus' teaching—might let in some much-needed light and air for local recovery and growth at ground level. Therein lies the hope. Rather than trying to evade the death of an out-of-touch, aloof hierarchical institution, future archbishops might embrace the end of the ecclesiastical establishment status theatre that hampers the Church of England in this kingdom. Let such things die a natural death; or opt for an assisted end.

Only then might the Church gain some purchase on that other kingdom, much closer to the one Jesus so often spoke of and practiced.

Present: A Law unto Themselves?

Debates over rules and regulations for religion are hardly new. When Jesus wriggles out of a trick question on tax evasion ("Render to Caesar what is to Caesar, and to God what is God's"; Mark 12:17),[157] he acknowledges that there are obligations to God, while others pertain to the state. So, to whom are religious bodies accountable? The answer from the church leaders for two millennia has been consistent: God. Yet it has never been that simple. In the aftermath of the revolutions that swept Europe across the eighteenth and nineteenth centuries, Catholics were left with two competing schools of thought on how the church was to be governed.

Some clung to what would eventually become known as ultramontanism (literally, "beyond the mountains"). This was a clerical political conception that maintained that the independent powers and prerogatives of the papacy came from beyond but could overrule in secular affairs. That the church was indeed a law unto itself. Others opted for the Galician school of thought, which maintained that secular authority—the state or the monarch—could trump Roman Catholic religious law.

English Anglicanism adopted a compromise, upholding the authority of the church in some spheres, while also affirming the primacy of common law in others. Many English people regarded this hybrid as a paragon of virtue. But as secularization began to gain a grip in the nineteenth century, the Church of England was plunged into internecine legal disputes over ritualism.

The Oxford Movement and its successors led to the reintroduction of surpliced choirs, candles, incense, bells, vestments, and other pre-Reformation practices into ordinary English parish churches. Some reacted with visceral horror to "Romish" influence. Some Church of England priests were actually jailed for ritualism, and there was even an attempt to put the bishop of Lincoln, Edward King, behind bars.

On the surface this was a theological war (of sorts). However, the underlying causes of the conflict lie in jurisprudence. Was the Church of England a self-governing, self-regulating body, or was it under the law of the land? What quickly became clear was that the secular courts were disinclined to rule on whether a priest or a congregation had decided to embrace smells and bells.

The government had to act in the wake of these bitter local disputes. A Royal Commission on Ecclesiastical Discipline was established between 1904 and 1906. In their final report, they recommended that the law on public worship should be devolved and the Church given powers to make such changes.

A revised constitutional settlement in 1919 created the first devolved parliament for the Church of England (then known as the Church Assembly). The General Synod eventually superseded it. This should mean that the Church of England was governed under a capacious dome of democracy. Today, however, on governance, safeguarding, equal marriage, gender, sexuality, transparency, and accountability, the Church of England has arrived at an entirely new impasse.

The General Synod of the Church of England ought to be the ecclesial parliament that delivers self-governing and self-regulation. But just as ritualism ripped the church apart over a century ago, General Synod now finds itself mired in disputes it cannot resolve. To make matters worse, its democratic processes have been undermined and depleted by the combined forces of episcopacy and unaccountable ecclesiocrats. General Synod has shown itself to be incapable of adopting standards of truthful conduct that are otherwise expected of normal public institutions.

Bishops have been seduced by ultramontanism. They have adopted the heresy of impeccability and believe that episcopal office and the church are to be without sin. Furthermore, in conflating their identity with God, they are omniscient too. So they function as though they cannot err, and there is nothing on which they are not experts.

Today's more Galician public doesn't buy this for a second. Standards of justice, HR, safeguarding, and accountability in the Church of England are many miles below the most basic protocols operating in the public sphere. The gulf between models of honesty and integrity within the Church and those in secular public bodies has become colossal.

This moment of crisis—an opportunity—has arrived. The Church of England's hierarchy can continue to be exceptional, a law unto itself. That road leads to disestablishment and to more devastating internal disputes. Alternatively, as a national church, it can become a law-abiding, fully transparent, and accountable institution like other public bodies.

At present, the Church of England hierarchy wants to have its cake and eat it. So it is run like a quasi-regal and elitist private fiefdom, covering up abuses of power and authority with endless opacity, yet enjoying all the privileges of a public platform. But when a national church no longer meets the bar for basic standards of conduct in public life, the time has come for a new Royal Commission.

The Church of England needs future archbishops of Canterbury who can lead it out of the self-imposed exile of being a law unto itself and into the responsible freedom of becoming a properly accountable public institution. The church must be subject to fully independent regulation and comply with customary secular law. Only then might it recover itself to serve the English nation as a body fit for purpose in the twenty-first century.

Future: A Postcolonial Archbishop of Canterbury?

In a recent article for *The Critic* ("More Than Just a Figurehead?," February 14, 2025), its influential Anglican columnist, the Revd. Marcus Walker, aimed at the alleged plans to strip the See of Canterbury of its international primatial symbolism. The arguments marshalled by Walker for the global significance—prestige, even—of the seat of Saint Augustine rested on some very English presumptions that assumed a certain pre-eminence. Awkwardly, rather like British prime ministers and American presidents, there is presupposed to be some "special relationship" between the pope and the archbishop of Canterbury that no other denomination enjoys.

Walker was at pains to highlight the various tokens and gifts that successive popes have bestowed on archbishops of Canterbury, as though these were expressions of how the papacy *really* thinks of and esteems the Church of England, rather than the "official" Roman Catholic position, which (uniquely) decreed Anglican claims to holy orders as "utterly null and void" (Pope Leo XIII, "Apostolicae Curae," 1896). Leo XIII was far from being some ecumenical reactionary. His papacy ushered in an era of transparency and democracy in the Catholic Church. Leo XIII commissioned the first Vatican Council and made strenuous political strides in promoting trade unions and rights for workers, and in improving health and social conditions across Europe for the working class, including the establishment of a hospice in the midst of a cholera epidemic. Leo XIII also elevated the Anglican convert John Henry Newman to the status of cardinal.

Facts tend to get in the way of arguments for esteem. Westminster Cathedral lists archbishops of Canterbury, but the roster stops at William Warham (1503–1532). The Roman Catholic Church does not recognize the presumptive occupants of the See of Saint Augustine after that date, since the Church of England broke away from Rome. The difficulty of English Anglicans talking up the "special relationship" with the papacy is that other denominations and their leaders also get special treatment, and receive warm, filial symbolic tokens connoting degrees of recognition and ecumenical hospitality.

The presumptive nature of English Anglicanism is infused—salted with—a kind of Empire-mythos, which even in the wake of the post-war settlements (i.e., after 1945) assumes that the status of Britain (but really England, in fact) retains some global significance that sets it apart from its near-competitors in Europe. In this Empire-mythos, the Second World War precipitated the weakening of British extensity but left its intensity of influence largely intact. While some case can be made for this outlook, most scholars would see the postwar world in a very different light.

For example, Ashley Jackson and Andrew Stewart carefully note in their *Superpower Britain: The 1945 Vision and Why It Failed*[158] that the British thought the very idea that China might be regarded as an emerging superpower was "poppycock." Eden, writing in 1942, opined that the American view that China ranked alongside Russia as a superpower was plainly erroneous. Churchill wrote to Eden in even more colorful terms, stating "that China is one of the four great world powers is an absolute farce" and "it is nonsense to talk of China as a great power." Peter Clarke (*The Last Thousand Days of the British Empire*, 2007) and John Darwin (*The Empire Project: The Rise and Fall of the British World System, 1830–1970*, 2009) concur that the strategic catastrophe of the Second World War had a devastating impact on Britain, and that any recovery after 1945 only amounted to the briefest remission. It is only with hindsight that this is now grasped; it was not seen at the time.[159]

Yet as historians of every stripe have shown, the British are still invested in the ongoing life and legacy of the Empire due to other factors. The English language is the "new Latin" of modernity. And in popular culture, as British political and economic fortunes declined, the nation reinvented itself as entertainers to the world. Through James Bond, Agatha Christie, J. K. Rowling, pop and rock music, film and television, and more recently video gaming, Britain punches above its weight. But this also masks the underlying ongoing decline.[160]

The British struggle in the post-war period was rooted in the global decline in deference towards the Empire, and the shaking off of imperialism in favor of national democracy. Britain was still casting herself as the mother of modern parliamentary democracy, yet only very begrudgingly setting aside the steady-state imperialism that it still used to rule over its territories, colonies, and dominions.

The global Anglican Communion held up a mirror to this polity too. Devolved authority, democracy, and independence—yes, of course; but not yet, and only when we give the green light. English Anglicanism, with its inherent class-based elitism, frequently operates with the same presumptions that shaped earlier British Empire mythos, which assumes models of hierarchical and quasi-imperial governance. In turn, in the episcopacy, this is often quasi-regal, presuming local deference and obedience to the hierarchy over democracy and devolution.

As with post-war Britain, the leadership of the Church of England cannot conceive of a global Anglican polity that is not infinitely better off with English Anglicans in charge, and Lambeth Palace central to the future direction of the denomination. Democracy and meritocracy are therefore subordinated to the ongoing culture of deference and elitism. The consequence of this (somewhat strange) worldview is that many English Anglicans overestimate their significance in Anglican global affairs, and are both puzzled and perturbed when ignored or snubbed by their denominational kith and kin.

The underlying fear for English Anglicans is comparable to that which overshadowed the postwar Empire and the end of imperialism. If Britain is no longer a global superpower, then it becomes (again) what it was under Henry VIII. Namely, a nation with some regional leverage, but by no means preeminent in wielding global power. That would be true for Britain and the English in the twenty-first century—and it lags behind China, Russia, Japan, and America, and in Europe, behind Germany and France.

For English Anglicans, the reality is similar. Despite a fondness for talking up the number of Anglican adherents globally to eighty-eight million, it is more likely to be fifty to fifty-five million. Numerically and in terms of extensity, it is likely that Presbyterians, Methodists, Baptists, and Lutherans can make comparable or better claims on numerical strength and range than Anglicans. In short, English Anglicanism is no longer a global ecclesial superpower. It is collapsing back into what it began as, namely a European Protestant national church, albeit with some regional denominational strengths. But that is a long, long way off being a global "Communion" (i.e., "ecclesial superpower"), in much the same way as the British Empire, or the successor Commonwealth, can no longer exist or rule by imperial decree in a post-war world. And certainly not in the twenty-first century.

In this, there are many in the Church of England who are adrift of the broader polity in the Anglican Communion. As Peter Clarke records of the British in 1948, most were unable to explain the difference between the Empire and the Commonwealth, and between a colony and a dominion. (The difference is in governance, with a colony under the direct rule of the Empire, whereas a dominion has attained a degree of self-governance, while yet remaining within the British family ethos.) In the same way, most English Anglicans would struggle to differentiate between autonomous provinces of the Anglican Communion, dioceses outside the Church of England that link directly to the archbishop of Canterbury, extra-provincial areas, churches in full communion with Canterbury but that are not in fact Anglican, and so forth.

Clarke goes on to note that many in Britain in 1948 could not contemplate national survival without the Empire's support.[161] I suspect the same pertains to the Church of England. It cannot imagine itself without the wider Anglican Communion, and it cannot conceive of a world in which it does not continue to be *primus inter pares*. To lose that status will seem unbearable to those who cling to the myth of being an ecclesial superpower. Somehow, to just regress into being a national Protestant church would mean it becoming some very "Small Thing." And yet that is exactly what it was in 1534—the Church of England. That, and that only. Not of Wales, Scotland, or Ireland, let alone some international ecclesiastical confection. The Church of England has, like the British Empire, eventually ceded its powers abroad, retired to being at home, and must now turn its attention to its own convoluted internal affairs.

The English Anglican Communion leaves behind an extraordinary global legacy. Moreover, some of those bonds remain powerful and vibrant, such as the Mothers' Union, and continue to shape local and regional initiatives. But like the British Empire of old, and more recently the Commonwealth, the Anglican Communion need not heed the bidding of the Church of England. Those days are over, and the once-upon-a-time preeminence of the global Anglican Communion now just a memory.

So, is the archbishop of Canterbury more than just a figurehead in the wider world? Probably not, although the answer may still partly depend on who you ask. Certainly, the GAFCON Declaration of October 2025 now flatly contradicts the official Anglican claim. That said, it does seem clearer now, more than ever, that the See of Canterbury is no longer pivotal to how Anglican polity thrives or survives in other parts of the world. Devolution and democracy are here to stay. The old order of White male English, elitist imperialistic deference has passed away. Anglicanism is not an ecclesial superpower, and no number of gifts and gestures from the papacy can occlude that. But what new forms of organization, federalism, and polity that will eventually take the place of this global Anglican Communion are yet to be born.

Conclusion

Looking ahead, the Church of England seems intent on constantly adding to its portfolio of tasks, as it has lost its core sense of purpose (i.e., basic function). That creates an extensive culture of frenetic exhaustion, with too much to do within poor and incomplete structures. This is what happens when the core function of a church is lost—the ecclesiology becomes an endless buffet of thin functionality. This is echoed in a recent essay from Mark Clavier,[162] looking back at the comprehensive review of the Church in Wales in 2012 led by Lord Harries. Clavier notes vocations- and ministry-"formation" has been replaced with "training," and in ministry, the church is at the mercy of short-term goal-oriented objectives.

The Church of England has fallen into a similar trap. It erects increasing amounts of scaffolding, but without any clear sense of the core form it is supporting, maintaining, repairing, or perhaps even seeking to extend. It neither understands the structures it occupies nor what needs to be done to conserve, improve, or extend them. Understanding the functions of the Church and thereby safeguarding its core form is lost in haphazard initiatives that erect more scaffolding with no obvious outcomes. Efforts in safeguarding serve as a prime example. But many mission initiatives face the same problems.

It was Newman who once quipped that the problem facing the Church of England was the absence of a soul. By this, he meant, I think, the lack of a rich and dense capacity for theological and spiritual critical reflection. This leaves it at the mercy of short-termism and pragmatism. The roots of the current crises always lie in the past. For example, it would be hard to find any recent holder of the See of Canterbury who brought a track record of fiscal prudence and wisdom to the table. Justin Welby, as the most recent incumbent, left successive deficits in his posts at Coventry, Liverpool, and Durham, mostly through financially speculative initiatives that failed. This was despite the much-vaunted reputation for business experience and financial leadership. (A treasurer at the French oil company Elf would not give the postholder a position of fiscal leadership or entrepreneurial business experience.) The expenditure at Lambeth Palace will probably never be audited appropriately, but the financial holes left behind are huge, and once again, the cupboard is now left bare for his successors to struggle with.

Welby somehow cast an aura of fiscal and missional assurance that few questioned, yet was hugely deficient in both spheres. Those who had the temerity to question this were denigrated and demonised. Yet all the evidence shows that clergy pensions and stipends are currently in a parlous state. At the same time, he removed statutory grants from dioceses and replaced those with competitive bids, rebranding the process as a "strategic initiative" geared to reversing the decline of the Church and promoting numerical growth.

There is some degree of vanity and folly regarding the incoherence of the proposed trajectory. The Church cannot afford to pay its own clergy or run its existing parish network. Welby's proposals would have added to the burden and debt by siphoning money to create more loss-making churches and new (so-called) missional congregations. (Literally cutting off one's nose to spite one's face.) Leaving aside the time, effort, and money required for each diocese to craft a bid to pile even more functions onto a deficit-making denomination, the effect has been to create a whole culture of rewarding "winners" (clergy, churches) for grants, which means 99 percent of the Church of England become losers by default.

Some dioceses have played the Church of England's version of the National Lottery Grants Applications game very well and have been handsomely rewarded. That makes it very hard for those inside the Church to be vocally critical. But when essential grants are all removed from the dioceses and turned into competitive beauty contests and missional bids, the morale of the rest of the Church of England was always bound to suffer and collapse. It surely has.

Put plainly, these are no longer kingdom values running the Church of England. Jesus did not reward winners. Nor did the early church. Welby's ill-conceived revolution was a thin version of Thatcherism.[163]

The fruits of it are already tasting bitter. And yes, the children's teeth have been set on edge.[164] The Church of England is now run by bureaucrats, managers, and executive officers, who in turn devise the job specifications and processes that select bishops, managers, and executives very much in the image of the ecclesiocrats who now lead the church.

But I end on a note of hope rooted in a practical, grounded ecclesiology. The Church of England and global Anglicanism have suffered their fair share of schism and hemorrhage over five hundred years. Methodism might be one of the larger cases. But the Church of England in South Africa (CESA—a split founded in 1938, now called REACH-SA), the Diocese of the Southern Cross (Sydney-sponsored), or the Anglican Church of North America (ACNA) point us to a history of fragmentation where Anglicanism arrived long ago at the point of conceding that such ordinations are "valid but illicit."

This is perhaps comparable to the ecclesiological tolerance, pragmatism, and forbearance that the Vatican has had to extend to Catholics in China. The Chinese Catholic Patriotic Association (CCPA) rejects the primacy of the Roman pontiff and has its own priests and bishops. On the other hand, the Bishops' Conference of the Catholic Church in China (BCCCC) is Vatican-approved, and Rome chooses its bishops. Following the establishment of modern China after the revolution (1949) and under the Chairman of the Chinese Communist Party, Mao Zedong, China broke off diplomatic relations with the Vatican in 1951. In fairness to Beijing, this was precipitated by the Holy See's 1950 statement that participation in certain Chinese Communist Party (CCP) organizations would result in excommunication from the Church. Several hundred Roman Catholic priests, nuns, and laity wrote to the Vatican to protest this interference in Chinese governance.

For some time, neither the BCCCC or CCPA could recognize the other as Chinese and authentically Catholic. To the great credit of Pope Benedict XVI and Pope Francis I, much has been done to repair the rifts with China from the last seventy-five years, restore some degree of mutual trust, and work together on common concerns. But it has meant Rome eventually conceding that CCPA ordinations and bishops are to be regarded as "valid," albeit "illicit." China has, likewise, made significant contributions and moves towards these developments. The faith is plainly common despite the differences in form and function, with two different kinds of Catholicism operating in China. The Chinese Takeaway (so to speak) for Anglicanism barely needs sketching here.[165]

What we can say by way of an ending is that Anglicanism needs to recover its theological roots, which are fundamentally Protestant in origin and ethos, as is its polity. And while it has many aesthetic and ritualistic-liturgical similarities with Roman Catholicism, Anglicanism is firmly a pan-Protestant polity that needs the institution to be organized around its theological-ecclesial identity. The leadership of the Church of England needs to find some way to escape its interminable searches for the proper forms that follow its ever-growing and increasingly incoherent legion of functions, and in the process conduct a thorough cleansing audit of those functions that were once essential (but no longer), those that are still mandatory, some that are desirable, and those that can now be safely discarded.

Only then will Anglicanism recover some degree of poise. The capacious home that is the Church of England, and the living edifice that is the building of wider global Anglicanism, can only be put in order when form finally follows function. That Chaucerian journey is yet to begin. As things currently stand, it is hard to see the pilgrims' progress.

Signs of the Times

A Sermon for Safeguarding Sunday

St. Andrew's Episcopal Cathedral, Aberdeen
Daniel 12:1–3; Hebrews 10:11–14, 18; and Mark 12:34–42

It is something of a heavy irony that Safeguarding Sunday in the Church of England fell in the same week that it was announced that the 105th archbishop of Canterbury, Justin Welby, resigned over his handling of the abuses perpetrated by John Smyth QC. This is without precedent in the five-hundred-year history of the Church of England.

John Smyth was one of the most prolific sexual abusers in recent Church-of-England history, yet with substantial evidence of cover-ups and inaction protecting him at the very highest levels. The report into the abuse was conducted by Keith Makin, and despite being subjected to lengthy delays by lawyers acting for Lambeth Palace, Justin Welby's position quickly became untenable. The *Makin Report* was published on November 7, 2024, providing forensic accounts of the failures and cover-ups, if not systemic corruption in the culture within the ecclesial hierarchy. Welby resigned on November 12.

Welby's tenure had failed to create a culture of transparency and accountability in the upper echelons of ecclesial governance. This is the protruding tip of a very large smoldering volcano. John Smyth QC died in 2018 without ever being brought to justice and represents "the Church of England's Jimmy Savile crisis." Smyth hailed from an impeccable elite public school and upper-class Oxbridge pedigree, and had been a prominent mover and shaker in the conservative Evangelical world from the 1970s. That culture had played a large part in forming Justin Welby's

Christian faith, his eventual arch-episcopal governance, and a whole generation of English bishops.

Historians will pick over this ecclesial car-crash in the generations to come. Imperialism and benign superiority is no longer a trusted mode of governance for the vast majority of Anglicans. Bishops and their senior advisors have no accountability, are aloof, and averse to external regulatory oversight. Bishops lecture the rest of the world on democracy and equality, but refuse to be subject to the laws that govern everyone else. Like ancient demi-gods, they invest in omniscient and omnicompetent myth-presumptions, as though by becoming a bishop they acquire sufficient knowledge to lecture the world on anything they hold a view about.

Our times are different. These days, people in the pews expect democratic accountability and transparency. They might consent to being under authority, but only provided it is subject to independent external scrutiny and regulation. Alas, the majority of Anglican bishops would prefer the hot fires of hell to such egalitarian answerability.

Welby's resignation might be seen as an updated episode of *1776 and All That*: no taxation without representation. Why should any punter in the pew fund governance rooted in autocracy with pretentions towards theocracy? Increasingly, the indications are that they won't put up with authority they did not elect, yet somehow presumes to rule them—and can even tap them for compliant semi-obligatory financial support.

Welby is arguably a representative harbinger of an ecclesial revolution. It has been coming for some while. As the former Labour Party MP Tony Benn (1925–2014) repeatedly asked of those in authority,

> What power have you got? Where did you get it from? In whose interests do you exercise it? To whom are you accountable? And how can we get rid of you?

If the answer to every one of those questions from the bishops and senior ecclesiocrats is "only God, or maybe the reigning monarch," then the stage is fully prepped for open revolt by those in the pews. In many respects, the story of global Anglicanism—not yet five hundred years old—is one of Protestant democratic polity vying with regalistic notions of autocracy and theocracy.

The regal model presumes it does not need to give an account of itself or even consult. It just rules and reigns, and when subjected to questions, ignores its people and the media as though they were insolent and unruly serfs. It will spurn democratic accountability and treat congregations as medieval monarchs might once have regarded lowly subjects.

This has not always been an English problem. Let us not forget that Samuel Seabury, the first American Anglican bishop to be consecrated (1784) without the approval of the Church of England, wore a specially made miter fashioned from beaver pelt and gold filigree wherever he went, in order to signal his self-proclaimed divine authority over a bemused American citizenry. Seabury believed his cathedral was wherever he happened to be celebrating the Eucharist, and he demanded monarchical deference.

Seabury did not believe the laity should have any say at all in the governance of the church, and his diocese, Connecticut, did not change that until later in the twentieth century. Seabury's lofty regal outlook matched his proslavery and high Tory leanings.

Yet these views have not prevailed. American Episcopalians are assiduously pro-democratic, and their ecclesial polity is progressively Protestant, albeit with some Catholic accents. That spells the end for English Anglican imperialism at home and abroad. Its time is up, and the resignation of the 105th archbishop of Canterbury demonstrated that the public have little patience with an institution that does not practice what it preaches. If democracy, equality, and accountability is good for the rest of the world, then English Anglicanism will need to model that too.

Until it does, dismissal by the public and decline will continue. To paraphrase Ernest Hemingway, bankruptcy happens in two ways: first very slowly, then all of sudden. Leading the Church of England from hereon will be like trying to ascend the proverbial glass cliff. Falling further and faster is the most likely result. But clinging on for dear life is hardly an option. The only future left for Anglicanism lies at ground level. The leadership needs to climb down, and as fast as possible.

The issue is simple. Any power imbalance always creates the space for power abuse. Bishops and their courtiers, advisors, and senior ecclesiocrats expect to rule and reign. Safeguarding in the Church of England is overseen by mercurial, unaccountable, unlicensed, non-transparent, and unregulated officers. Every bishop refuses to level the playing field by balancing power and becoming subject to independent external professional regulation and oversight. The result is inevitable. Nothing in such a safeguarding system can ever be safe. It is wide open to abuse, incompetence, and cover-ups. All the evidence for that is lengthy and legion. But bishops and their officers will still not cede their power. So they cannot and will not be trusted.

Our readings this morning have a rich theme. The lectionary always does. Roughly, they connect through fecundity (the parable—or sign—of the fig tree), the importance of sacrifice, and the need for perseverance. The readings remind us that judgment always comes, and truth will always out. The systems of governance, even in the church, that think they have a God-given right to endure will perish.

I don't think we know, yet, if Justin Welby's resignation has any point to it. The establishment has a habit of making expedient examples of individuals and sacrificing them to preserve the status quo and thereby maintain the power, privilege, and patrimony of an aloof institution. But I want to leave you this morning with a reminder of our hope. Like Jonah in the belly of the whale, good things are born in the darkness. It is there that God laughs deeply. The resurrection is a laugh freed forever; and this crisis in the Church of England, never before seen in its five-hundred-year history, might be an opportunity for a completely new beginning.

In the meantime, we remain at the mercy of episcopal hubris. But more importantly, we are at the mercy and judgment seat of God. As the Gospel has it, "heaven and earth will pass away," as will the Church and its governance. Only God's word is eternal. Nobody knows the day or the hour of judgment. But this week, it does feel like that end-time for the Church has come much closer. These are but birth pangs; the beginning of some new creation. Thanks be to God. Amen.

Acknowledgements

THIS BOOK WOULD NOT have been possible without the help and support of friends and colleagues at Virginia Theological Seminary (VTS). In particular, thanks go to Dean Markham, president of the Seminary. I also especially want to thank the staff in the library and archives—notably David Buresh and Denton Waits—together with support from Rachel Sanderson, Riley Temple '14, and Joseph Thompson. Thank you to them for enabling the treasures of one of the finest collections of Anglican Studies in the world to be open and accessible, and with such warmth. Special thanks also to Nicky Burridge, vice president for alumni engagement and communications at VTS for her support.

The development of this book would not have been achievable without significant support and contributions. To my family, and especially to Emma, my unending gratitude belongs.

Endnotes

1. Burke, *Reflections on the Revolution*, 5.
2. Percy, *Crisis of Colonial Anglicanism*; Percy, "Christmas in the Anglican Tradition"; Percy, "Passionate Coolness."
3. Marshall, *One Catholic and Apostolic*; Rowthorn, *Samuel Seabury*; Porter, *Samuel Seabury*.
4. Thoms, *Seabury*; Hebb, *Samuel Seabury and Charles Inglis*; Cameron, *Samuel Seabury*; Steiner, *Samuel Seabury*.
5. Kornblith, *Slavery and Sectional Strife*.
6. For a fuller discussion of the concept of *terroir*, see Percy, *Engaging with Contemporary Culture*. See also Healy, *Church, World and Christian Life*.
7 See my *Crisis of Colonial Anglicanism*.
8. Gibbon, *History of the Decline and Fall*.
9. Brendon, *Decline and Fall of the British Empire*.
10. Lindbeck, *Nature of Doctrine*.
11. Greengrass, *Christendom Destroyed;* Wigley, *Rise and Fall of the Victorian Sunday*.
12. Barker, *Regeneration*. However, as readers will detect, I am effectively following the line taken by Diamond, *Collapse*.
13. Wilkinson, *Church of England*. This text contains several fine discussions of the classism embedded in attitudes to the conflict, the role of chaplains, and the elitism of some bishops matching that of the generals. The bishop of London at the time, Arthur Foley Winnington Ingram, was a noted supporter of the war and argued that conscientious objectors be imprisoned in areas most likely to be bombed by zeppelins, so as to change the minds of conflict-averse shirkers. Other senior clergy adopted rhetoric that had not been witnessed since medieval crusades to the Holy Lands.
14. Moral injury describes experiences of stress, trauma, and disorientation, where someone in leadership holding responsibility and legitimate authority betrays the ethical core and moral values of those acting in a stressful critical incident. The betrayal can result in the psychological, social, and spiritual trauma of colleagues. In caring contexts or combat zones, for example, those experiencing moral injury report disorientation, alienation, dislocation, and mental collapse.

15. Banner, *Britain's Slavery Debt.*
16. Niebuhr, *Social Sources of Denominationalism.* This text, published in 1929, is an unsurpassed study of class, race, and hierarchy in churches.
17. Reed, *Glorious Battle*; Pickering, *Anglo-Catholicism.* These are good sources for readers wishing to examine specific studies of the history of classism in English Anglicanism.
18. Faulkner, *Requiem for a Nun.*
19. Orwell, *Nineteen Eighty-Four*, 162.
20. Winchester, *Krakatoa*; Winchester, *Crack in the Edge of the World*; Parker, *One Fine Day.*
21. Sanghera, *Empireworld.*
22. Grzymała-Busse, *Sacred Foundations.*
23. Grzymała-Busse, *Nations Under God.*
24. Compton, *End of Empathy.*
25. Sanghera, *Empireland.* See particularly chapters 11 and 12 on selective amnesia. See also Sanghera, *Empireworld*, with a particular focus on the inherent contradictions within English and British colonialism that one encounters in non-governmental expressions of the Empire, such as the Church of England.
26. Ward, *Untied Kingdom.*
27. Elkins, *Legacy of Violence*; Linstrum, *Age of Emergency.*
28. Peckham, *Fear*; Stern, *Empire Incorporated*; Ibrahim, *Authoritarian Century*; Manville and Ober, *Civic Bargain.* See that the Enlightenment led to concepts of citizenship, civic society, agreement, and pacts on decision-making, and sounded the death-knell for monarchical and authoritarian powers.
29. Hobson, *Imperialism.* Hobson claimed that capitalist business activity brought about imperialism.
30. Marzouki et al., *Saving the People.*
31. Matovski, *Popular Dictatorships.* Some readers may think of Russia, Turkey, Venezuela, or Egypt here, though the presidency of Donald Trump and the prime ministerial era of Boris Johnson may also qualify for consideration. In an alleged crisis, "Make America Great Again" or "Take Back Control" are barely concealed bids for a narrow nationalism of self-interest.
32. Gibbon, *History of the Decline and Fall*; cf. Percy, *Crisis of Colonial Anglicanism.*
33. Williams, "Stones Revived," 2.
34. Williams, "Stones Revived," 4.
35. Steiner, *Samuel Seabury*, 65–66. See also White, "Consecration of Bishop Seabury."
36. Steiner, *Samuel Seabury*, 65.
37. Subrahmanyam, *Europe's India*; Asher and Talbot, *India Before Europe.* See the above for two recent and fine treatments of English imperialism in India.
38. Tharhoor, *Inglorious Empire.*
39. Evans, *Nation of Shopkeepers*; Vogler, *Scoff*; Vogler, *Stuffed.* At its peak, the sugar boycotts amounted to over three hundred thousand people, including many children foregoing confectionary in order to protest against the slave-based production.
40. Renton, *Blood Legacy*, 57. Snowden, *Epidemics and Society.*

41. Renton, *Blood Legacy*, 178–79.
42. Renton, *Blood Legacy*, 174–75.
43. Costa, *Crowns of Glory;* Høgsbjerg, *Atlantic History in Fifteen Slave Revolts.*
44. Fergusson, *Empire*, 45ff.
45. Brekke, *Faithonomics*, 229–34. In fact, the British Census of India in 1871 split the Muslim, Christian, Jain, Sikh, Buddhist, and "Hindoo" communities into somewhat artificial categories, knowing full well that many regions were ambiguous and flexible in their religious orientation. To be fair, the British knew their categories were imprecise, haphazard, and divisive, but the silos were imposed nonetheless. However, for many in India, it was simply meaningless to ask if they were Hindu or Jain, as they were both, just as followers of Sikh, Hindu, Jain, and Buddhist faiths also shared practices and customs.
46. Tharoor, *Inglorious Empire.*
47. Lester, *Truth About Empire.*
48. Percy, *Shaping the Church.* In this approach, I simply draw on Niebuhr, *Social Sources of Denominationalism*, which asks us to attend to how class, race, and wealth shapes denominational identity.
49. Snowden, *Epidemics and Society.*
50. Jenkins, *Climate Catastrophe and Faith*, 33ff; Fagan, *Great Warming.*
51. Snowden, *Epidemics and Society*; Davis, *Late Victorian Holocausts*; Fagan, *Little Ice Age*; Fagan, *Floods, Famines and Emperors*; Degroot, *Frigid Golden Age*; Blom, *Nature's Mutiny.* Ferguson, *Empire*; Parker, *One Fine Day.* To be sure, there are (relatively speaking) glowing accounts of the legacy of English expansionism, which tend to gloss over the classism and racism embedded in the "civilising project." Indeed, that expansionism was only to reach its peak a century ago, in 1923. Healey, *Blazing World*; Gatiss, *Tragedy of 1662*; Keay, *Restless Republic.*
52. Snowden, *Epidemics and Society.*
53. Sarmiento, "Southwark Election News."
54. Whatmore, *End of Enlightenment.*
55. Dalrymple, *Anarchy*; Olusoga, *Black and British*; Whatmore, *End of Enlightenment.* These texts expose Britain's history in this respect.
56. Fagan, *Little Ice Age*, 91–97.
57. Bramen, *American Niceness.*
58. Bramen, *American Niceness*, 251–53.
59. Bremner, "Colonial Themes in Stained Glass."
60. Bramen, *American Niceness*, 40–95.
61. Frankopan, *Silk Roads.*
62. Frankopan, *Silk Roads*, 215–16.
63. Scruton, *Our Church.* I find Scruton's analysis of the origins and development of the Church of England to be overly romantic and historically naïve.
64. Frankopan, *Silk Roads*, 277.
65. Carson, *East India Company.*
66. Reid, *Fighting Retreat.*
67. Platt, *Subscribing to Faith?*; Yamaguchi, *Daughters of the Anglican Clergy.*
68. Small advertisements for such lost property pepper the local newspapers of the

mid–late eighteenth century, across the colonies. In Connecticut alone, dozens appear in the editions of *Connecticut Gazette* (New Haven, founded 1755), *New London Gazette* (New London, established 1763), *Connecticut Courant* (Hartford, published from 1764), *Connecticut Journal* (New Haven, from 1767) and *The Norwich Packet* (published from 1773 in Norwich, Connecticut). $10 was the standard sum for reward.

69. Laslett, *John Locke.*

70. Edwards, *Faithful Tribe*; Jess, *Orange Order*; Blacker and Wallace, *Formation of the Orange Order.*

71. Keay, *Restless Republic.*

72. Pittock, *Jacobitism*; Szechi, *1715.*

73. McDonald, *Jacobean Kirk.*

74. Nye, *Understanding International Conflicts.* This paved the way for Nye to write several more reflections on the uses of hard and soft power, including *The Paradox of American Power* and *The Powers to Lead.*

75. Percy, *Humble Church;* Percy, *Precarious Church.*

76. Berger, *Sacred Canopy*, 144. Oligarchies tend to protect or promote religious monopolies, a point not lost on Peter Berger, who notes that the tendency of such nations and rulers is to reproduce "oligopolistic" faiths that are hierarchical in character, and dominate any other rivals or alternatives. The Church of England would qualify as an oligopolistic denomination (in effect the head of a religious cartel), presuming to rule on behalf of others nationally and internationally. See Brekke, *Faithonomics*, 202–3, which also discussed how this legitimates discrimination.

77. Gross, *War Against Catholicism.* This is a fine and penetrating study focussing on one country.

78. Welch, *Feminist Ethic of Risk*, 111ff.

79 For a discussion of my work in the field of ecclesiology, see Markham and Daniels, *Reasonable Radical?*

80. Sandeman, "Figures Show a Gentle Decline."

81. Porter, *Sydney Anglicans*; Porter, *New Puritans*; Porter, *New Exile?*

82. Morgan, *Snobbery.*

83. Percy, *Clergy;* Kater, *Ministry in the Anglican Tradition.* Kater's historical survey of and account for four hundred years of Anglican ministry is unsurpassed in depth and coverage.

84. Whitley, *Blinded Eagle;* Bennett, *Edward Irving Reconsidered.*

85. Thompson et al., eds., *Domestic Violence*, 31.

86. Ogden, *Violence, Entitlement and Politics*; Kimmel, *Angry White Men.*

87. Hammond, *In Understanding Be Men.*

88. Du Mez, *Jesus and John Wayne.*

89. Du Mez, *Jesus and John Wayne*, 87.

90. Morgan, *Snobbery.*

91. Greider, "Too Militant?"; Gill-Austern, "Love Understood as Self-Sacrifice"; Harrison and Robb, *Making the Connections.* See these texts for more on the suppression of female voices in church settings, including expressions of righteous anger.

92. Berkowitz, *Sex and Punishment*; Meek, *Sex, Politics and Society*; Stone, *Family, Sex and Marriage*; Meek, *Queer Trades;* Jones, *Sexual Politics.* There is a considerable

amount of Christian literature that approaches homosexuality from theological perspectives. While some are nuanced, many represent a "thesis-directing-facts" approach to human biology, culture, and history. Readers will be better-served by studies, such as those I have listed above, that avoid confessional politics and posturing within church-sponsored debates.

93. Porter, *Sydney Anglicans*; Porter, *New Puritans.*

94. Percy, *Words, Wonders and Power*; Percy and Jones, *Fundamentalism, Church and Society*; Percy, "Anatomy of Fundamentalism."

95. Keillor, *Lake Wobegon Days.* Readers interested in following up these themes are directed especially to chapter 3 on "Protestant." See also Keillor et al., "Secret Life of Lutherans."

96. Barton, *History of the Bible*; Schmid and Schröter, *Making of the Bible*; Wright, *Why the Bible Began.* Some Christian traditions include the Apocryphal books within the Old Testament; others treat them as a kind of semi-detached appendix; and others do not regard them as Scripture at all. The Bible is a bounded collection of Scriptures, but the contents and ordering are subject to some modest variables. The core of the Old and New Testaments is largely agreed. The Protestant Old Testament is thirty-nine books, while the Roman Catholic Church recognizes forty-six books, with many parts of the Eastern Orthodox Churches recognizing an additional six books. Catholics, Protestants, and Orthodox have the same twenty-seven-book New Testament canon. Temporal, regional, and cultural variations in the make-up of authorised Scriptures are relatively minor, and need not concern us here. There is no need to debate the finer points of Psallms 151–155, 1 and 2 Esdras, or the texts known as Prayer of Manasseh or the Apocalypse of Baruch, nor 3 Maccabees (let alone 4 Maccabees, which is only used by the Georgian Churches). Sydney Anglicans, I suspect, would rather you did not meditate on such things.

97. Achebe, *Things Fall Apart.*

98. Haidt, *Righteous Mind.*

99. Bloom, *Restless Revolutionaries.*

100. Franklin, Benjamin Franklin to Lord Kames.

101. Brennan, *US Constitution and Related Documents*; Thomas, *Common Sense.*

102. Levithan, "Forgotten Founder."

103. Berlin, *Four Essays on Liberty*, 118–72.

104. Author's translation.

105. Spielberg, *Bridge of Spies.*

106. Anna Reid, *Nasty Little War.* We can presume that if the Russian Revolution of 1917 had failed, the British would have responded differently to the demands for change at home.

107. As one senior churchman has recently opined, "When the (English Anglican) House of Bishops meets in private we vote on a show of hands. Then the Secretariat will often say not to bother with us counting, as they will handle that for us and send the results. Well, I sit at the back, and I do count. I can tell you that the Secretariat's counting of hands and mine are different. We make a decision as Bishops, and are then told a week later in the minutes that we actually voted quite differently for something else we did not actually decide upon" (private correspondence, 2024). Democracy does not depend on a system of one person, one vote. It is at the mercy of who counts the votes, and who says which votes count.

108. Black Presence Project, "Reverend Samuel Seabury."
109. Tyson, *Theology and Climate Change.*
110. Tyson, *Theology and Climate Change*, 38.
111. Arendt, *Eichman in Jerusalem.*
112. Tisby, *Color of Compromise.*
113. Irons, *Origins of Proslavery Christianity.*
114. Maqbool and Swann, "Priest Thought to Pose Risk."
115. Maqbool and Swann, "Church of England Struggle."
116. Maqbool and Swann, "Church of England Struggle."
117. Strong, *Partisan Anglicanism*, 144; United Grand Lodge, *Freemasons Chronicle*, 518, 375.
118. Apollo University Lodge No. 357, founded in 1818. The Sherwood family appear to have prominent Oxfordshire and Berkshire Freemasonry connections dating from the nineteenth century. See Carr, *Ars Quatuor Coronatorum*; Freemasons United Grande Lodge, *Masonic Year Book Historical Supplement*; Dyer, *Grand Stewards and Their Lodge.* The Archbishops' Council decline to comment on whether they, the senior legal officers, law firms, and senior staff serving Lambeth Palace are influenced by freemasonry. It would not be surprising given other high-profile safeguarding cases, but without a proper Register of Interests operating, the extent of Masonic influence cannot be known.
119. IICSA, "IICSA Peter Ball Investigation"; IICSA, "IICSA Inquiry Anglican Church Investigation," 13; Wood, "Religious Power"; Parsons, "Toxic Masculinity."
120. Martin, "Risk Assessment Should Suffice."
121. Martin, "Philip North's Nomination." Even in the case of Bishop North's own nomination to the See of Sheffield (withdrawn), and then Blackburn, normal processes were side-stepped or somehow subverted.
122. BBC News, "Church of England Criticised."
123. See the determination of Lyndsey de Mestre KC in Diocese of Oxford vs. Revd. Canon Richard Peers, para 9.4., p. 7, The bishop of Llandaff and the archbishop of Wales, alerted to the alleged falsification of risk assessments by Peers after he became dean of Llandaff, also declined to act, stating that investigation of a potential forgery of a church document by one of their clergy "was not in the interests of the Church in Wales." See Gadd, *In the Matter of a Complaint.*

    "Four risk assessments were subsequently prepared on the basis of the conclusions in the Wood Report. These and other safeguarding processes put in place at the time have been criticised. For the avoidance of doubt, the Tribunal is not concerned with the details of how those operated or with evaluating their appropriateness."

    The respondent was not licensed, authorised, or approved to write or commission risk assessments, and the church court presided over by Lyndsey de Mestre KC declined to consider the manufacture of bogus risk assessments, which the bishop of Oxford, for the plaintiff, had previously endorsed. Later in her determination, de Mestre praises Canon Peers' "professionalism" in safeguarding, having decided to ignore serious evidence to the contrary.
124. Recent examples include an alleged £40,000 payoff on behalf of the bishop of Blackburn, and £100,000 payoff on behalf of a southern diocese, with both victims forced to agree to NDAs. The bishop of Blackburn was given several opportunities to confirm, deny, or comment on this, but declined to respond.

125. Percy, *Power and the Church*; Percy, *Salt of the Earth.*

126. For example, in one recent CDM case in 2022–23, the bishop of Oxford was simultaneously writing a supportive written witness statement for the respondent (Canon Richard Peers) when at the same time the bishop and Diocese of Oxford were meant to be prosecuting a case against Peers for weaponizing safeguarding against a third party. The case went ahead, but the bishop and Diocese were able to secure the weakest possible prosecuting counsel, rendering the case pointless.

127. Fraser, "Dying the Christian Science Way."

128. Percy, *Exiled Church.*

129. See *The Makin Review.* For a summary of the history of safeguarding in Church of England, see Collier, "Safeguarding in Church and State over the Last 50 Years." See also Graystone, *Bleeding for Jesus*; and Fife and Fife, *Letters to a Broken Church.*

130. Chomsky and Polychroniou, *Precipice.*

131. Northcott, *Political Theology of Climate Change.*

132. Bryson, *Notes from a Small Island.*

133. Fox, *Watching the English.*

134. Percy, *Anglicanism.*

135. Harrison, *Secret Leviathan.*

136. Strong, *Anglicanism and the British Empire.*

137. Snow, *Mission, Race, Empire.*

138. Hunt, *Republic.*

139. Reece, *Fall.*

140. Ong, *Orality and Literacy.*

141. Tilby, "Schismatics."

142. Brittain and McKinnon, *Anglican Communion at a Crossroads*; Hobson, "What the Church of England Should Say."

143. See Mahlburg, "'We Are the Anglican Communion.'"

144. It cannot be "The Penitent's Tale" or the "Repenter's Tale," since Mr. Welby showed regret for his inactions but not remorse, and there has been no change in structures over the scandal, and the victims of Smyth remain shunned by the safeguarding hierarchies and senior leadership of the Church of England. See Bash and Percy, *Forgiveness, Reparation, and Remorse.*

145. *Conclave* is a 2024 political thriller film directed by Edward Berger and written by Peter Straughan, based on the 2016 novel by Robert Harris.

146. *The Two Popes* is a 2019 biographical drama film directed by Fernando Meirelles and written by Anthony McCarten, adapted from McCarten's play *The Pope* which premiered at Royal and Derngate Theatre in 2019.

147. *Racing Demon* (Faber & Co.) is a 1990 play by English playwright David Hare. Part of a trio of plays about British institutions (*Murmuring Judges* and *The Absence of War*), it focuses on the Church of England, and tackles issues such as gay ordination, and the role of evangelism in inner city communities. The play debuted at the National Theatre. Through comedy-drama, Hare's play follows clergymen struggling to make sense of their purpose, mission, and ultimate vocation.

148. ACNS, "To Lead and to Serve"; ACNS, "Hurd Review."

149. On Lord Hurd's Report, *To Lead and to Serve* (published September 2001) see: ACNS, "To Lead and to Serve"; ACNS, "Hurd Review."
150. ACNS, "Review of the See of Canterbury."
151. Keillor, *Life Among the Lutherans*, 92.
152. See Percy, "Passionate Coolness."
153. Coffey, "Make Christianity Cool Again."
154. See Festinger, *Theory of Cognitive Dissonance*.
155. Percy, *Crisis of Colonial Anglicanism*.
156. See Gregersen, *Louis Sullivan and His Mentor*, ix.
157. Author's translation.
158. Jackson and Stewart, *Superpower Britain*, 214–15.
159. Clarke, *Last Thousand Days*; and Darwin, *Empire Project*.
160. Sandbrook, *Great British Dream Factory*.
161. Clarke, *Last Thousand Days*, 506.
162. Clavier, "Beyond the Scaffolding."
163. This is extensively discussed in Percy, *Future Shapes of Anglicanism*.
164. Cf., Jer 31:29 and Ezek 18:2–4.
165. See Editorial Committee, "Catholic Church in China."

Bibliography

Seabury Primary Sources

Essays and Books (in date order)

The Errors of Calvinism. n.p. 1766.

Letters of a Westchester Farmer [written using the pseudonym A. W. Farmer]. n.p. 1774–75.

Hamilton's View of the Controversy Between Great Britain and Her Colonies [written as "A. W. Farmer"]. n.p. 1775.

The Communion-Office, or Order for the Administration of the Holy Eucharist or Supper of the Lord with Private Devotions. n.p. 1786.

"Forms of Prayer for the United States in Congress Assembled 1786." (NB: only a fragment survives).

The Communion-Office, or Order for the Administration of the Holy Eucharist or Supper of the Lord. With Private Devotions. Recommended to the Episcopal Congregations in Connecticut. New London, 1786.

An Earnest Persuasive to Frequent Communion. n.p. 1789.

An Earnest Persuasive to Frequent Communion; Addressed to Those Professors of the Church of England, in Connecticut, Who Neglect That Holy Ordinance. New Haven, 1789.

Discourses on Several Subjects. New York, 1793.

A Burial Office for Infants Who Depart This Life Before They Have Polluted Their Baptism by Actual Sin. n.p. 1795.

The Psalter or Psalms of David, Pointed as They Are to Be Sung or Said in Churches. with the Order for Morning and Evening Prayer Daily Throughout the Year (Also Containing the Athanasian Creed, the Litany, Prayers for Special Occasions, Thanksgivings, and a Catechism). New London, 1795.

Discourses on Several Important Subjects. New York, 1798.

Pamphlets and Addresses (in date order)

A View of the Controversy between Great-Britain and Her Colonies. New York, 1774.

Free Thoughts on the Proceedings of the Continental Congress. New York, 1774.

The Congress Canvassed. New York, 1774.

An Alarm to the Legislature of the Province of New-York, Occasioned by the Present Political Disturbances. New York, 1775.

Samuel, by Divine Permission, Bishop of the Episcopal Church in the State of Connecticut [injunction regarding political prayers]. n.p. 1785.

Bishop Seabury's First Charge, to the Clergy of His Diocese, Delivered at Middletown, August 4, 1785. With a List of the Succession of Scot's Bishops, from the Revolution 1688, to the Present Time. New Haven, 1786.

Bishop Seabury's Second Charge, to the Clergy of His Diocese, Delivered at Derby, in the State of Connecticut, on the 22d of September, 1786. New Haven, 1786.

An Address to the Ministers and Congregations of the Presbyterian and Independent Persuasions in the United States of America, by a Member of the Episcopal Church. New Haven, 1790.

A Discourse Delivered Before the Triennial Convention of the Protestant Episcopal Church at Trinity Church, New York, on the Twelfth Day of September, One Thousand Seven Hundred and Ninety-Two. New York, 1792.

Samuel, by Divine Permission, Bishop of Connecticut and Rhode Island [regarding the deposition of James Sayre] n.p. 1793 Broad-side.

A Discourse Delivered in St. James' Church, in New-London, on Tuesday the 23d of December, 1794, Before an Assembly of Free and Accepted Masons, Convened for the Purpose of Installing a Lodge in That City. New London, 1794.

A Discourse Delivered Before an Assembly of Free and Accepted Masons, Convened for the Purpose of Installing a Lodge in the City of Norwich, in Connecticut, on the Festival of St. John the Baptist, 1795. Norwich, 1795.

Samuel, By Divine Permission, Bishop of Connecticut and Rhode-Island. . . [charitable fund] New London, 1795.

Samuel, By Divine Permission, Bishop of Connecticut and Rhode-Island. . . [Algerian Captives] New London, 1795.

Sermons and Homilies (in date order)

"A Discourse on Brotherly Love, Preached Before the Honorable Fraternity of Free and Accepted Masons, of Zion Lodge, at St. Paul's Chapel, in New York, on the Festival of St. John the Baptist, One Thousand Seven Hundred and Seventy-Seven." New York, 1777.

"A Discourse on II Tim. III.16. Delivered in St. Paul's and St. George's Chapels, in New-York, on Sunday the 11th of May, 1777." New York, 1777.

"St. Peter's Exhortation to Fear God and Honor the King, Explained and Inculcated: in a Discourse Addressed to His Majesty's Provincial Troops, in Camp at King's Bridge, on Sunday the 28th Sept. 1777." New York, 1777 (attributed to Seabury, but uncertain).

"A Sermon Preached Before the Grand Lodge, and the Other Lodges of Ancient Freemasons, in New-York, at St. Paul's Chapel, on the Anniversary of St. John the Evangelist, 1782." New York, 1783.

"The Address of the Episcopal Clergy of Connecticut, to the Right Reverend Bishop Seabury, with the Bishop's Answer and, a Sermon, Before the Convention at Middletown, August 3d, 1785." n.p. 1785.

"A Sermon Delivered before the Boston Episcopal Charitable Society in Trinity Church; at Their Anniversary Meeting on Easter Tuesday March 25, 1788. Boston, 1788.

"A Sermon Preached in Christ Church, Philadelphia, Before the Corporation for the Relief of the Widows and Children of Clergymen at their Anniversary Meeting, October 7, 1789." Philadelphia, 1789.

"The Duty of Considering Our Ways. A Sermon Preached in Saint James Church, New-London, on Ash Wednesday, 1789." New London, 1789.

"A Discourse, Delivered in St. John's Church, in Portsmouth, New Hampshire, at the Conferring the Order of Priesthood on the Rev. Robert Fowle, A.M. of Holderness, on the Festival of St. Peter, 1791." 1791.

Other Sources

Achebe, Chinue. *Things Fall Apart*. New York: Bantam, Doubleday & Dell, 1958.

ACNS. "Hurd Review: Major Recommendations for the See of Canterbury." September 7, 2001. https://www.anglicannews.org/news/2001/09/hurd-review-major-recommendations-for-the-see-of-canterbury.aspx.

———. "Review of the See of Canterbury." September 7, 2001. https://www.anglicannews.org/news/2001/09/review-of-the-see-of-canterbury.aspx.

———. "To Lead and to Serve: The Report of the Review of the See of Canterbury." September 6, 2001. https://www.anglicannews.org/news/2001/09/to-lead-and-to-serve-the-report-of-the-review-of-the-see-of-canterbury.aspx.

Arendt, Hannah. *Eichmann in Jerusalem: A Report on the Banality of Evil*. 1963. Reprint, London: Penguin Random House, 2022.

Asher, Catherine E. B., and Cynthia Talbot. *India Before Europe*. Cambridge: Cambridge University Press, 2022.

Banner, Michael. *Britain's Slavery Debt: Reparations Now!* Oxford: Oxford University Press, 2024.

Barker, Pat. *Regeneration*. London: Penguin, 1992.

Barton, John. *A History of the Bible: The Book and Its Faiths*. London: Penguin, 2019.

BBC News. "Church of England Criticised over Suicide of Falsely Accused Priest." BBC News, July 16, 2021. https://www.bbc.co.uk/news/uk-england-london-57780729.

———. "Church of England 'Regret' over Suicide of Falsely Accused Priest." BBC News, August 25, 2021. https://www.bbc.co.uk/news/uk-england-london-58326903.

Bash, Anthony, and Martyn Percy. *Forgiveness, Reparation, and Remorse: Reckoning with Truthful Apology*. York: Ethics Press International, 2025.

Bennett, David M. *Edward Irving Reconsidered: The Man, His Controversies, and the Pentecostal Movement*. Eugene, OR: Wipf & Stock, 2014.

Berger, Peter. *The Sacred Canopy: Elements of a Sociological Theory of Religion*. Garden City, NY: Anchor, 1969.

Berkowitz, Eric. *Sex and Punishment: 4000 Years of Judging Desire*. London: Westbourne, 2012.

Berlin, Isaiah. *Four Essays on Liberty*. Oxford: Oxford University Press, 1969.

Black Presence Project. "Reverend Samuel Seabury." Winter 2019. https://blackpresence.episcopalny.org/person/reverend-samuel-seabury/.

Blacker, William, and Robert Hugh Wallace. *The Formation of the Orange Order, 1795–1798: The Edited Papers of Colonel William Blacker and Colonel Robert H. Wallace.* Belfast: Education Committee of the Grand Orange Lodge of Ireland, 1994.

Blom, Philipp. *Nature's Mutiny: How the Little Ice Age of the Long Seventeenth Century Transformed the West and Shaped the Present.* London: Liverlight, 2019.

Bloom, Clive. *Restless Revolutionaries: A History of Britain's Fight for a Republic.* Cheltenham, UK: History, 2007.

Bramen, Carrie Tirado. *American Niceness: A Cultural History.* Cambridge: Harvard University Press, 2017.

Brekke, Torkel. *Faithonomics: Religion and the Free Market.* London: Hurst, 2016.

Bremner, G. A. "Colonial Themes in Stained Glass, Home and Abroad: A Visual Survey." *The Journal of Interdisciplinary Studies in the Long Nineteenth Century* 30 (2020) 1–23.

Brendon, Piers. *The Decline and Fall of the British Empire, 1781–1997.* New York: Vintage, 2008.

Brennan, Stephen, ed. *The US Constitution and Related Documents.* New York: Skyhorse, 2012.

Brittain, Christopher Craig, and Andrew McKinnon. *The Anglican Communion at a Crossroads: The Crises of a Global Church.* Philadelphia: Penn State University Press, 2018.

Bryson, Bill. *Notes from a Small Island.* London: HarperCollins, 1995.

Burke, Edmund. *Reflections on the Revolution in France.* Vol. 2 of *Select Works of Edmund Burke.* London: James Dodsley, Pall Mall, 1790.

Cameron, Kenneth Walker. *Samuel Seabury, 1729–1796: Election, Consecration, and Reception—A Documentary History.* Hartford, CT: Transcendental, 1978.

Carr, Harry, ed. Ars Quatuor Coronatorum: Transactions of the Quatuor Coronati Lodge No. 2076, Vol. 82 for the year 1969.

Carson, Penelope. *The East India Company and Religion, 1698–1858.* Rochester, NY: Boydell & Brewer, 2012.

Chesterton, G. K. *St Thomas Aquinas.* London: Macmillan, 1933.

Chomsky, Noam, and C. J. Polychroniou. *The Precipice: Neoliberalism, the Pandemic and the Urgent Need for Social Change.* London: Penguin, 2021.

Clarke, Peter. *The Last Thousand Days of the British Empire.* London: Allen Lane, 2007.

Clavier, Mark. "Beyond the Scaffolding: What the Church in Wales's Harries Report Missed and Why It Still Matters." Well-Tempered, April 22, 2025. https://markclavier.substack.com/p/beyond-the-scaffolding.

Coffey, Helen. "Make Christianity Cool Again: Why Gen Z Is Flocking to Church." Independent, April 20, 2025. https://www.independent.co.uk/life-style/church-christianity-gen-z-young-people-faith-god-easter-b2734957.html.

Collier, Peter. "Safeguarding in Church and State over the Last 50 Years: 'From Ball and Banks to Beech via Bell.'" *Journal of Ecclesiastical Law* 22 (2020) 156–93.

Compton, John W. *The End of Empathy: Why White Protestants Stopped Loving Their Neighbours.* Oxford: Oxford University Press, 2020.

Costa, Emilia Viotta da. *Crowns of Glory, Tears of Blood: The Demerara Slave Rebellion of 1823.* Oxford: Oxford University Press, 1997.

Dalrymple, William. *The Anarchy: The Relentless Rise of the East India Company.* London: Bloomsbury, 2019.

Darwin, John. *The Empire Project: The Rise and Fall of the British World System, 1830–970.* Cambridge: Cambridge University Press, 2009.

Davis, Mike. *Late Victorian Holocausts: El Niño Famines and the Making of the Third World*. London: Verso, 2017.

Degroot, Dagamor. *The Frigid Golden Age: Climate Change, the Little Ice Age, and the Dutch Republic, 1560–720*. Cambridge: Cambridge University Press, 2018.

Diamond, Jared. *Collapse: How Societies Choose to Fail or Survive*. London: Penguin, 2005.

Du Mez, Kristin Kobes. *Jesus and John Wayne: How White Evangelicals Corrupted a Faith and Fractured a Nation*. New York: Liveright, 2020.

Dyer, Colin. *The Grand Stewards and Their Lodge*. London: Grand Stewards' Lodge, 1985.

Editorial Committee. "'The Catholic Church in China in 2002: An Analysis' and 'Statistics and Major Events of the Catholic Church in China, 2002.'" *Tripod* 202 (2023) 149–90.

Edwards, Ruth Dudley. *The Faithful Tribe: An Intimate Portrait of the Loyal Institutions*. London: HarperCollins, 2000.

Elkins, Caroline. *Legacy of Violence: A History of the British Empire*. New York: Vintage, 2023.

Evans, Dan. *A Nation of Shopkeepers: The Unstoppable Rise of the Petite Bourgeoisie*. London: Repeater, 2023.

Fagan, Brian. *Floods, Famines, and Emperors: El Nino and the Fate of Civilizations*. New York: Basic, 1999.

———. *The Great Warming: Climate Change and the Rise and Fall of Civilizations*. London: Bloomsbury, 2009.

———. *The Little Ice Age: How Climate Made History 1300–1850*. New York: Basic, 2000.

Faulkner, William. *Requiem for a Nun*. London: Chatto & Windus, 1919.

Fergusson, Niall. *Empire: The Rise and Demise of the British World Order and the Lessons for Global Power*. New York: Basic, 2004.

Festinger, Leon. *A Theory of Cognitive Dissonance*. Stanford, CA: Stanford University Press, 1957.

Fife, Janet, and Gilo Fife. *Letters to a Broken Church*. Edinburgh: Ekklesia, 2019 (2nd ed. 2026).

Fox, Kate. *Watching the English: The Hidden Rules of English Behaviour*. London: Hodder & Stoughton, 2004.

Franklin, Benjamin. Benjamin Franklin to Lord Kames, February, 25 1767. National Archives, Founders Online. https://founders.archives.gov/documents/Franklin/01-14-02-0032.

Frankopan, Peter. *The Silk Roads: A New History of the World*. London: Bloomsbury, 2015.

Fraser, Caroline. "Dying the Christian Science Way: The Horror of My Father's Last Days." *The Guardian*, August 6, 2024. https://www.theguardian.com/world/2019/aug/06/christian-science-church-medicine-death-horror-of-my-fathers-last-days.

The Freemasons Chronicle, December 13, 1884. https://masonicperiodicals.org/periodicals/fcn/issues/fcn_13121884/.

Freemasons United Grand Lodge of England. *The Masonic Year Book Historical Supplement*. 2nd ed. London: United Grand Lodge of England, 1969, with a Supplement in 1976.

Gadd, Karen. *In the Matter of a Complaint Under the Clergy Discipline Measure 2003 Before the Bishop's Disciplinary Tribunal for the Diocese of Oxford*. https://www.churchofengland.org/sites/default/files/2024-23/peers-determination.pdf.

Gatiss, Lee. *The Tragedy of 1662: The Ejection and Persecution of the Puritans*. Cambridge: Latimer House, 2007.

Gibbon, Edward. *History of the Decline and Fall of the Roman Empire*. 6 vols. New York: Everyman, 1995.

Gill-Austern, Barbara. "Love Understood as Self-sacrifice and Self-Denial: What Does It Do to Women?" In *Through the Eyes of Women: Insights for Pastoral Care*, edited by Jeanne S. Moessner, 81–102. Minneapolis: Fortress, 1996.

Graystone, Andrew. *Bleeding for Jesus: John Smyth and the Cult of the Iwerne Camps*. London; DLT, 2021 (2nd ed. 2026).

Greengrass, Mark. *Christendom Destroyed: Europe 1517–1648*. London: Allen Lane, 2014.

Gregersen, Charles E. *Louis Sullivan and His Mentor, John Herman Edelmann, Architect*. Bloomington, IN: Author-House, 2013.

Greider, Kathleen. "Too Militant? Aggression, Gender, and the Construction of Justice." In *Through the Eyes of Women: Insights for Pastoral Care*, edited by Jeanne S. Moessner, 123–42. Minneapolis: Fortress, 1996.

Gross, Michael. *The War Against Catholicism: Liberalism and the Anti-Catholic Imagination in Nineteenth-Century Germany*. Ann Arbor: Michigan University Press, 2005.

Grzymała-Busse, Anna. *Nations Under God: How Churches Use Moral Authority to Influence Policy*. Princeton: Princeton University Press, 2015.

———. *Sacred Foundations: The Religious and Medieval Roots of the European State*. Princeton: Princeton University Press, 2023.

Haidt, Jonathan. *The Righteous Mind: Why Good People Are Divided by Politics and Religion*. London: Penguin, 2013.

Hammond, T. C. *In Understanding Be Men: A Handbook of Christian Doctrine*. Nottingham, UK: IVP, 1936.

Harrison, Barbara, and Celia Robb. *Making the Connections: Essays in Feminist Social Ethics*. Boston: Beacon, 1985.

Harrison, Mark. *Secret Leviathan: Secrecy and State Capacity Under Soviet Communism*. Redwood, CA: Stanford University Press, 2023.

Healy, Jonathan. *The Blazing World: A New History of Revolutionary England, 1603–1689*. London: Vintage, 2023.

Hebb, Ross. *Samuel Seabury and Charles Inglis: Two Bishops, Two Churches*. Vancouver, BC: Fairleigh Dickinson University Press, 2010.

Hobson, John A. *Imperialism: A Study*. New York: Trott, 1902.

Hobson, Theo. "What the Church of England Should Say to Its Conservative Rebels." *The Spectator*, August 13, 2024. https://www.spectator.co.uk/article/what-the-church-of-england-should-say-to-its-conservative-rebels/.

Høgsbjerg, Christian. *Atlantic History in Fifteen Slave Revolts: Resistance, Rebellion and Abolition from Below*. London: Bloomsbury, 2023.

Hunt, Alice. *Republic: Britain's Revolutionary Decade 1649–1660*. London: Faber, 2025.

Ibrahim, Azeem. *Authoritarian Century: Omens of a Post-Liberal Future*. London: Hurst, 2022.

IICSA. "The Anglican Church Case Studies: The Diocese of Chichester and the Response to Allegations Against Peter Ball. Investigation Report, May 2019. A Report of the Inquiry Panel Professor Alexis Jay OBE, Professor Sir Malcolm Evans KCMG OBE, Ivor Frank, and Drusilla Sharpling CBE." https://www.iicsa.org.uk/document/anglican-church-case-studies-chichesterpeter-ball-investigation-report.html.

———. "IICSA Inquiry Anglican Church Investigation Hearing, Day 5." September 2018. Archived December 15, 2022. https://webarchive.nationalarchives.gov.uk/ukgwa/20221215002350/https://www.iicsa.org.uk/key-documents/6346/view/public-hearing-transcript-27-july-2018.pdf.

Irons, Charles. *The Origins of Proslavery Christianity*. Chapel Hill: University of North Carolina Press, 2008.

Jackson, Ashley, and Andrew Stewart. *Superpower Britain: The 1945 Vision and Why It Failed*. Oxford: Oxford University Press, 2025.

Jenkins, Philip. *Climate Catastrophe and Faith: How Changes in Climate Drive Religious Upheaval*. Oxford: Oxford University Press, 2021.

Jess, Mervyn. *The Orange Order*. Dublin: O'Brien, 2007.

Jones, Timothy W. *Sexual Politics in the Church of England 1857–1957*. Oxford: Oxford University Press, 2012.

Kater, John L. *Ministry in the Anglican Tradition from Henry VIII to 1900*. London: Lexington/Fortress Academic, 2022.

Keay, Anna. *The Restless Republic: Britain Without a Crown*. London: HarperCollins, 2022.

Keillor, Garrison. *Lake Wobegon Days*. New York: Viking, 1985.

———. *Life Among the Lutherans*. Minneapolis: Augsburg, 2010.

———, et al. "The Secret Life of Lutherans." Radio Heartland, January 18, 2014. YouTube, 5:28. https://www.youtube.com/watch?v=sSeiDPZ1jNA.

Kimmel, Michael. *Angry White Men: Masculinity at the End of an Era*. New York: Bold, 2012.

Kornblith, Gary J. *Slavery and Sectional Strife in the Early American Republic, 1776–1821*. Lanham, MD: Rowman & Littlefield, 2010.

Labaree, Leonard W. *The Papers of Benjamin Franklin, Vol 14. January 1 Through December 31, 1767*. New Haven: Yale University Press, 1970.

Laslett, Peter, ed. *John Locke: Two Treatises of Government*. Cambridge: Cambridge University Press, 1988.

Lester, Alan, ed. *The Truth About Empire: Real Histories of British Colonialism*. London: Hurst, 2024.

Levitan, Jon. "Forgotten Founder: William Ewald on Justice James Wilson, the Constitution and the Declaration of Independence." SCOTUSblog, December 7, 2017. https://www.scotusblog.com/2017/12/forgotten-founder-william-ewald-justice-james-wilson-constitution-declaration-independence/.

Lindbeck, George. *The Nature of Doctrine: Religion and Theology in a Postliberal Age*. Louisville, KY: Westminster John Knox, 1984.

Linstrum, Erik. *Age of Emergency: Living with Violence at the End of the British Empire*. Oxford: Oxford University Press, 2023.

Mahlburg, Kurt. "'We Are the Anglican Communion': GAFCON Declares Formal Split from Canterbury, Founds Global Anglican Communion." The Daily Declaration, October 17, 2025: https://dailydeclaration.org.au/2025/10/17/gafcon-canterbury-split/.

The Makin Review. https://www.churchofengland.org/sites/default/files/2024-11/independent-learning-lessons-review-john-smyth-qc-november-2024.pdf.

Manville, Brook, and Josh Ober. *The Civic Bargain: How Democracy Survives*. Princeton: Princeton University Press, 2023.

Maqbool, Aleem, and Steve Swann. "Priest Thought to Pose Risk to Children Is Paid Off." BBC News, August 13, 2024. https://www.bbc.co.uk/news/articles/cv2gj77pvwwo.

———. "Why Does the Church of England Struggle to Deal with Child Abuse Allegations?" BBC InDepth, August 15, 2024. https://www.bbc.co.uk/news/articles/cr5n2542q82o.

Marshall, Paul Victor. *One Catholic and Apostolic: Samuel Seabury and the Early Episcopal Church*. New York: Church Publishing, 2004.

Martin, Francis. "Philip North's Nomination to Blackburn Was Legitimate, Reviewer Concludes." *Church Times*, April 12, 2024. https://www.churchtimes.co.uk/articles/2024/19-april/news/uk/philip-north-s-nomination-to-blackburn-was-legitimate-reviewer-concludes.

———. "Risk Assessment Should Suffice to Remove a Cleric from Office, Bishop of Blackburn Argues." *Church Times*, August 16, 2024. https://www.churchtimes.co.uk/articles/2024/23-august/news/uk/risk-assessment-should-suffice-to-remove-a-cleric-from-office-bishop-of-blackburn-argues.

Marzouki, Nadia, et al., eds. *Saving the People: How Populists Hijack Religion*. London: Hurst & Co., 2016.

Matovski, Aleksandar. *Popular Dictatorships: Crises, Mass Opinion, and the Rise of Electoral Authoritarianism*. Cambridge: Cambridge University Press, 2022.

McDonald, Alan. *The Jacobean Kirk, 1567–1625: Sovereignty, Polity and Liturgy*. London: Routledge, 1998.

Meek, Jeffrey. *Queer Trades, Sex and Society: Male Prostitution and the War on Homosexuality in Interwar Scotland*. London: Routledge, 2023.

———. *Sex, Politics and Society: The Regulation of Sexuality Since 1800*. 2nd ed. London: Longman, 1989.

Morgan, David. *Snobbery: The Practices of Distinction*. Bristol, UK: Policy, 2016.

Morgan, Stephen. *John Henry Newman and the Development of Doctrine: Encountering Change, Looking for Continuity*. Washington, DC: Catholic University of America Press, 2021.

Newman, J. H. *An Essay in Aid of a Grammar of Assent*, London: Burns & Oates, 1870.

———. *An Essay on the Development of Christian Doctrine*. London: James Toovey, 1845.

Niebuhr, H. Richard. *The Social Sources of Denominationalism*. New York: Meridian, 1957.

Norris, Thomas J. *Newman and His Theological Method: A Guide for the Theologian Today*. Leiden: Brill, 1977.

Northcott, Michael. *A Political Theology of Climate Change*. Grand Rapids: Eerdmans, 2013.

Nye, Joseph S. *The Paradox of American Power*. Oxford: Oxford University Press, 2003.

———. *The Powers to Lead*. Oxford: Oxford University Press, 2008.

———. *Understanding International Conflicts: An Introduction to Theory and History*. London: Pearson, 1997.

Ogden, Steven. *Violence, Entitlement and Politics*. London: Routledge, 2022.

Olusoga, David. *Black and British: A Forgotten History*. London: Pan Macmillan, 2016.

Omrani, Bijan. *God Is an Englishman: Christianity and the Creation of England*. London: Forum, 2025.

Ong, Walter. *Orality and Literacy*. London: Routledge, 1982.

Orwell, George. *Nineteen Eighty-Four*. London: Secker & Warburg, 1949.

Paine, Thomas. *Common Sense Addressed to the Inhabitants of America*. 1776. Reprint, New York: Cosimo Classics, 2006.

Parker, Matthew. *One Fine Day: Britain's Empire on the Brink*. London: Abacus, 2023.

Parsons, Stephen. "Toxic Masculinity: A Problem for the Church?" Surviving Church, September 30, 2018. https://survivingchurch.org/2018/09/30/toxic-masculinity-a-problem-for-the-church/.

Peckham, Robert. *Fear: An Alternative History of the World*. London: Profile, 2023.

Percy, Martyn. "The Anatomy of Fundamentalism." In *Fundamentalisms: Threats and Ideologies in the Modern World*, edited by James Dunn, 47–68. London: I. B. Taurus, 2016.

———. *Anglicanism: Confidence, Commitment and Communion*. Farnham, UK: Ashgate, 2013.

———. "Christmas in the Anglican Tradition." In *The Oxford Handbook of Christmas*, edited by Timothy Larsen, 153–66. Oxford: Oxford University Press, 2020.

———. *Clergy: The Origin of Species*. London: Bloomsbury/T&T Clark, 2006.

———. "Credo." *The Times*, January 4, 2025.

———. *The Crisis of Colonial Anglicanism: Empire, Slavery and Revolt in the Church of England*. London: Hurst, 2025.

———. *The Exiled Church*. London: SCM-Canterbury, 2025.

———. *The Humble Church: Becoming the Body of Christ*. London: SCM-Canterbury, 2021.

———. "Passionate Coolness: Exploring Mood and Character in Ecclesial Polity." In *Theologically-Engaged Anthropology*, edited by Derrick Lemons, 296–314. Oxford: Oxford University Press, 2018.

———. *Power and the Church: Ecclesiology in an Age of Transition*. London: Cassell, 1997.

———. *The Precarious Church: Redeeming the Body of Christ*. London: SCM-Canterbury, 2023.

———. *Salt of the Earth: Religious Resilience in a Secular Age*. London: Continuum, 2002.

———. *Shaping the Church: The Promise of Implicit Theology*. London: Routledge, 2010.

———. *Words, Wonders and Power: Understanding Contemporary Christian Fundamentalism and Revivalism*. London: SPCK, 1996.

Percy, Martyn, and Ian Jones, eds. *Fundamentalism, Church and Society*. London: SPCK, 2002.

Pickering, W. S. F. *Anglo-Catholicism: A Study in Religious Ambiguity*. London: Routledge, 1980.

Pittock, Murray. *Jacobitism*. London: Palgrave Macmillan, 1988.

Platt, Jane. *Subscribing to Faith? The Anglican Parish Magazine 1859–1929*. London: Macmillan, 2015.

Porter, H. Boone. *Samuel Seabury: Bishop in a New Nation*. The National Council, 1962.

Porter, Muriel. *A New Exile? The Future of Anglicanism.* Northcote, Australia: Morning Star, 2016.

———. *The New Puritans: The Rise of Fundamentalism in the Anglican Church.* Melbourne: Melbourne University Press, 2007.

———. *Sydney Anglicans and the Threat to World Anglicanism: The Sydney Experiment.* London: Routledge 2011.

Pui-Lan, Kwok. *The Anglican Tradition from a Postcolonial Perspective.* New York: Seabury, 2023.

———. *Postcolonial Imagination and Feminist Theology.* Louisville, KY: Westminster John Knox, 2005.

———. *Postcolonial Politics and Theology: Unravelling Empire for a Global World.* Louisville, KY: Westminster John Knox, 2021.

Reece, Henry. *The Fall: The Last Days of the English Republic.* New Haven: Yale University Press, 2024.

Reed, John Shelton. *Glorious Battle: The Cultural Politics of Victorian Anglo-Catholicism.* Nashville, TN: Vanderbilt University Press, 1996.

Reid, Anna. *A Nasty Little War: The West's Fight to Reverse the Russian Revolution.* London: John Murray, 2023.

Reid, Walter. *Fighting Retreat: Churchill and India.* London: Hurst, 2024.

Renton, Alex. *Blood Legacy: Reckoning with a Family's Story of Slavery.* London: Canongate, 2021.

Rowthorn, Anne W. *Samuel Seabury: A Bicentennial Biography.* New York: Seabury, 1988.

Sandbrook, Dominic. *The Great British Dream Factory: The Strange History of Our National Imagination.* London: Allen Lane, 2015.

———. *White Heat: A History of Britain in the Swinging Sixties.* London: Little, Brown: 2006.

Sandeman, John. "Figures Show a Gentle Decline in Sydney Anglicans' Attendance Plus Three Letter Writing Campaigns and a Call to Support the Voice." Anglican.ink, September 18, 2023. https://anglican.ink/2023/09/18/figures-show-a-gentle-decline-in-sydney-anglicans-attendance-plus-three-letter-writing-campaigns-and-a-call-to-support-the-voice/.

Sanghera, Sathnam. *Empireworld: How British Imperialism Has Shaped the Globe.* London: Penguin, 2024.

———. *Empireland: How Imperialism Has Shaped Modern Britain.* London: Penguin, 2021.

Sarmiento, Simon. "Southwark Election News: Jeffrey John Rejected." Thinking Anglicans, July 7, 2010. https://www.thinkinganglicans.org.uk/4494–92/.

Schmid, Konrad, and Jens Schröter. *The Making of the Bible: From the First Fragments to Sacred Scripture.* Cambridge: Belknap for Harvard University Press, 2021.

Scruton, Roger. *Our Church: A Personal History of the Church of England.* London: Atlantic, 2012.

Snow, Jennifer C. *Mission, Race, Empire: The Episcopal Church in Global Context.* Oxford: Oxford University Press, 2024.

Snowden, Frank. *Epidemics and Society: From the Black Death to the Present.* New Haven: Yale University Press, 2019.

Spielberg, Stephen, director. *Bridge of Spies.* 20th Century Fox, 2015.

Steiner, Bruce. *Samuel Seabury, 1729–1796: A Study in the High Church Tradition.* Athens: Ohio University Press, 1972.

Stern, Philip. *Empire Incorporated: The Corporations That Built British Colonialism.* Cambridge: Harvard University Press, 2023.

Stone, Lawrence. *The Family, Sex and Marriage in England, 1500–1800.* London: Penguin, 1981.

Strong, Rowan. *Anglicanism and the British Empire, 1700–1850.* Oxford: Oxford University Press, 2007.

———, ed. *Partisan Anglicanism and Its Global Expansion 1829–c.* 1914. Vol. 3 of *The Oxford History of Anglicanism.* Oxford: Oxford University Press, 2017.

Subrahmanyam, Sanjay. *Europe's India: Words, People, Empires, 1500–1800.* Cambridge: Harvard University Press, 2017.

SWITALSKIS. "IICSA Peter Ball investigation 23–27 July 2018." Child Abuse Law, November 6, 2018. https://www.childabuselaw.co.uk/2018/07/iicsa-peter-ball-investigation-23-27-july-2018/.

Szechi, Daniel. *1715: The Great Jacobite Rebellion.* New Haven: Yale University Press, 2006.

Tharhoor, Shashi. *Inglorious Empire: What the British Did to India.* London: Penguin, 2016.

Thompson, Mark, et al., eds. *Domestic Violence: A Starting Point in Supporting Victims.* Sydney, NSW: Moore-Women, 2018. https://moore.edu.au/supporting-domestic-violence-victims.

Thoms, Herbert. *Seabury: Priest and Physician, Bishop of Connecticut.* Nottingham, UK: Shoestring, 1963.

Tilby, Angela. "Angela Tilby: Schismatics in the C of E Go Up a Gear." *Church Times,* August 2, 2024. https://www.churchtimes.co.uk/articles/2024/2-august/comment/columnists/angela-tilby-schismatics-in-the-c-of-e-go-up-a-gear.

Tisby, Jemar. *The Color of Compromise.* Grand Rapids: Zondervan, 2021.

Tyson, Paul. *Theology and Climate Change.* London: Routledge, 2021.

Vogler, Pen. *Scoff: A History of Food and Class in Britain.* London: Atlantic, 2020.

———. *Stuffed: A History of Good Food and Hard Times in Britain.* London: Atlantic, 2023.

Ward, Stuart. *Untied Kingdom: A Global History of the End of Britain.* Cambridge: Cambridge University Press, 2023.

Welch, Sharon. *A Feminist Ethic of Risk.* Minneapolis: Fortress, 2000.

Whatmore, Richard. *The End of Enlightenment: Empire, Commerce, Crisis.* London: Penguin, 2023.

White, Gavin. "The Consecration of Bishop Seabury." *Scottish Historical Review* 63 (1984) 37–49.

Whitley, H. C. *Blinded Eagle: Introduction to the Life & Teaching of Edward Irving.* London: SCM, 1955.

Wigley, John. *The Rise and Fall of the Victorian Sunday.* Manchester: Manchester University Press, 1980.

Wilkinson, Alan. *The Church of England and the First World War.* London: SPCK, 1980.

Williams, John. "'The Stones Revived. A Sermon Preached on the Centenary of the Consecration of Bishop Samuel Seabury', by Rt. Revd. John Williams DD, Bishop of Connecticut." New Haven, CT: Turtle, Morehouse & Taylor, 1884. https://anglicanhistory.org/usa/jwilliams/stones1884.html.

Winchester, Simon. *A Crack in the Edge of the World: The Great American Earthquake of 1906*. London: Penguin, 2006.

———. *Krakatoa: The Day the World Exploded: August 27, 1883*. London: Penguin, 2004.

Wood, Keith Porteous. "Religious Power and Privilege Failed the Victims in the Peter Ball Affair." *National Secular Society*, August 11, 2018. https://www.secularism.org.uk/opinion/2018/08/religious-power-and-privilege-failed-the-victims-in-the-peter-ball-affair.

Wright, Jacob L. *Why the Bible Began: An Alternative History of Scripture and Its Origins.* Cambridge: Cambridge University Press, 2023.

Yamaguchi, Midori. *Daughters of the Anglican Clergy: Religion, Gender and Identity in Victorian England*. London: Macmillan, 2014.

Index

www.ingramcontent.com/pod-product-compliance
Lightning Source LLC
LaVergne TN
LVHW100521110826
845146LV00002B/733

* 9 7 9 8 3 8 5 2 2 9 3 2 1 *